Prentice Hall LITERATURE

PENGUIN EDITION

Unit Three
Resources

Grade Seven

PEARSON

Upper Saddle River, New Jersey
Boston, Massachusetts
Chandler, Arizona
Glenview, Illinois
Shoreview, Minnesota

BQ Tunes Credits
Keith London, Defi ned Mind, Inc., Executive Producer
Mike Pandolfo, Wonderful, Producer
All songs mixed and mastered by Mike Pandolfo, Wonderful
Vlad Gutkovich, Wonderful, Assistant Engineer
Recorded November 2007 – February 2008 in SoHo, New York City, at
Wonderful, 594 Broadway

13-digit ISBN: 978-0-13-366438-6
10-digit ISBN: 0-13-366438-4

1 2 3 4 5 6 7 8 9 10   12 11 10 9 8

PEARSON

CONTENTS

"Snowflake Bentley" by Barbara Eaglesham

"No Gumption" by Russell Baker

"The Eternal Frontier" by Louis L'Amour

"All Together Now" by Barbara Jordan

"Alligator" by Bailey White

"The Creamation of Sam McGee" by Robert Service

BQ Tunes

The Expert, performed by Hydra

Yeah... Unh... yea... Hydra... yea... Blitzkrieg... yea....

I want it all
From the cars, to the bikes to the planes,
To the books, to the stars, to the mike, to the games,
First I'll learn how to get it, that's just one of the perks.
Cus' I also want to learn how they work.
Call me the expert.

Nah, you can't give me a car and just hand me the keys /
I need to learn how to drive it not to crash into trees /
And aside from my safety, there's something else that's got me /
Exploring more about it that's just my **curiosity** /
So I pop open the hood and **analyze** the parts /
The radiator keeps it cool, the engine makes it start /
I want the **knowledge** to build it or tear it apart /
To repair it if it breaks down out of town in the dark /
So no Mr. Mechanic, can't overcharge me for parts /
Or sell me things I don't need please I've studied the art /
I **understand** the diagrams and the tune up charts /
So change your tune up man, I'm way too smart! Yup!

I want it all
From the cars, to the bikes to the planes,
To the books, to the stars, to the mike, to the games,
First I'll learn how to get it, that's just one of the perks.
Cus' I also want to learn how they work.
Call me the expert.

I'll learn it all
But **evaluate** things that you learn / some things are more important than others
of more concern /
I'll learn it all

Continued

Investigate to reach your objective / find out all the details like a good detective /

I'll learn it all

Inquire with those well informed on the topic / if they don't know what they're saying information is toxic

I'll learn it all

Y'all know what I mean, don't let somebody tell you what's true, find out for yourself... Feel me?

See ever since I was a freshman (yes then)

If there was something I wanted to know I'd go and ask a **question** /

Jus' because I got an answer doesn't mean I would accept them /

To be sure it was right, the truth and nothing less than /

I might set up an **experiment**, prep them and test them /

Research gave me **information** in a note book I kept them /

Examine findings carefully like a doctors dissection /

Once I knew I had the right answer I could get some rest then /

Everybody was impressed an' yeah I liked how it felt /

But the real reason I did it is was to get the facts for myself /

That's what's gonna help me keep putting platinum plaques on my shelf /

Discover everything I can that'll keep me on top /

If you don't seek out the knowledge you'll eventually flop /

It's better not to be so foolish / Nah, it's not the way /

Who wants to **interview** somebody with nothing to say? Huh, huh?

I want it all

From the cars, to the bikes to the planes,

To the books, to the stars, to the mike, to the games,

First I'll learn how to get it, that's just one of the perks.

Cus' I also want to learn how they work.

Call me the expert.

I want it all

From the cars, to the bikes to the planes,

To the books, to the stars, to the mike, to the games,

First I'll learn how to get it, that's just one of the perks.

Cus' I also want to learn how they work.

Call me the expert.

The Expert, *continued*

Song Title: **The Expert**

Artist / Performed by Hydra

Vocals: Rodney "Blitz" Willie

Lyrics by Rodney "Blitz" Willie

Music composed by Keith "Wild Child" Middleton

Produced by Keith "Wild Child" Middleton

Technical Production: Mike Pandolfo, Wonderful

Executive Producer: Keith London, Defined Mind

Name _____ Date _____

Unit 3: Types of Nonfiction
Big Question Vocabulary—1

The Big Question: What should we learn?

analyze: *v.* to study something's pieces and parts in order to understand it better; other forms: *analyzing, analyzed, analysis*

curiosity: *n.* a desire to learn about or know something; other form: *curious*

facts: *n.* pieces of information that are known to be true; other forms: *fact, factual*

interview: *n.* a meeting in which a person is asked questions

　　　　　v. to ask a person questions for a specific purpose; other form: *interviewed*

knowledge: *n.* information and understanding that someone gains through learning or experience; other form: *know*

DIRECTIONS: *List three items as instructed. Then answer each question.*

1. List three questions that arouse your *curiosity*.

   _____   _____   _____

   What might you do to satisfy your curiosity about one of these things? _____

   _____

2. List three famous people whom you would like to *interview*.

   _____   _____   _____

   What would be your first question to one of these people? _____

   _____

3. What *facts* would you use to help a child gain *knowledge* about your state?

   _____   _____   _____

   Which fact would be most interesting to the child? Explain. _____

   _____

4. What three steps might help a student to *analyze* a poem?

   _____   _____   _____

   Why is it important to work carefully when you *analyze* something? _____

   _____

Unit 3: Types of Nonfiction
Big Question Vocabulary—2

The Big Question: What should we learn?

discover: *v.* to uncover information that you did not know before; other forms: *discovery, discovered, discovering*

evaluate: *v.* to decide how good, useful, or successful something is; other forms: *evaluation, evaluating, evaluated*

experiment: *n.* a test that shows why things happen or why something is true

　　　　　　v. to perform a test to gather new information; other form: *experimenting*

explore: *v.* to discuss or think about something thoroughly; other form: *exploration*

inquire: *v.* to ask someone for information about a topic; other forms: *inquired, inquiring*

A. DIRECTIONS: *Underline the* **synonym** *(the word or phrase closest in meaning) to each vocabulary word.*

1. **discover**	a. test	b. try to see	c. find out
2. **evaluate**	a. judge	b. criticize	c. uncover
3. **experiment**	a. find	b. visualize	c. test
4. **explore**	a. overlook	b. analyze	c. decide
5. **inquire**	a. question	b. consider	c. respond

B. DIRECTIONS: *Complete each sentence by writing the correct vocabulary word in the blank space. Three possible choices are shown in parentheses.*

1. To begin his research on the rings of Saturn, Ramon went to the school librarian to _____ about the facts. *(experiment, inquire, evaluate)*

2. Cheryl performed two tests to _____ the purity of the water. *(experiment, inquire, evaluate)*

3. You can _____ many facts about animals by studying how they interact. *(experiment, discover, explore)*

4. To _____ for clues about its meaning, Jeb and I examined the strange painting carefully. *(explore, evaluate, inquire)*

5. To make his salad more delicious, the chef decided to _____ with different seasonings. *(discover, explore, experiment)*

Unit 3: Types of Nonfiction
Big Question Vocabulary—3

The Big Question: What should we learn?

examine: *v.* to look at something carefully in order to learn more about it; other forms: *examined, examining, examination, exam*

information: *n.* facts and details about a topic; other forms: *informative, inform*

investigate: *v.* to try to find out the truth about something, such as the details of a crime; other forms: *investigation, investigating, investigated*

question: *n.* a sentence or phrase used to ask for information

     v. to have doubts about something; other forms: *questioning, questioned*

understand: *v.* to know how or why something happens or what it is like; other forms: *understood, understanding*

A. DIRECTIONS: *Review the vocabulary words and their definitions. Then write the one that belongs in each group of related words.*

1. knowledge, wisdom, truths, _____

2. check, explore, inquire, _____

3. inspect, study, watch, _____

4. know, learn, grasp, _____

5. challenge, debate, ask, _____

B. DIRECTIONS: *On the line before each sentence, write True if the statement is true, or False if it is false. If the statement is false, rewrite the sentence so that it is true.*

_____1. Most *information* is based on opinions that cannot be proved true.

_____

_____2. If you *examine* the stars through a telescope, you will see them clearly.

_____

_____3. If you don't *understand* the question, you'll probably get the right answer.

_____

_____4. A person who *investigates* a crime is often guilty.

_____

_____5. It is rude and unnecessary to *question* the claims in an advertisement.

_____

Unit 3 Resources: Types of Nonfiction
3

Name _____ Date _____

Unit 3: Types of Nonfiction
Applying the Big Question

What should we learn?

DIRECTIONS: *Complete the chart below to apply what you have learned about what we should learn. One row has been completed for you.*

Example	Type of knowledge	Why it is important	Effect it will have	What I learned
From Literature	Understanding different cultures, as in "Conversational Ballgames."	To be able to better relate to people who are different from us.	More tolerance and better relationships.	When with people from another culture, don't assume that your own customs are the norm.
From Literature				
From Science				
From Social Studies				
From Real Life				

Name _____

Unit 3: Types of Nonfiction   Skills Concept Map—1
What should we learn?

Words you can use to discuss the Big Question

Reading Skills and Strategies:
Predictions

You can identify the main idea → by → *adjusting your reading rate to recognize main ideas and key points* → and by → *making connections between key points and supporting details*

Informational Text:
Essay

You can use a checklist → to → *analyze the author's argument*

(demonstrated in this selection)
Selection name: _____

Literary Analysis:
Types of Nonfiction

Nonfiction → includes → *expository essays* → and → *reflective essays*

(demonstrated in this selection)
Selection name: _____

(demonstrated in this selection)
Selection name: _____

Basic Elements of Nonfiction Writing
- Organization
- Author's Purpose

Types of Nonfiction
- Letters
- Journals
- Biographies
- Autobiographies

Comparing Literary Works:
Biography and Autobiography

→ developed through → *supporting details* / *character traits*

(demonstrated in these selections)
Selection names:
1. _____
2. _____

Student Log

Complete this chart to track your assignments.

Writing	Extend Your Learning	Writing Workshop	Other Assignments

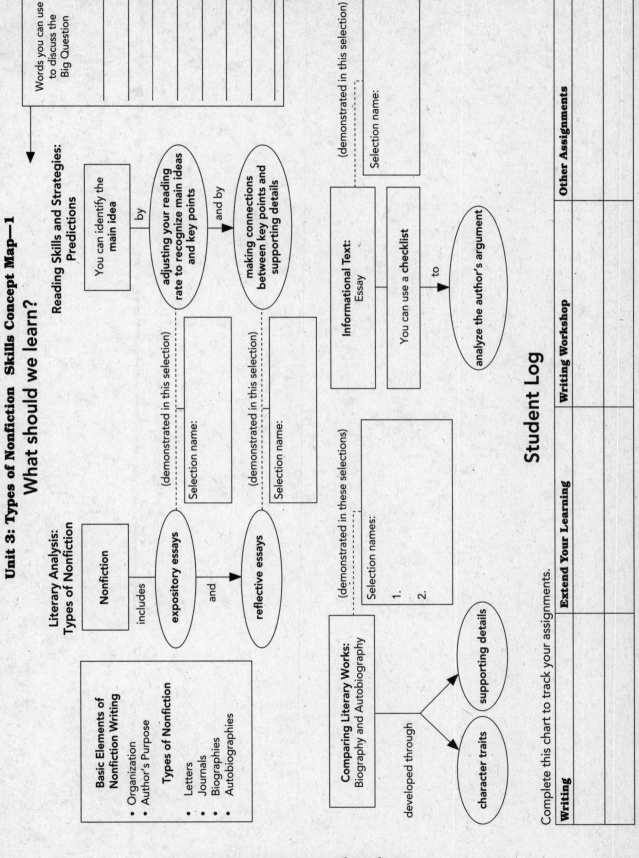

5

Vocabulary Warm-up Word Lists

Study these words. Then, complete the activities that follow.

Word List A

details [dee TAYLZ] *n.* the small secondary parts of something
   Denise added <u>details</u> of lace and sequins to her plain dress.

emblems [EM bluhmz] *n.* objects that stand for or suggest other things; symbols
   Four flags were displayed as <u>emblems</u> of four countries.

glorious [GLAWR ee uhs] *adj.* deserving great praise; magnificent
   The autumn colors of those trees are <u>glorious</u> reds and yellows.

military [MIL uh te ree] *adj.* having to do with the army, the armed forces, or warfare
   The <u>military</u> objective was to take possession of the bridge.

opportunity [op er TOO nuh tee] *n.* a chance to do something
   Wanda regarded the essay test as her <u>opportunity</u> to show what she knew about the subject.

ordinarily [awrd uhn E ruh lee] *adv.* usually; as a rule
   Frank wears tennis shoes <u>ordinarily</u>, but today he is wearing sandals.

portrait [PAWR trit] *n.* a painting, drawing, or a photograph of a person
   Hanging over the mantel is a <u>portrait</u> of William's great-grandfather.

standard [STAN duhrd] *adj.* conforming to what is usual
   The hotel served the <u>standard</u> breakfast of a buttered roll or muffin with coffee or tea.

Word List B

contrasting [kuhn TRAST ing] *v.* showing differences when compared
   By <u>contrasting</u> the dark trim with the white walls, George achieved an interesting look.

former [FAWR mer] *adj.* belonging to the past; earlier
   The <u>former</u> mayor of the city visited the seventh-grade class.

impress [im PRES] *v.* to affect the mind or feelings of
   Sandra wanted to <u>impress</u> the judges with her graceful dancing.

individuals [in duh VIJ oo uhlz] *n.* single human beings; persons
   Ten <u>individuals</u> tried out for the team, but only five would be chosen.

rivals [RY vuhlz] *n.* persons or things you compete with; competitors
   For the past five years, the two schools have been <u>rivals</u> for the league championship.

sash [SASH] *n.* a band or ribbon worn around the waist or over the shoulder
   The Girl Scout had ten badges sewn to the <u>sash</u> she wore over her shoulder.

sheen [SHEEN] *n.* a glistening brightness; shininess; gloss
   Erin brushes her horse's coat to bring out its natural <u>sheen</u>.

traditional [truh DISH uh nuhl] *adj.* conforming to long-established customs or practices
   For her wedding, Celeste wore a <u>traditional</u> white gown and veil.

Name _____ Date _____

Vocabulary Warm-up Exercises

Exercise A *Fill in each blank in the paragraph below with an appropriate word from Word List A. Use each word only once.*

After seeing a [1] _____ of her grandfather during his army days, Carla thought that she might like to have a [2] _____ career. She thought it would be a [3] _____ thing to serve her country in this way. She liked the idea of wearing [4] _____ of honor in the form of stripes and medals. Other [5] _____ of the uniform, however, did not appeal to her. [6] _____, Carla was a stylish dresser. She did not think she would like wearing the [7] _____ uniform. If given the [8] _____, Carla would design a new, more flattering uniform for women in the service.

Exercise B *Decide whether each statement below is true or false. Circle T or F. Then, explain your answer.*

1. If you are <u>contrasting</u> colors when you paint a room, you are using several shades of the same color.
   T / F _____

2. To bring out the <u>sheen</u> in a table, you might polish it with wax.
   T / F _____

3. <u>Rivals</u> cheer for each other's successes.
   T / F _____

4. A <u>traditional</u> costume would be modern and newly designed.
   T / F _____

5. If you write to a <u>former</u> teacher, you write to the teacher you will have next year.
   T / F _____

6. If you wanted to <u>impress</u> a panel of judges, you would perform to the best of your ability.
   T / F _____

7. A team is made up of a group of <u>individuals</u> working together.
   T / F _____

8. The winner of a competition might be given a colorful <u>sash</u> as a mark of honor.
   T / F _____

"What Makes a Rembrandt a Rembrandt?" by Richard Mühlberger
Reading Warm-up A

Read the following passage. Pay special attention to the underlined words. Then, read it again, and complete the activities. Use a separate sheet of paper for your written answers.

When Sara had the <u>opportunity</u> to go on a guided tour at the art museum, she jumped at it. <u>Ordinarily</u>, she just wandered from room to room on her own, looking at the paintings and other art. She would try her best to understand each piece. On Wednesday morning, however, a guided tour was offered with the price of a <u>standard</u> admission. Sara was happy to join the small group that followed the guide and listened to what the guide said.

The first painting the guide spoke about was a <u>portrait</u> of a young woman. The guide pointed out how the artist had used light to draw attention to certain parts of the painting. Light from a window shone on her pearls, her rings, and other jewelry. The young woman wore hair combs made of gold. These objects suggested that the woman came from a rich family.

Sara was interested in the next painting explained by the guide. It was an oil painting with a <u>military</u> theme. Men in uniforms rode on strong, healthy horses. Other men marched proudly, heads held high. An audience watched the soldiers from the sidelines. This audience was made up of women, children, and older people. It was clear that the officers and soldiers were expecting a <u>glorious</u> return from battle. It was also clear that some of the old men on the sidelines were worried about the soldiers. A few of the old men wore <u>emblems</u>, showing that they had fought in earlier wars. That probably explained why they seemed worried about the young men in uniform. The guide explained that the painting was not only telling a story but also expressing a mood.

By the time the tour was over, Sara had learned a great deal. She realized that examining the <u>details</u> of works of art is often the best way to understand them.

1. Underline the words that describe the <u>opportunity</u> Sara had. What is another word for *opportunity*?

2. Underline the words that tell what Sara <u>ordinarily</u> did when she went to a museum. What do you *ordinarily* do on Saturdays?

3. Sara paid for a <u>standard</u> admission. What is another way of saying *standard* admission? What other kinds of admission might there be?

4. Underline the words that tell about the subject of the first <u>portrait</u>. If an artist were making a *portrait* of you, how would you pose?

5. The second painting has a military theme. Underline the words in the paragraph that suggest the <u>military</u> theme. What does *military* mean?

6. Circle the words that show that the men were expecting a <u>glorious</u> return from battle. What does *glorious* mean?

7. Underline the words that tell what the old men's <u>emblems</u> showed. What kinds of *emblems* might they have been wearing?

8. Circle two <u>details</u> that Sara examined during the guided tour. Use *details* in a sentence.

"What Makes a Rembrandt a Rembrandt?" by Richard Mühlberger
Reading Warm-up B

Read the following passage. Pay special attention to the underlined words. Then, read it again, and complete the activities. Use a separate sheet of paper for your written answers.

The *Mona Lisa* by Leonardo da Vinci is probably the world's most famous portrait. In that painting, a young woman dressed in the fashion of her day is seated in a traditional pose. Her right hand gracefully rests on her left wrist as she sits. Behind her is a dreamlike setting. The woman's mysterious expression is contrasting the impressions of friendliness and distance. Arranged over her left shoulder is what appears to be a sash of some kind. Her straight hair is parted in the middle and falls to her shoulders. Leonardo's use of light gives a sheen to the rich fabric of her sleeves.

The painting, also known as *La Gioconda*, is named for the former Mona Lisa. This young woman from Florence, Italy, married Francesco del Giocondo in 1495. Known as la Gioconda after her marriage, she posed for the famous portrait sometime between 1503 and 1505. The painting was a favorite of Leonardo's. He carried it with him for many years as he moved from one city to another.

Many individuals have wondered how Leonardo managed to make the Mona Lisa look alive. How is it possible that she seems to change as we look at her? How can she seem to look a little different each time we see her? The answer lies in a technique Leonardo invented. Using the technique, Leonardo blurred outlines and mellowed colors. The technique causes various forms in the painting to seem to blend with other forms. By leaving the outlines and colors somewhat unclear, Leonardo forces a viewer to use imagination more than any of his rivals ever did.

So the next time you want to impress your friends, talk about Leonardo when the discussion gets around to art.

1. Underline the sentence that gives some details about what a traditional pose might be. Use *traditional* in a sentence.

2. Circle the words that describe the impressions that the woman's expression is contrasting. What does *contrasting* mean?

3. Circle the words that show how the woman is wearing the sash. How would you wear a *sash*?

4. How does Leonardo make the fabric seem to have a sheen? Would a *sheen* show up in the dark? Explain.

5. Why is the woman called the former Mona Lisa? Use the word *former* in a sentence.

6. Underline the words that tell what many individuals wondered. Define *individuals*.

7. What profession do you think Leonardo's rivals were in? Use *rivals* in a sentence.

8. Underline the words that suggest a way to impress your friends. If you wanted to *impress* someone, what would you do?

Richard Mühlberger
Listening and Viewing

Segment 1: Meet Richard Mühlberger
- Why do you think Richard Mühlberger chose to write art history books?
- Do you agree with the writing advice given to Mühlberger by a fellow writer "to stick to the masters"?

_____

_____

_____

Segment 2: The Essay
- According to Richard Mühlberger, what are some characteristics of essays?
- When would you write an essay, and why?

_____

_____

_____

Segment 3: The Writing Process
- Why is it very important to Richard Mühlberger to write in precise, detailed language when writing about a painting?
- Why do you think Richard Mühlberger chooses to write his books in a "conversational tone"?

_____

_____

_____

Segment 4: The Rewards of Writing
- What does Richard Mühlberger hope that his readers will gain by reading books about art?
- Why do you think books about art are important?

_____

_____

_____

_____

Learning About Nonfiction

An author has a specific **purpose for writing** an essay or article. Often, that purpose is to explain, to entertain, to inform, or to persuade. An essay or an article uses one or more of these **formats:**

- Expository writing: presents facts, discusses ideas, or explains a process
- Persuasive writing: attempts to persuade the reader to adopt a particular point of view or take a particular course of action
- Reflective writing: addresses an event or experience and gives the writer's insights about its importance
- Humorous writing: entertains the audience by evoking laughter
- Narrative writing: tells about real-life experiences
- Descriptive writing: appeals to the reader's senses of sight, hearing, taste, smell, and touch
- Analytical writing: breaks a large idea into parts to help the reader see how they work together as a whole

A. DIRECTIONS: *The following are titles of nonfiction essays or articles. Circle the letter of the answer choice that shows the best format for each title. Then, circle the letter of the answer choice that shows the purpose that the author probably had for writing the article.*

1. "How to Build a Doghouse"
   Format: A. persuasive   **B.** expository   **C.** narrative   **D.** reflective
   Purpose: A. to explain   **B.** to entertain

2. "Don't Throw That Cardboard and Paper in the Trash!"
   Format: A. persuasive   **B.** analytical   **C.** narrative   **D.** humorous
   Purpose: A. to entertain   **B.** to persuade

3. "Moving to Tucson Changed My Life"
   Format: A. persuasive   **B.** expository   **C.** analytical   **D.** reflective
   Purpose: A. to persuade   **B.** to share insights

B. DIRECTIONS: *Below are essay topics and their purpose. Write the format that you would use to write each essay. Explain your choice. Refer to the bulleted list above as needed for help.*

Topic: how to draw a face   Purpose: to explain
Format choice/reason: <u>expository; it explains a process</u>.

1. Topic: a strange animal   Purpose: to entertain
   Format choice/reason: _____

2. Topic: vote for a certain candidate   Purpose: to persuade
   Format choice/reason: _____

3. Topic: The Civil War   Purpose: to present ideas
   Format choice/reason: _____

Name _____ Date _____

"What Makes a Rembrandt a Rembrandt?" by Richard Mühlberger
Model Selection: Nonfiction

Nonfiction writing is about real people, places, objects, ideas, and experiences. Here are some common types:

Type of Nonfiction	Description
Biography	the life story of a real person, written by another person
Autobiography	the author's account of his or her own life
Media Accounts	true stories written for newspapers, magazines, television, or radio
Essays and Articles	short nonfiction works about a particular subject

Nonfiction writing must be organized to present information logically and clearly. Writers use **chronological organization** (they present details in time order); **comparison-and-contrast organization** (they show similarities and differences); **cause-and-effect organization** (they show relationships among events); and **problem-and-solution organization** (they identify a problem and present a solution).

DIRECTIONS: *On the lines below, answer these questions about "What Makes a Rembrandt a Rembrandt?"*

1. What type of nonfiction writing is "What Makes a Rembrandt a Rembrandt?" Explain.

   _____

2. How is the first paragraph in "Two Handsome Soldiers" organized? Explain.

   _____

   _____

3. What two real people are the most important in this article?

   _____

4. Why does Richard Mühlberger use an expository format for sections of "What Makes a Rembrandt a Rembrandt?"

   _____

5. Often, nonfiction writers have more than one purpose for writing an article or essay. Which *two* purposes did Richard Mühlberger have for writing this article? Check your choices.

   _____ **A.** to persuade his city to form a militia company as a social club

   _____ **B.** to entertain readers with a humorous event

   _____ **C.** to explain Rembrandt's painting techniques

   _____ **D.** to explain why Banning Cocq was a great Dutch soldier

   _____ **E.** to inform readers with facts about the painting *Night watch*

"What Makes a Rembrandt a Rembrandt?" by Richard Mühlberger
Open-Book Test

Short Answer *Write your responses to the questions in this section on the lines provided.*

1. You are reading the personal thoughts and reflections of a real person and his or her real experiences. Are you reading a nonfiction journal or a persuasive essay? Explain.

   _____
   _____
   _____
   _____

2. You are about to read an essay that is expository writing. What type of information do you expect to find in this essay?

   _____
   _____
   _____

3. Which nonfiction format for an essay addresses an event or experience and includes the writer's insights about its importance? Explain your answer.

   _____
   _____
   _____

4. How would you expect an article claiming wind power is better than solar power to be organized? Would chronological organization be more likely, or comparison and contrast? Explain your answer.

   _____
   _____
   _____
   _____

5. In "What Makes a Rembrandt a Rembrandt?" the author states that instead of just painting portraits of the militia members, as other artists did, Rembrandt chose to show them in action. Why did Rembrandt do this?

   _____
   _____
   _____

6. Based on "What Makes a Rembrandt a Rembrandt?" what is the main reason that Rembrandt's painting is remarkable? Use details from the article to support your answer.

7. According to the end of "What Makes a Rembrandt a Rembrandt?" one of Rembrandt's students said that *Night Watch* would "outlive all its rivals." What did he mean by this?

_____

_____

_____

_____

8. Nonfiction tells about real people, places, ideas, or experiences. In the chart, give an example of this information as found in "What Makes a Rembrandt a Rembrandt?" Then, answer the question that follows.

Nonfiction	"What Makes a Rembrandt a Rembrandt?"
Real person	
Real place	
Real idea	

What experience does the author, Richard Mühlberger, hope the reader will gain by reading his article? _____

_____

9. In addition to being an analytical article, "What Makes a Rembrandt a Rembrandt?" also blends two other kinds of nonfiction formats, descriptive and expository. Give an example of this kind of information found in the article.

Descriptive: _____

Expository: _____

10. What is the most likely reason that Richard Mühlberger wrote "What Makes a Rembrandt a Rembrandt?" Explain your answer.

_____

_____

_____

_____

Name _____ Date _____

Essay

Write an extended response to the question of your choice or to the question or questions your teacher assigns you.

11. Based on "What Makes a Rembrandt a Rembrandt?" what do you think is the most dramatic detail or figure in Rembrandt's painting *Night Watch*? In an essay, explain which part of the painting most demands a viewer's attention and is something you would remember.

12. The title of this article is "What Makes a Rembrandt a Rembrandt?" Author Richard Mühlberger refers to members of a militia company as "citizen soldiers." In a short essay, explain his meaning. Use details from the article to support your explanation.

13. According to "What Makes a Rembrandt a Rembrandt?" Rembrandt's painting of a militia company was different from other such paintings. In an essay, explain in what ways it was different and in what ways it was similar. How did its differences make it stand out? Use at least two details from the article to support your ideas.

14. **Thinking About the Big Question: What should we learn?** In "What Makes a Rembrandt a Rembrandt?" author Richard Mühlberger gives information about the painter of *Night Watch*. In an essay, explain what you think is most important to know about Rembrandt, and tell why it is important. Use details from the essay to support your answer.

Oral Response

15. Go back to question 5, 6, or 7 or to the question your teacher assigns you. Take a few minutes to expand your answer and prepare an oral response. Find additional details in "What Makes a Rembrandt a Rembrandt?" that support your points. If necessary, make notes to guide your oral response.

Name _____ Date _____

Selection Test A

Learning About Nonfiction *Identify the letter of the choice that best answers the question.*

___ 1. Which is the *best* definition of nonfiction?
 A. stories that tell about imaginary people
 B. textbooks that inform students
 C. writing that tells about real people and experiences
 D. writing that attempts to persuade or describe

___ 2. Which is the *best* definition for essays and articles?
 A. short nonfiction works about a subject
 B. short nonfiction works that entertain
 C. short nonfiction works that persuade
 D. short nonfiction works of two or more pages

___ 3. Which is a *main* function of expository writing?
 A. to persuade
 B. to create characters
 C. to make people laugh
 D. to present facts

___ 4. Which format would a nonfiction writer be *most likely* to use to tell about a personal experience?
 A. persuasive
 B. narrative
 C. expository
 D. analytical

___ 5. Which format would a nonfiction writer be *most likely* to use to put into words the sounds and appearance of a wild bird?
 A. expository
 B. analytical
 C. descriptive
 D. persuasive

Critical Reading

___ 6. Which is the correct classification for "What Makes a Rembrandt a Rembrandt?"
 A. journal entry
 B. article
 C. biography
 D. media account

___ 7. According to "What Makes a Rembrandt a Rembrandt?" why did the cities of the Netherlands need the militia?
   A. to paint portraits
   B. to do business
   C. to defend the city
   D. to elect officials

___ 8. Who was Rembrandt?
   A. a Dutch artist
   B. a Dutch king
   C. a night watchman or guard
   D. the captain of a militia company

___ 9. According to "What Makes a Rembrandt a Rembrandt?" who was the leader of the militia company?
   A. Captain Amsterdam
   B. Captain Rembrandt
   C. Captain Netherlands
   D. Captain Banning Cocq

___ 10. Based on "What Makes a Rembrandt a Rembrandt?" which is the BEST description of Rembrandt's painting?
   A. The militia men are posed as if they are preparing for a parade.
   B. The militia men are bravely fighting a battle against an enemy.
   C. The militia men are standing in an even row, wearing colorful hats.
   D. The militia men are discussing battle plans while studying a map.

___ 11. Based on "What Makes a Rembrandt a Rembrandt?" what is the BEST description of how Rembrandt chose to paint the painting?
   A. He used bright colors and symbols of peace.
   B. He used dramatic contrasts of light and dark.
   C. He made the painting very thick and dark.
   D. He surrounded the men with mythical figures.

___ 12. Based on "What Makes a Rembrandt a Rembrandt?" why did Rembrandt choose to dress the men in historic costumes?
   A. to show that they were old men
   B. to add humor and color
   C. to give the company special honor
   D. to use some of his costumes

____ 13. What does the author state about the title *Night Watch* in "What Makes a Rembrandt a Rembrandt?"

  A. It is a great title, because it speaks of the men's bravery.

  B. Rembrandt tried to change the title but failed.

  C. It is a mistake. There is no clock or watch in the picture.

  D. It is a mistake. The scene takes place during the day.

____ 14. According to "What Makes a Rembrandt a Rembrandt?" what art term means "an intense contrast of light and dark"?

  A. musket

  B. chiaroscuro

  C. composition

  D. organization

____ 15. "What Makes a Rembrandt a Rembrandt?" follows a blend of two nonfiction formats. It is expository, because it provides facts. What other format does it follow?

  A. persuasive

  B. humorous

  C. reflective

  D. descriptive

Essay

16. According to "What Makes a Rembrandt a Rembrandt?" in 1678, one of Rembrandt's students said that *Night Watch* would "outlive all its rivals." Is he saying the painting could not be destroyed? Is he saying that it is a good or a bad painting? In a short essay, explain what he meant.

17. Based on "What Makes a Rembrandt a Rembrandt?" what do you think is the most dramatic detail or figure in Rembrandt's painting *Night Watch?* Which part of the painting demands a viewer's attention and is something you would remember? In a short essay, explain your choice.

18. **Thinking About the Big Question: What should we learn?** In "What Makes a Rembrandt a Rembrandt?" Richard Mühlberger gives information about the painter of *Night Watch*. In an essay, explain what you think is most important to know about Rembrandt, and tell why it is important. Use details from the essay to support your answer.

"What Makes a Rembrandt a Rembrandt?" by Richard Mühlberger
Selection Test B

Learning About Nonfiction *Identify the letter of the choice that best completes the statement or answers the question.*

_____ 1. Which is the *best* definition of essays and articles?
   A. nonfiction that tells about someone's life
   B. nonfiction that entertains the audience
   C. nonfiction that presents information on a subject
   D. nonfiction that explains how to complete a process

_____ 2. Which of the following is a format for essays and articles?
   A. expository writing
   B. science fiction writing
   C. short story writing
   D. playwriting

_____ 3. Which of the following is a function of expository writing?
   A. to entertain with humor
   B. to persuade readers
   C. to present facts
   D. to discuss one's insights

_____ 4. Which statement is always true about nonfiction?
   A. It attempts to persuade the reader to adopt a point of view.
   B. It may contain imaginary people, objects, or places.
   C. It is written for newspapers, magazines, television, or radio.
   D. It is about real people, places, ideas, and experiences.

_____ 5. Which nonfiction format addresses an event or experience and includes the writer's insights about its importance?
   A. expository writing
   B. reflective writing
   C. persuasive writing
   D. analytical writing

_____ 6. Which of the following is a function of nonfiction descriptive writing?
   A. to describe the appearance of a magic elf
   B. to describe the spicy smell of pizza baking
   C. to describe a creature from another planet
   D. to describe how to build a bookcase

Critical Reading

_____ 7. Which statement is true about "What Makes a Rembrandt a Rembrandt?"
   A. It is about the adventures of a militia company.
   B. It explains how to paint a portrait.
   C. It presents facts about a famous painting.
   D. It is about the childhood of a famous person.

_____ 8. In "What Makes a Rembrandt a Rembrandt?" the author repeats the phrase
        "a Rembrandt" in his title. What does the phrase mean?
        A. a Dutch artist
        B. a painting by Rembrandt
        C. a militia company
        D. a parade

_____ 9. According to "What Makes a Rembrandt a Rembrandt?" what is the best descrip-
        tion of a militia company?
        A. a group of artists who paint together often
        B. a group of men who come together for parades
        C. a group of men who are trained to pose for pictures
        D. a group of men who are trained to defend their city

_____ 10. Based on "What Makes a Rembrandt a Rembrandt?" how is Rembrandt's painting
        different from most portraits of militia companies?
        A. He used oil paints, but most artists didn't at the time.
        B. He lined up all the men in an even line, but most artists didn't.
        C. He showed the men in action, but most artists didn't.
        D. He used many colors, and most artists used only black and white.

_____ 11. According to "What Makes a Rembrandt a Rembrandt?" why did Captain Banning
        Cocq choose Rembrandt to paint his militia company?
        A. He wanted to impress everyone with his choice of an artist.
        B. He wanted to have each member of the militia pay Rembrandt a fee.
        C. He felt sorry for Rembrandt because the artist was not successful.
        D. He wanted the painting to be very large and bright.

_____ 12. Based on "What Makes a Rembrandt a Rembrandt?" what is the main reason that
        Rembrandt's painting is remarkable?
        A. It features real men in a real setting.
        B. It uses many sharp contrasts of dark and light.
        C. It was completed in the year 1642.
        D. It features weapons and armor from the past.

_____ 13. According to "What Makes a Rembrandt a Rembrandt?" how did Rembrandt add
        realism to the painting?
        A. He used only one bright color instead of several.
        B. He immediately named it _Night Watch_.
        C. He added people who were watching the parade.
        D. He dressed most of the people in fancy costumes.

_____ 14. Who is the female in the painting who has a dead chicken, according to "What
        Makes a Rembrandt a Rembrandt?"
        A. a cook who provides food for the militia and their families
        B. a mascot who holds the militia's emblem, the claws of a bird
        C. the wife of Captain Banning Cocq, who wanted to be in it
        D. the owner of the dog that has just killed the chicken

____ 15. Based on "What Makes a Rembrandt a Rembrandt?" what did Rembrandt include in the painting in order to bring special dignity to the company?
   A. The king of the Netherlands looks on with interest from the sidelines.
   B. The men are dressed in costumes that speak of the country's glorious past.
   C. A drummer stands ready to call the people to order with a drum roll.
   D. Warships in the background suggest the might and power of the militia.

____ 16. According to "What Makes a Rembrandt a Rembrandt?" what is true about the painting's title *Night Watch*?
   A. The name shows that the men in the militia company are on guard.
   B. The name was Rembrandt's idea, as expressed in his will.
   C. It is the official title of the painting, named by Captain Banning Cocq.
   D. It is a mistake because the scene definitely does not occur at night.

____ 17. What is *Night Watch* said to be, according to "What Makes a Rembrandt a Rembrandt?"
   A. the largest Dutch painting of all time
   B. the oldest Dutch painting that still exists
   C. the most famous Dutch painting of all time
   D. the best Dutch painting of all time

____ 18. Which is the most likely reason that Mühlberger wrote "What Makes a Rembrandt a Rembrandt?"
   A. to reflect on a personal experience in which he saw the painting at a museum
   B. to provide details about the life of one of the world's greatest artists
   C. to persuade readers that Rembrandt was as important as Vincent Van Gogh
   D. to describe and analyze the many interesting features of *Night Watch*

____ 19. This article follows a blend of two nonfiction formats. What are they?
   A. persuasive and descriptive
   B. descriptive and expository
   C. narrative and humorous
   D. expository and reflective

Essay

20. The title of this article is "What Makes a Rembrandt a Rembrandt?" The author refers to members of a militia company as "citizen soldiers." In a short essay, explain his meaning. Use details from the article to support your explanation.

21. According to "What Makes a Rembrandt a Rembrandt?" Rembrandt's painting of a militia company was different from other such paintings. In what ways was it different? In what ways was it similar? Use at least two details from the article to support your response to these questions.

22. **Thinking About the Big Question: What should we learn?** In "What Makes a Rembrandt a Rembrandt?," author Richard Mühlberger gives information about the painter of *Night Watch*. In an essay, explain what you think is most important to know about Rembrandt, and tell why it is important. Use details from the essay to support your answer.

Study these words. Then, complete the activities that follow.

Word List A

effort [EF uhrt] *n.* the use of energy to get something done
　Jake made an <u>effort</u> to be friendly to Steven.

installed [in STAWLD] *v.* fixed in position for use
　The electrician <u>installed</u> overhead lighting in the kitchen.

gravity [GRAV i tee] *n.* in physics, the force by which any two bodies attract each other
　The moon has weaker <u>gravity</u> than Earth because it is smaller.

missions [MISH uhnz] *n.* important jobs given to a person or organization
　After accomplishing three <u>missions</u> in a year, the team took a break.

orbit [AWR bit] *n.* the path traveled by an object moving around a larger object
　The moon is in <u>orbit</u> around the Earth.

organized [AWR guh nyzd] *adj.* arranged in an orderly way
　Paul's tool chest is well <u>organized</u>.

relax [ri LAKS] *v.* to make or become less tight or firm
　Suzanne's tired muscles started to <u>relax</u> in the hot bath.

securely [si KYOOR lee] *adv.* firmly; strongly
　The knots were tied so <u>securely</u> that we could not untie them.

Word List B

disks [DISKS] *n.* in the spine, layers of connective tissue
　Damage to one's <u>disks</u> can cause severe pain.

downright [DOWN ryt] *adv.* thoroughly; utterly
　After two hours of exercise, Carmen was <u>downright</u> exhausted.

feeble [FEE buhl] *adj.* weak; not strong
　The <u>feeble</u> man surprised us by lifting the heavy package.

overcome [oh vuhr KUM] *v.* to master; prevail over; surmount
　Darla's greatest challenge was to <u>overcome</u> her shyness.

percent [puhr SENT] *n.* a hundredth part
　Harry puts 30 <u>percent</u> of his income into a savings account.

stuffy [STUF ee] *adj.* having the nasal passages stopped up, as from a cold
　Because of her <u>stuffy</u> nose, Angela had trouble pronouncing the word *murmur*.

tissue [TISH oo] *n.* the material forming plant or animal cells
　Calcium, as found in milk and cheese, makes bone <u>tissue</u> stronger.

unexpected [un ek SPEKT id] *adj.* not anticipated; unforeseen
　Seeing Marie again was an <u>unexpected</u> pleasure for George.

Name _____ Date _____

"Life Without Gravity" by Robert Zimmerman
Vocabulary Warm-up Exercises

Exercise A *Fill in each blank in the paragraph below with an appropriate word from Word List A. Use each word only once.*

It took some [1] _____, but finally the powerful telescope was

[2] _____ in the observatory. Ricardo checked all the nuts and bolts

and made sure it was [3] _____ in place. At last, he could

[4] _____ and enjoy his evenings by looking at the stars. Ricardo liked

nothing more than gazing at the heavenly bodies, seeing how they seemed to be

[5] _____ in a wonderful pattern. He enjoyed observing the moon as it

moved across the sky in its [6] _____ around the Earth. He marveled at

the fact that the moon's [7] _____ affects the tides on Earth. Ricardo

resolved that one of the [8] _____ of his life would be to educate others

about the wonders of astronomy.

Exercise B *Revise each sentence so that the underlined vocabulary word is used in a logical way. Be sure to keep the vocabulary word in your revision.*

1. Sylvia thought the roller-coaster ride was <u>downright</u> boring.

   _____

2. Stanley found it easy to breathe deeply through his <u>stuffy</u> nose.

   _____

3. Myra's skin <u>tissue</u> was not even damaged by her serious sunburn.

   _____

4. After winning fourteen games in a row, the team had an <u>unexpected</u> win.

   _____

5. Josh needs an operation to repair the healthy <u>disks</u> in his spine.

   _____

6. Mark's <u>feeble</u> muscles allowed him to lift 200 pounds.

   _____

7. It took no courage for Heather to <u>overcome</u> her fear of flying.

   _____

8. The two friends split the money evenly, each one taking 10 <u>percent</u>.

   _____

"Life Without Gravity" by Robert Zimmerman
Reading Warm-up A

Read the following passage. Pay special attention to the underlined words. Then, read it again, and complete the activities. Use a separate sheet of paper for your written answers.

In the summer of 1969, one of President John F. Kennedy's great visions was fulfilled. Eight years earlier, Kennedy had said that the United States would put a man on the moon before the decade was over. On the morning of July 16, 1969, *Apollo 11* astronauts Neil Armstrong, Buzz Aldrin, and Michael Collins were ready for one of the greatest <u>missions</u> in history. They sat in their seats in the spaceship *Columbia*, <u>securely</u> strapped in, awaiting blastoff. At 9:32 A.M., they were propelled into space.

Within twelve minutes, the crew was in <u>orbit</u> around the Earth. They circled the Earth one and a half times. Then they headed for the moon. It took them three days to get into the lunar orbit. The next day, Armstrong and Aldrin climbed into the lunar module, the *Eagle*. Collins stayed in the *Columbia* while the other two astronauts descended to the surface of the moon. They landed at a place called the Sea of Tranquility.

Right away, Armstrong radioed NASA headquarters. He said, "Houston, Tranquility Base here. The *Eagle* has landed." The team <u>organized</u> for the mission was finally able to <u>relax</u>. One controller told the crew, "You got a bunch of guys about to turn blue. We're breathing again."

A little over six hours later, Armstrong was ready to walk on the moon. More than half a billion people watched on television. He climbed down the ladder from the *Eagle*. Setting foot on the surface, he said, "That's one small step for man, one giant leap for mankind."

Soon Aldrin joined him. They explored the surface for about two and a half hours. They noticed that it took little <u>effort</u> to move, given the moon's weak <u>gravity</u>. They <u>installed</u> a U.S. flag and a plaque on the moon's surface. The plaque reads, "Here men from the planet Earth first set foot upon the moon. July 1969 A.D. We came in peace for all mankind."

1. Underline the words that explain what one of the greatest <u>missions</u> in history was. Name one other great *mission* in history.

2. The men were <u>securely</u> strapped in. What is another way of saying that?

3. Circle the words that describe the two kinds of <u>orbit</u> in which the *Columbia* found itself. Use *orbit* in a sentence.

4. Circle the word that tells what was <u>organized</u> for the mission. What does *organized* mean?

5. Circle the sentence that shows that the controllers were able to <u>relax</u>. What do you like to do to *relax*?

6. Underline the words that tell why Armstrong and Aldrin used little <u>effort</u> on the moon. Name two activities that take a lot of *effort*.

7. Underline the word that describes the <u>gravity</u> on the moon. Use *gravity* in a sentence.

8. Underline the two things that Armstrong and Aldrin <u>installed</u> on the moon's surface. What are some things that are *installed* in your classroom?

"Life Without Gravity" by Robert Zimmerman
Reading Warm-up B

Read the following passage. Pay special attention to the underlined words. Then, read it again, and complete the activities. Use a separate sheet of paper for your written answers.

Most people can come up with many excuses for avoiding exercise. You might say you are too young or too old. You might complain of being too busy or too tired. You might say you have a <u>stuffy</u> nose. You might use the excuse that something <u>unexpected</u> just came up that requires your immediate attention. The fact is that all those excuses are <u>downright</u> <u>feeble</u>! It is important to <u>overcome</u> your own laziness, get up on your feet, and move those muscles for better health.

When you get ready to start a physical fitness program, you need to have correct information. If you just start exercising muscles you have never exercised before, you could damage muscle <u>tissue</u>. It is even possible to damage the <u>disks</u> in your spine by lifting weights that are too heavy. Find out before you begin just how much exercise is suitable for your age and level of fitness. It is a good idea to see a doctor before changing your routine.

A good physical fitness program includes aerobic exercise. Such exercise strengthens your cardiovascular (heart and lung) system. A good method for measuring intensity during aerobic exercise is the heart rate. The term *heart rate* refers to the number of times your heart beats per minute. To improve cardiovascular fitness, you must raise your heart rate to a certain level. Then you must keep it there for 20 minutes. You should do that at least three times a week.

The heart rate you should maintain is called your target heart rate. Here is a simple formula to find out your target heart rate: the maximum heart rate (220 minus your age) multiplied by 70 <u>percent</u>. So for a twelve-year-old the maximum heart rate would be 220 minus 12, or 208, multiplied by 70 percent, or .70: 145.6. Your goal, therefore, during a session of aerobic exercise would be to get your heart rate up to 145 or 146 for 20 minutes. Do not forget to check with a doctor first, though.

1. Circle the word that is described by <u>stuffy</u>. Name another thing that might be described as **stuffy**.

2. Underline the words that hint at the meaning of <u>unexpected</u>. Describe an **unexpected** event that happened recently at school or at home.

3. Circle the word that is described by <u>downright</u>. Use **downright** in a sentence.

4. Underline the noun that is described by the word <u>feeble</u>. What does **feeble** mean?

5. Circle the words that explain what is important to <u>overcome</u>. Name one difficulty someone might have to **overcome**.

6. Underline the word that describes <u>tissue</u>. What is **tissue**?

7. Circle the words that explain where <u>disks</u> are in your body. Use **disks** in a sentence.

8. To find your target heart rate, you use a formula that involves 70 <u>percent</u>. What does **percent** mean?

"Life Without Gravity" by Robert Zimmerman
Writing About the Big Question

What should we learn?

Big Question Vocabulary

analyze	curiosity	discover	evaluate	examine
experiment	explore	facts	information	inquire
interview	investigate	knowledge	question	understand

A. *Choose one word from the list above to complete each sentence. There may be more than one right answer.*

1. Anna's _____ about other people helped her learn about different cultures.

2. It can be fun to _____ new neighborhoods in your hometown.

3. Try to ask each new acquaintance at least one _____ about her life.

B. *Follow the directions in responding to each of the items below.*

1. List two different times that you learned something outside of school. Write your response in complete sentences.

   _____

   _____

2. Choose one of the experiences you listed in number 1. Write two sentences describing that experience. Use at least two of the Big Question vocabulary words. You may use the words in different forms (for example you can change *analyze* to *analyzing*).

   _____

   _____

C. *Complete the sentence below. Then, write a short paragraph in which you connect this sentence to the big question.*

   Our assumptions about unfamiliar experiences are _____

   _____

   _____

Name _____ Date _____

"Life Without Gravity" by Robert Zimmerman
Reading: Adjust Your Reading Rate to Recognize Main Ideas and Key Points

The **main idea** is the central point of a passage or text. Most articles and essays have a main idea. Each paragraph or passage in the work also has a main idea, or **key point.**

The main idea of a paragraph is usually stated in a **topic sentence.** The paragraph then supplies **supporting details** that give examples, explanations, or reasons.

When reading nonfiction, **adjust your reading rate to recognize main ideas and key points.**

- **Skim** the article to get a sense of the main idea before you begin reading. Look over the text quickly, looking for text organization, topic sentences, and repeated words.
- **Scan** the text when you need to find answers to questions or to clarify or find supporting details. Run your eyes over the text, looking for a particular word or idea.
- **Read closely** to learn what the main ideas are and to identify the key points and supporting details.

A. DIRECTIONS: *Scan each paragraph below to find answers to the questions that follow.*

Our bodies are adapted to Earth's gravity. Our muscles are strong in order to overcome gravity as we walk and run. Our inner ears use gravity to keep us upright. And because gravity wants to pull all our blood down into our legs, our hearts are designed to pump hard to get blood up to our brains.

1. What parts of the body are discussed in this paragraph?

    _____

In microgravity, you have to learn new ways to eat. Don't pour a bowl of cornflakes. Not only will the flakes float all over the place, the milk won't pour. Instead, big balls of milk will form. You can drink these by taking big bites out of them, but you'd better finish them before they slam into a wall, splattering apart and covering everything with little tiny milk globules.

2. What foods are mentioned in this paragraph?

    _____

B. DIRECTIONS: *Now, read the paragraphs closely. Answer these questions.*

1. What is the main idea of the first paragraph?

    _____

2. What are two details that support that main idea?

    _____

3. What is the main idea of the second paragraph?

    _____

4. What are two details that support that main idea?

    _____

"Life Without Gravity" by Robert Zimmerman
Literary Analysis: Expository Essay

An **expository essay** is a short piece of nonfiction that explains, defines, or interprets ideas, events, or processes. The way in which the information is organized and presented depends on the specific topic of the essay. Writers organize the main points of their essays logically, to aid readers' comprehension. They may organize information in one of these ways or in a combination of ways:

- Comparison and contrast
- Cause and effect
- Chronological order
- Problem and solution

"Life Without Gravity" is an expository essay that explains an idea. It uses cause and effect to make the explanation clear. In the paragraph below, the details help readers understand some of the effects of weightlessness.

> Worse, weightlessness can sometimes be downright unpleasant. Your body gets upset and confused. Your face puffs up, your nose gets stuffy, your back hurts, your stomach gets upset, and you throw up.

DIRECTIONS: *The left-hand column of the following chart names parts of the human body that are affected by weightlessness. In the right-hand column, write the effect—in your own words—as it is described in "Life Without Gravity." If one effect causes yet another effect, describe the second effect as well.*

Body Part	Effects of Weightlessness
The blood	Weightlessness causes _____ _____
The spine	Weightlessness causes _____ _____
The bones	Weightlessness causes _____ _____
The muscles	Weightlessness causes _____ _____
The stomach	Weightlessness causes _____

"Life Without Gravity" by Robert Zimmerman
Vocabulary Builder

Word List

blander   feeble   globules   manned   readapted   spines

A. DIRECTIONS: *On the short line, write* T *if the following statement is true and* F *if it is false. Then, explain your answer in a complete sentence.*

____ 1. Animals' *spines* are very strong.

_____

____ 2. A *feeble* voice is one that can be heard across a room.

_____

____ 3. Foods made without pepper are *blander* than the same foods prepared with pepper.

_____

____ 4. All astronauts have successfully *readapted* to life on Earth.

_____

____ 5. *Manned* space flight is considered too dangerous at this time.

_____

____ 6. Floating *globules* help astronauts exercise their muscles in space.

_____

B. WORD STUDY: *The suffix -ness from Old English means "the condition or quality of being." Read the following sentences. Use your knowledge of the suffix -ness to write a full sentence to answer each question. Include the italicized word in your answer.*

1. What are some of the ways that *weightlessness* is enjoyable?

_____

2. How can living in space cause *feebleness*?

_____

3. Why is it important for astronauts to have a *willingness* to try new things?

_____

Name _____ Date _____

Enrichment: Astronaut Training

Astronauts go through a difficult training process. To qualify for the program sponsored by the National Aeronautics and Space Administration (NASA), an applicant must have a bachelor's degree in science or engineering. Trainees take classes in computer science, mathematics, geology, meteorology, navigation, oceanography, astronomy, and physics. They learn about survival on land and at sea, and they are trained in scuba diving. They are exposed to microgravity in aircraft and in a water tank. They experience low and high atmospheric pressure. They fly in jets fifteen hours a month and learn to eject and use a parachute. Then they learn to operate the space shuttle. Among the chores they must master are managing the payload (what the shuttle carries), keeping house, stowing waste, and operating the television machinery.

A. DIRECTIONS: *Answer these questions. Base your answers on the preceding passage.*

1. Why might someone want to train to be an astronaut?

   _____

   _____

2. What aspect of astronaut training do you think would be the most difficult? Why?

   _____

   _____

B. DIRECTIONS: *Imagine that you are training to be an astronaut. Write a letter to a friend or family member describing a typical day in your training.*

_____

_____

_____

_____

_____

_____

_____

_____

_____

Name _____ Date _____

"Life Without Gravity" by Robert Zimmerman
Open-Book Test

Short Answer *Write your responses to the questions in this section on the lines provided.*

1. In "Life Without Gravity," the space tourist Dennis Tito says, "Living in space is like . . . living in a different world." What does he mean by this?

   _____

   _____

   _____

2. What percent of bone tissue do astronauts lose after several months in microgravity? What main idea in the first half of "Life Without Gravity" does this detail support?

   _____

   _____

   _____

3. If it said in "Life Without Gravity" that after long months in space, an astronaut's handshake was feeble, how would the handshake feel? Why might it feel that way? Base your answer on the meaning of *feeble*.

   _____

   _____

   _____

4. The main idea of a paragraph in the middle of "Life Without Gravity" is that astronauts' stomach problems are the worst thing about being weightless. Many astronauts have three symptoms. What are the symptoms, or details, that support this main idea?

   _____

   _____

   _____

5. In the middle of "Life Without Gravity," author Robert Zimmerman writes that food in a weightless environment tastes blander than usual. Why do you think this is true? Base your answer on the meaning of *blander*.

   _____

   _____

   _____

   _____

6. In the chart below, write on detail that supports each main idea from "Life Without Gravity." Then, respond to the statement that follows the chart.

Main Idea	Detail
Weak gravity in space changes the body.	
You have to learn new ways to eat in microgravity.	

Using the information in the chart, write a key point that tells what this essay is about. _____
_____

7. Toward the end of "Life Without Gravity," astronaut Jerry Linenger says his body felt like a 500-pound barbell. What does he mean by this?
_____
_____
_____

8. What kind of essay is "Life Without Gravity"? Is it expository, reflective, or persuasive? How do you know? Explain.
_____
_____
_____

9. In "Life Without Gravity," author Robert Zimmerman organizes his information as cause and effect. He also uses problem and solution. Give an example from the essay to illustrate each type of organization.
_____
_____
_____
_____

10. According to "Life Without Gravity," the author disagrees with the statement that "everything is fun, nothing is hard" in space. What reasons does he have for disagreeing?
_____
_____
_____

Essay

Write an extended response to the question of your choice or to the question or questions your teacher assigns you.

11. What might happen if gravity on Earth disappeared for a day? In an essay, describe a few hours in a day without gravity. How might you eat, sleep, and exercise? How might your body react to weightlessness? Use three details from "Life Without Gravity" to support your description.

12. "Life Without Gravity" considers the advantages and disadvantages of weightlessness. In an essay, name two of the advantages and two of the disadvantages. Then, state your opinion of the effects of weightlessness on the human body. Use details from the essay to support your opinion.

13. In an essay, explain the problems that author Robert Zimmerman describes astronauts facing in "Life Without Gravity." How do these problems affect the astronauts? How have they solved the problems? Explain whether you feel that the problems astronauts face in microgravity will prevent extended space travel in the future. Support your opinion with details from the essay.

14. **Thinking About the Big Question: What should we learn?** In "Life Without Gravity," the author provides many ideas and details about living in microgravity. What do you consider the most important idea in "Life Without Gravity"? In an essay, describe the idea you think is most important and explain its importance. Support your claim with details from the essay.

Oral Response

15. Go back to question 2, 3, or 7 or to the question your teacher assigns you. Take a few minutes to expand your answer and prepare an oral response. Find additional details in "Life Without Gravity" that support your points. If necessary, make notes to guide your oral response.

Name _____ Date _____

"Life Without Gravity" by Robert Zimmerman
Selection Test A

Critical Reading *Identify the letter of the choice that best answers the question.*

____ 1. According to "Life Without Gravity," how does weightlessness affect the circulation of blood?
A. It causes blood to flow more slowly.
B. It causes blood to flow to the head.
C. It causes blood to flow more quickly.
D. It causes blood to flow to the legs.

____ 2. According to "Life Without Gravity," why can astronauts' muscles become weak?
A. Without gravity, the blood is rerouted from the legs to the head.
B. Without gravity, the body "grows" by as much as several inches.
C. Without gravity, eating is difficult, so the body does not get proper nutrition.
D. Without gravity, the muscles do not push or pull on the body's bones.

____ 3. According to "Life Without Gravity," what might happen if astronauts' bones became very weak?
A. The astronauts would throw up when they returned to Earth.
B. Their bones would snap when they returned to Earth.
C. The astronauts would continue to grow when they returned to Earth.
D. Their hearts would pump harder when they returned to Earth.

____ 4. Which detail from "Life Without Gravity" supports the main idea that weightlessness makes bones "thin and spongy"?
A. Astronauts "grow" taller.
B. Astronauts lose bone tissue.
C. Astronauts develop straight spines.
D. Astronauts enjoy weightlessness.

____ 5. Which sentence is the topic sentence of this paragraph from "Life Without Gravity"?

> Worst of all is how their stomachs feel. During the first few days in space, the inner ear—which gives people their sense of balance—gets confused. Many astronauts become nauseous. They lose their appetites. Many throw up. Many throw up a lot!

A. Worst of all is how their stomachs feel.
B. Many astronauts become nauseous.
C. They lose their appetites.
D. Many throw up a lot!

___ 6. According to "Life Without Gravity," when does weightlessness become "fun"?
   A. when you try to eat while experiencing nausea
   B. when you walk on a treadmill twice a day
   C. when your heart and spine adjust to its effects
   D. when food you ordinarily dislike tastes bland

___ 7. According to "Life Without Gravity," what happens if you pour milk in a weight-less environment?
   A. It splatters on the floor.
   B. It stays in the container.
   C. It forms into balls.
   D. It turns into cream.

___ 8. According to "Life Without Gravity," what happens if you do not have a clamp on the straw you are drinking through in a weightless environment?
   A. Liquid flows out after you stop drinking.
   B. The straw becomes clogged with liquid.
   C. The straw bursts apart.
   D. You choke on the liquid.

___ 9. Why did the astronaut Jerry Linenger say his body "felt like a 500-pound barbell"?
   A. He had gained weight.
   B. He was not used to gravity.
   C. He had been very sick.
   D. He had not eaten properly.

___ 10. Which title best describes "Life Without Gravity"?
   A. "How Astronauts Eat"
   B. "How to Become an Astronaut"
   C. "The Ups and Downs of Weightlessness"
   D. "The Difficulties of Outer Space"

___ 11. Which of the following statements about "Life Without Gravity" explains why it is an expository essay?
   A. It is a short work of nonfiction that does not express the writer's opinion.
   B. It is a short work of nonfiction that uses examples to make its points.
   C. It is a short work of nonfiction that explains something in an amusing way.
   D. It is a short work of nonfiction that explains the effects of weightlessness.

Vocabulary and Grammar

____ **12.** In which sentence is the word *blander* used logically?

    A. The cook added spices to make the food taste blander.

    B. If you do not like hot food, you should choose blander dishes.

    C. In ordinary circumstances, hot sauce makes foods taste blander.

    D. The blander dishes were marked with red flames on the menu.

____ **13.** How might a *feeble* cry sound?

    A. weak and hard to hear   **C.** high pitched

    B. extremely loud   **D.** low and rumbling

____ **14.** Which of these sentences contains a conjunction?

    A. Astronauts bounce about from wall to wall, flying!

    B. Weightlessness can sometimes be downright unpleasant.

    C. The heart and spine adjust.

    D. In microgravity, you have to learn new ways to eat.

____ **15.** How many conjunctions are there in the following sentence?

    These men and women faced the discomforts of weightlessness and overcame them.

    A. 0

    B. 1

    C. 2

    D. 3

Essay

16. What might happen if the gravity on Earth disappeared for a day? In an essay, describe a few hours in a day without gravity. Use three details from "Life Without Gravity" to support your description.

17. What makes "Life Without Gravity" an expository essay? In an essay of your own, answer that question. First, define an expository essay. Then, give one example from "Life Without Gravity" to illustrate your definition.

18. Thinking About the Big Question: What should we learn? In "Life Without Gravity," the author provides many ideas and details about living in microgravity. What do you consider the most important idea in "Life Without Gravity"? In an essay, discuss the idea you think is most important Support your answer with details from the essay.

"Life Without Gravity" by Robert Zimmerman
Selection Test B

Critical Reading *Identify the letter of the choice that best completes the statement or answers the question.*

_____ 1. According to "Life Without Gravity," why does the author disagree with the statement that "everything is fun, nothing is hard" in space?
   A. because weightlessness has unpleasant effects on the body
   B. because astronauts have to memorize a great deal of information
   C. because learning to fly the space shuttle requires hours of training
   D. because life on a space station can be extremely lonely

_____ 2. Why does the "space tourist" Dennis Tito say, "Living in space is like . . . living in a different world"?
   A. Life without gravity is strange and hard to get used to.
   B. Astronauts travel to completely different worlds.
   C. It is extremely difficult to eat in a weightless environment.
   D. Astronauts are so far from their lives and families on Earth.

_____ 3. According to "Life Without Gravity," what effect does weightlessness have on blood?
   A. It causes blood to flow more slowly.
   B. It causes blood to flow to the head.
   C. It causes blood to thin out.
   D. It causes blood to form clots.

_____ 4. "Life Without Gravity" suggests that astronauts' muscles become weak because
   A. blood stops flowing to the muscles.
   B. it is difficult to eat nutritious meals.
   C. the disks in the spine relax, causing the astronauts to "grow" taller.
   D. the muscles do not have the opportunity to push and pull on the bones.

_____ 5. Which detail supports the main idea that microgravity weakens astronauts' bones?
   A. Astronauts grow one to three inches taller.
   B. Astronauts' legs become thin and sticklike.
   C. Astronauts lose 10 percent of their bone tissue after several months.
   D. Astronauts get used to living without gravity after about one week.

_____ 6. According to "Life Without Gravity," what is the cause of astronauts' nausea?
   A. too much blood flowing to the head
   B. the weakening of the muscles
   C. the lengthening of the spine
   D. an upset in the sense of balance

_____ 7. According to "Life Without Gravity," weightlessness becomes "fun"
   A. when you eat spicy food that tastes bland.
   B. when you exercise to maintain your strength.
   C. when your heart and spine adjust.
   D. when food gets splattered everywhere.

_____ 8. According to "Life Without Gravity," if you point your head to the left, you will
   A. turn upside-down.
   B. feel intense nausea.
   C. move to the right.
   D. move to the left.

_____ 9. According to "Life Without Gravity," when milk is poured in a weightless environment,
   A. it covers everything with tiny globules.
   B. it remains in the container and hardens.
   C. it forms big floating balls.
   D. it separates from the cream.

_____ 10. The astronaut Jerry Linenger says that his body "felt like a 500-pound barbell" because
   A. he had gained a great deal of weight.
   B. he was weak and unused to gravity.
   C. he had felt nausea for a long time.
   D. he had not been able to eat properly.

_____ 11. What is the topic sentence of this paragraph from "Life Without Gravity"?

   And yet, Linenger recovered quickly. In fact, almost two dozen astronauts have lived in space for more than six months, and four have stayed in orbit for more than a year. These men and women faced the discomforts of weightlessness and overcame them. And they all readapted to Earth's gravity without problems, proving that voyages to Mars are possible . . . even if it feels like you are hanging upside down the whole time!

   A. And yet, Linenger recovered quickly.
   B. In fact, almost two dozen astronauts have lived in space . . .
   C. These men and women faced the discomforts of weightlessness and overcame them.
   D. And they all readapted . . . , proving that voyages to Mars are possible.

_____ 12. Which of the following statements about "Life Without Gravity" explains why it is an expository essay?
   A. It describes the negative effects of weightlessness before it describes the positive effects.
   B. It is a short work of nonfiction that explains the effects of weightlessness on astronauts.
   C. It uses an informal tone to convey factual information.
   D. It uses real-life examples to explain the main points.

_____ 13. Which title best describes "Life Without Gravity"?
   A. "How Astronauts Eat in Outer Space"
   B. "What Astronauts Have to Do"
   C. "The Ups and Downs of Weightlessness"
   D. "The Challenge of Living in Outer Space"

_____ 14. What is the main idea of "Life Without Gravity"?
   A. Weightlessness has a negative effect on the bones.
   B. Weightlessness causes astronauts to grow taller.
   C. Weightlessness has advantages and disadvantages.
   D. Weightlessness can be fun once one adjusts to it.

Vocabulary and Grammar

____ 15. In which sentence is the word *feeble* used logically?
   A. The man's shout was strong and feeble.
   B. The astronaut's handshake was limp and feeble.
   C. The astronaut took feeble pictures of the beautiful sunset.
   D. The runner's feeble legs carried her swiftly over the finish line.

____ 16. The claim that food in a weightless environment tastes *blander* than usual means that
   A. it is more tasteless.
   B. it has more texture.
   C. it is fresher.
   D. it is processed.

____ 17. Which sentence from "Life Without Gravity" contains two conjunctions?
   A. "Worse, weightlessness can sometimes be downright unpleasant."
   B. "Our muscles are strong in order to overcome gravity as we walk and run."
   C. "The bones in the spine and the disks between them spread apart and relax."
   D. "Air currents will then blow them into nooks and crannies."

____ 18. How many conjunctions are there in this sentence from "Life Without Gravity"?
   In weightlessness you choose to move up or down and left or right simply by pointing your head.
   A. 0
   B. 1
   C. 2
   D. 3

Essay

19. "Life Without Gravity" considers the advantages and the disadvantages of weightlessness. In an essay, name two of the advantages and two of the disadvantages. Then, state your opinion of the effects of weightlessness on the human body. If you had the opportunity to travel in space, would you be willing to do it? Why or why not?

20. In an essay, describe the characteristics of an expository essay, and explain why "Life Without Gravity" is considered an expository essay. Cite three examples from "Life Without Gravity" to illustrate your explanation.

21. **Thinking About the Big Question: What should we learn?** In "Life Without Gravity," the author provides many ideas and details about living in microgravity. What do you consider the most important idea in "Life Without Gravity"? In an essay, describe the idea you think is most important and explain its importance. Support your claim with details from the essay.

Name _____ Date _____

"Conversational Ballgames" by Nancy Masterson Sakamoto
Vocabulary Warm-up Word Lists

Study these words. Then, complete the activities that follow.

Word List A

challenge [CHAL uhnj] *v.* to question or dispute the truth or correctness of something
We <u>challenge</u> your idea that skateboarders should not wear knee guards.

confused [kuhn FYOOZD] *adj.* mixed up; bewildered
After being awakened from a deep sleep, Heather felt <u>confused</u>.

consider [kuhn SID uhr] *v.* to regard as; think to be
Most people <u>consider</u> it rude if you sneeze without covering your mouth.

conversation [kahn vuhr SAY shuhn] *n.* an exchange of ideas by informal talk
Matt and Sylvia had a <u>conversation</u> about the tennis game.

extremely [ek STREEM lee] *adv.* much more than usual or common; very
Please be <u>extremely</u> careful when you cross that rickety bridge.

interesting [IN trist ing] *adj.* exciting curiosity or attention
Agnes's antics made the party much more <u>interesting</u>.

lack [LAK] *n.* the condition of not having enough; shortage
Surprisingly, Barry's <u>lack</u> of talent did not keep him from performing.

tennis [TEN is] *n.* a game played by striking a ball back and forth with rackets over a net
Although she rarely wins, Monica enjoys playing <u>tennis</u>.

Word List B

cultural [KUL chuhr uhl] *adj.* having to do with the way of life of a particular people, including their customs, religions, ideas, and so on
Our country is made strong by <u>cultural</u> diversity.

discussion [di SKUSH uhn] *n.* argument on or consideration of a subject
The topic under <u>discussion</u> is after-school activities.

formal [FAWR muhl] *adj.* requiring elaborate dress and manners
Jan's <u>formal</u> gown was made of silk.

occasional [uh KAY zhuh nuhl] *adj.* occurring now and then
Don made <u>occasional</u> comments as he observed the game.

powerful [POW uhr fuhl] *adj.* strong; mighty
Alphonse's <u>powerful</u> play in the last quarter won the game.

refer [ri FUHR] *v.* to call attention to; to speak of
Marsha's comments <u>refer</u> to Angela's previous statement.

response [ri SPAHNS] *n.* a reply or reaction
The audience's <u>response</u> to the performance consisted of wild clapping.

suitable [SOOT uh buhl] *adj.* proper for the purpose or occasion
A <u>suitable</u> response is a simple thank you.

"**Conversational Ballgames**" by Nancy Masterson Sakamoto
Vocabulary Warm-up Exercises

Exercise A *Fill in each blank in the paragraph below with an appropriate word from Word List A. Use each word only once.*

At first, Allie felt [1] _____ by what Charlie had said. Then she took some time to [2] _____ his exact words. As she thought about it, it became clear that he had issued a [3] _____. It seemed that he wanted to play a game of [4] _____ with her to determine who was the better player. Allie already knew that Charlie was [5] _____ poor at the game. It was [6] _____ that he would choose this game to prove his superiority. Why not a game of checkers, at which he was clearly the better player? His [7] _____ of talent at tennis was obvious to everyone who knew him. Just then, Allie remembered a [8] _____ she had recently overheard. It seemed that Charlie had been taking tennis lessons lately.

Exercise B *Answer the questions with complete explanations.*

1. Would it be <u>suitable</u> to give a twelve-year-old a car for his or her birthday?
_____

2. If you were told that a dog exhibits <u>occasional</u> bursts of violence, would you want to be around that dog?
_____

3. What might you expect to see and hear at a <u>cultural</u> event?
_____

4. What would you wear to a <u>formal</u> event, such as a wedding?
_____

5. What is your <u>response</u> when you are introduced to someone for the first time?
_____

6. What is the difference between a <u>discussion</u> and a speech?
_____

7. Suppose you are doing research on a certain topic, and ten sources <u>refer</u> to a certain book. Would you try to find that book?
_____

8. Do you think that a <u>powerful</u> flea powder would kill fleas on a dog?
_____

Name _____ Date _____

"**Conversational Ballgames**" by Nancy Masterson Sakamoto
Reading Warm-up A

Read the following passage. Pay special attention to the underlined words. Then, read it again, and complete the activities. Use a separate sheet of paper for your written answers.

Listen in on the conversation of historians talking about the origins of tennis. You will find that they do not all agree. In fact, they seem confused about how the game began. Some think that an early form of the game was played by the ancient Egyptians, Greeks, and Romans. No one has ever found any ancient drawings or descriptions of tennislike games. However, a few Arabic words dating from ancient Egypt have interesting sounds. For example, consider the Egyptian town of Tinnis on the Nile. Also, think about the Arabic word *rahat*. It means "palm of the hand." Notice how close it is to the word *racquet*.

Other than those two words, there is a complete lack of evidence of any form of tennis before the year 1000. Most historians agree that the game was started by French monks. That would have been in the 1200s or 1300s. There is evidence that they played a crude form of handball. Sometimes they would play against their monastery walls. Other times they would string a rope across a courtyard and play over the rope. They called the game *jeu de paume*, meaning "game of the hand." Historians who challenge the idea of more ancient origins point to the French word *tenez* as proof. The word means "take this." It was said when one player served the ball.

As the game grew in popularity, indoor courts began to be used. The ball was still played off the walls. To protect their hands, players started using a glove. At first the glove had webbing between the fingers. It evolved into a handle with webbing attached—the first racquet.

The monks introduced the game to the nobility. Among them it became extremely popular. According to some accounts, there were as many as 1,800 tennis courts in France by the thirteenth century. Soon the game became popular in England, where over the years it evolved into the game we know today.

1. Underline the word that tells who is having a conversation about tennis. Write a short *conversation* between two or more characters.

2. Circle the words that explain what about tennis is the subject of the discussion. Use *tennis* in a sentence.

3. Underline the words that tell what historians are confused about. What does *confused* mean?

4. Circle the word that tells what is interesting about the Arabic words. Define *interesting*.

5. Underline the two words that you are asked to consider. Use *consider* in a sentence.

6. Circle the words that tell what there is a lack of. What would you like to see in your classroom that there is a *lack* of now?

7. Underline the words that tell what the historians challenge. Use *challenge* in a sentence.

8. Circle the words that tell what became extremely popular among the nobility. What does *extremely* mean?

Name _____ Date _____

Read the following passage. Pay special attention to the underlined words. Then, read it again, and complete the activities. Use a separate sheet of paper for your written answers.

The Japanese tea ceremony is a <u>cultural</u> tradition that follows a basic format. The host usually wears a kimono, a traditional Japanese costume. Guests have the choice of a kimono or other <u>formal</u> wear. After walking quietly and calmly through a garden, guests are met by the host, who silently greets them with a silent bow. Each guest's <u>response</u> is a similar bow. Everyone then removes his or her shoes and goes through a small door to enter the teahouse.

Once inside, guests admire the kettle, the flowers, and other decorations. The decorations, <u>suitable</u> to the season or the occasion, are always simple. Then the guests kneel on mats made of rice straw, resting on their heels. They watch as the host performs the various ceremonies. If no meal is offered, the host will serve small sweets. Then each utensil for the tea is cleaned in front of the guests in a precise way. The tea is prepared by whisking powdered green tea into hot water with a bamboo whisk. With much ceremony, bowing, and wiping of the bowl's rim, the bowl is passed among the guests.

After the guests have had the tea, the host cleans each utensil again. Again, much ceremony goes along with this. Guests take turns examining and admiring each item, often using a special cloth to handle each one. After the host collects the utensils, the guests depart. The host stands at the door and bows, ending the ceremony.

The ceremony is a time for the host and the guests to be spiritually refreshed. <u>Discussion</u> is limited. Guests relax, enjoying the atmosphere. They listen to the sounds of the water and the fire. They smell the incense and the tea. They make <u>occasional</u> comments. They might <u>refer</u> to the beauty of the teahouse as they enjoy one another's company. The ceremony is a <u>powerful</u> reminder of the importance of slowing down our hectic lives.

1. Circle the word that is described by <u>cultural</u>. Use *cultural* in a sentence.

2. Underline the word that names a Japanese garment that can be worn on a <u>formal</u> occasion. Describe what you would wear on a *formal* occasion.

3. Circle the words that describe each guest's <u>response</u> to the host's bow. Use *response* in a sentence.

4. Underline the noun that is described by <u>suitable</u>. What does *suitable* mean?

5. Circle the word that describes the amount of <u>discussion</u> at a tea ceremony. What is another word for *discussion*?

6. Underline the word that <u>occasional</u> describes. What does *occasional* mean?

7. Circle the words that explain what guests might <u>refer</u> to in their discussion. Use *refer* in a sentence.

8. Circle the root word in <u>powerful</u>. Define *powerful*.

Name _____ Date _____

"Conversational Ballgames" by Nancy Masterson Sakamoto
Writing About the Big Question

What should we learn?

Big Question Vocabulary

analyze	curiosity	discover	evaluate	examine
experiment	explore	facts	information	inquire
interview	investigate	knowledge	question	understand

A. *Choose one word from the list above to complete each sentence. There may be more than one right answer.*

1. _____ an older person in your family to learn about history.

2. _____ is often gained after a lifetime of experience.

3. It can take time to learn to _____ someone from another culture.

B. *Follow the directions in responding to each of the items below.*

1. List two different times that you learned something about a person from another culture. Write your response in complete sentences.

   _____

   _____

2. Choose one of the experiences you listed in number 1. Write two or more sentences describing that experience. Use at least two of the Big Question vocabulary words in your answer. You may use the words in different forms (for example, you can change *analyze* to *analyzing*).

   _____

   _____

C. *Complete the sentence below. Then, write a short paragraph in which you connect this sentence to the big question.*

   Cultural knowledge can _____

   _____

   _____

Unit 3 Resources: Types of Nonfiction

"Conversational Ballgames" by Nancy Masterson Sakamoto
Reading: Adjust Your Reading Rate to Recognize Main Ideas and Key Points

The **main idea** is the central point of a passage or text. Most articles and essays have a main idea. Each paragraph or passage in the work also has a main idea, or **key point.**

The main idea of a paragraph is usually stated in a **topic sentence**—a sentence that identifies the key point. The paragraph then supplies **supporting details** that give examples, explanations, or reasons.

When reading nonfiction, **adjust your reading rate to recognize main ideas and key points.**

- **Skim** the article to get a sense of the main idea before you begin reading. Look over the text quickly, looking for text organization, topic sentences, and repeated words.
- **Scan** the text when you need to find answers to questions or to clarify or find supporting details. Run your eyes over the text, looking for a particular word or idea.
- **Read closely** to learn what the main ideas are and to identify the key points and supporting details.

A. DIRECTIONS: *Scan each paragraph below to find answers to the questions that follow.*

A western-style conversation between two people is like a game of tennis. If I introduce a topic, a conversational ball, I expect you to hit it back. If you agree with me, I don't expect you simply to agree and do nothing more. I expect you to add something—a reason for agreeing, another example, or an elaboration to carry the idea further. But I don't expect you always to agree. I am just as happy if you question me, or challenge me, or completely disagree with me. Whether you agree or disagree, your response will return the ball to me.

1. What game does the author discuss in this paragraph? _____

A Japanese-style conversation, however, is not at all like tennis or volleyball. It's like bowling. You wait for your turn. And you always know your place in line. It depends on such things as whether you are older or younger, a close friend or a relative stranger to the previous speaker, in a senior or junior position, and so on.

2. What game does the author discuss in this paragraph? _____

B. DIRECTIONS: *Now, read the paragraphs closely for main ideas and supporting details.*

1. What is the main idea of the first paragraph?

_____

2. What are two details that support that main idea?

_____

3. What is the main idea of the second paragraph?

_____

4. What are two details that support that main idea?

_____

"Conversational Ballgames" by Nancy Masterson Sakamoto
Literary Analysis: Expository Essay

An **expository essay** is a short piece of nonfiction that explains, defines, or interprets ideas, events, or processes. The way in which the information is organized and presented depends on the specific topic of the essay. Writers organize the main points of their essays logically, to aid readers' comprehension. They may organize information in one of these ways or in a combination of ways:

- Comparison and contrast
- Cause and effect
- Chronological order
- Problem and solution

"Conversational Ballgames" is an expository essay that explains two processes. It uses comparison and contrast to make the explanation clear. In the paragraph below, the details set up the differences between Japanese and western styles of conversation.

Japanese-style conversations develop quite differently from western-style conversations. And the difference isn't only in the languages. I realized that just as I kept trying to hold western-style conversations even when I was speaking Japanese, so my English students kept trying to hold Japanese-style conversations even when they were speaking English.

DIRECTIONS: *Use this chart to compare and contrast Japanese-style conversation and western-style conversation. In the left-hand column, write five characteristics of western-style conversations as those conversations are described in "Conversational Ballgames." In the right-hand column, describe how the Japanese style differs from, or is similar to, each characteristic described on the left.*

Western-Style Conversation	Japanese-Style Conversation
1.	
2.	
3.	
4.	
5.	

Name _____ Date _____

"**Conversational Ballgames**" by Nancy Masterson Sakamoto
Vocabulary Builder

Word List

elaboration   indispensable   murmuring   parallel   suitable   unconsciously

A. DIRECTIONS: *Think about the meaning of the italicized word in each sentence. Then, answer the question.*

1. If two lines run *parallel* to each other, what do you know about them?

   _____

2. If a speaker is *murmuring,* what might he or she be asked to do?

   _____

3. Why might someone who is learning Japanese say that a dictionary is *indispensable*?

   _____

4. If you were engaged in a conversation about cultural differences, and someone asked you for *elaboration,* what would you do?

   _____

5. If two cultures had different ideas about *suitable* times for serious conversation, would holding a meeting be simple or difficult?

   _____

6. Why is it hard to stop doing something if you do it *unconsciously*?

   _____

B. WORD STUDY: *The suffix -able means "capable or worthy of being." Read the following sentences. Use your knowledge of the suffix -able to write a full sentence to answer each question.*

1. Does a *capable* person need help?

   _____

2. If an experience is *enjoyable*, are you eager to have it end?

   _____

3. Is a *breakable* plate a good choice for a picnic?

   _____

Name _____ Date _____

Enrichment: Writing Dialogue

From reading "Conversational Ballgames," you know how western-style and Japanese-style conversations differ. Work with a partner to write a conversation in each style. Decide which of you will be speaker 1 and which will be speaker 2. Then, write your parts. Write about one of these topics:

- The best time to do homework
- The best way to spend summer vacation
- My favorite musician

Western-style conversation

Speaker 1: _____

_____

Speaker 2: _____

_____

Speaker 1: _____

_____

Speaker 2: _____

_____

Japanese-style conversation

Speaker 1: _____

_____

Speaker 2: _____

_____

Speaker 1: _____

_____

Speaker 2: _____

_____

"Life Without Gravity" by Robert Zimmerman
"Conversational Ballgames" by Nancy Masterson Sakamoto
Integrated Language Skills: Grammar

Conjunctions

Conjunctions connect words or groups of words. **Coordinating conjunctions,** such as *but, and, nor, for, so, yet,* and *or,* connect words or groups of words that have a similar function in a sentence. They might connect two or more nouns, adjectives, adverbs, groups of words, or sentences. In the following examples, the coordinating conjunctions are in bold type. The words they connect are underlined.

Connecting nouns:	<u>Bones</u> **and** <u>muscles</u> become weak in outer space.
Connecting verbs:	How can people <u>talk</u> **and** <u>eat</u> at the same time?
Connecting adjectives:	A conversation can be <u>interesting</u>, <u>exciting</u>, **or** <u>boring</u>.
Connecting sentences:	<u>Becoming an astronaut is difficult</u>, **but** <u>it is also rewarding</u>.

A. PRACTICE: *Circle the coordinating conjunction in each sentence. Then, underline the words, groups of words, or sentences that the conjunction connects.*

1. Some astronauts adjust well to living without gravity, but others have problems.
2. Zero gravity is hard on the bones and the muscles.
3. Astronauts are not surprised by zero gravity, for they are trained to expect it.
4. Sakamoto had mastered Japanese, yet she was having trouble communicating.
5. In western conversations, someone may agree, question, or challenge.
6. Sakamoto learned the art of Japanese conversation, so she was able to participate fully.

B. Writing Application: *Complete the following instructions by writing sentences about "Life Without Gravity" or "Conversational Ballgames." In each sentence that you write, use the coordinating conjunction in the way described.*

1. Join two nouns with the conjunction *and.* _____

   _____

2. Join two verbs with the conjunction *or.* _____

   _____

3. Join two sentences with the conjunction *but.* _____

   _____

4. Join two groups of words with the conjunction *or.* _____

   _____

5. Join two adjectives with the conjunction *yet.* _____

   _____

Name _____ Date _____

Integrated Language Skills:
Grammar Support for Writing an Analogy

An **analogy** makes a comparison between two or more things that are similar in some ways, but otherwise unalike. A good analogy can spice up your writing, make the reader smile, or explain a difficult concept.

Analogies often take the form of a compound sentence with two parts joined by the phrase "is like." For example, A is like B. The two halves of the sentence usually have a parallel structure. For example,

A NOUN without a NOUN is like A NOUN without a NOUN.

___{first half}_____connector _____{second half____.

Before you write an analogy of your own, practice by completing this chart.

A	connector	B
Life without gravity	is like	French fries without ketchup.
Life without gravity	is like	spaghetti without _____.
Life without gravity	is like	noun without _____.
	is like	
Communicating with someone from another culture	is like	hiking blindfolded.
Communicating with someone from another culture	is like	singing _____.
Communicating with someone from another culture	is like	_____.

Now, use a separate piece of paper to write three complete analogies. Use the beginning phrases provided in the chart or come up with your own.

Name _____ Date _____

"Life Without Gravity" by Robert Zimmerman
"Conversational Ballgames" by Nancy Masterson Sakamoto

Integrated Language Skills: Support for Extend Your Learning

Listening and Speaking: "Life Without Gravity"

Use a chart like this one to prepare an **oral summary** of "Life Without Gravity." First, summarize the four most important ideas in the article. Then, for each idea, write down supporting details and a quotation that illustrates the idea. Next, note a visual aid that you might use to illustrate the idea graphically. Finally, write a concluding statement.

Main Idea	Supporting Details	Quotations That Support Main Idea	Visual Aids That Illustrate Main Idea
1.			
2.			
3.			
4.			

Concluding statement expressing the main message: _____

_____

Listening and Speaking: "Conversational Ballgames"

Use a chart like this one to prepare an **oral summary** of "Conversational Ballgames." First, summarize the most important ideas in the article. Then, for each idea, write down supporting details and a quotation that illustrates the idea. Next, note a visual aid that you might use to illustrate the idea graphically. Finally, write a concluding statement.

Main Idea	Supporting Details	Quotations That Support Main Idea	Visual Aids That Illustrate Main Idea
1.			
2.			
3.			

Concluding statement expressing the main message: _____

_____

"Conversational Ballgames" by Nancy Masterson Sakamoto
Open-Book Test

Short Answer *Write your responses to the questions in this section on the lines provided.*

1. Toward the beginning of "Conversational Ballgames," author Nancy Masterson Sakamoto compares western conversations to tennis. In what two ways are western-style conversations and tennis similar?

   _____

   _____

   _____

2. In the middle of "Conversational Ballgames," the author states that Japanese-style conversations are "not at all like tennis or volleyball. It's like bowling." What two details in the paragraph with this statement support this main idea?

   _____

   _____

   _____

3. In the middle of "Conversational Ballgames," the author says that in Japanese conversations, all the conversational "balls run parallel." What does she mean by this? Base your answer on the meaning of *parallel*.

   _____

   _____

   _____

   _____

4. In the middle of "Conversational Ballgames," the author says she "was playing the wrong game" when she took part in Japanese conversation. What does she mean by this? Explain.

   _____

   _____

   _____

5. What custom do Japanese people and westerners agree about at the end of "Conversational Ballgames"? How does this custom affect dinner conversation?

   _____

   _____

   _____

   _____

6. In "Conversational Ballgames," the author gives details of two different conversational styles. Fill in this chart with two details about each type of conversation. Then, provide an appropriate title for your chart.

Japanese-style Conversation	Western-style Conversation

Title:_____

7. What kind of essay is "Conversational Ballgames"? Explain your answer.

_____

_____

_____

8. What two processes does "Conversational Ballgames" explain? Is the organization of the information in this essay comparison and contrast, or is it problem and solution? Explain your answer.

_____

_____

_____

9. An essay's title often reflects its main idea. What other title could describe "Conversational Ballgames"? Explain your answer.

_____

_____

_____

10. The author of "Conversational Ballgames" compares Japanese-style conversation to the game of bowling. How is this conversation like bowling? Do people take turns speaking? Do people interrupt each other?

_____

_____

_____

_____

Essay

Write an extended response to the question of your choice or to the question or questions your teacher assigns you.

11. In an essay, describe an advantage and a disadvantage of one of the styles of conversation described in "Conversational Ballgames." First, briefly describe the conversational style. Then, explain one advantage and one disadvantage. Use examples from the selection to support your points.

12. Most Americans are used to the western style of conversation described in "Conversational Ballgames." Imagine a conversation in the Japanese style. How would that conversation be different from the conversations you are used to? In an essay, describe what would be different about the Japanese-style conversation. Cite details from Sakamoto's essay to support your points.

13. Toward the end of "Conversational Ballgames," Nancy Masterson Sakamoto says it is no easier for her to "just listen" during a conversation than it is for her Japanese students to "just relax" when speaking with foreigners. What does she mean by this? How does the statement reflect the subject of her essay? In an essay of your own, explain the statement and the author's meaning. Support your explanation with details from the essay.

14. **Thinking About the Big Question: What should we learn?** In discussing the differences in two conversational styles in "Conversational Ballgames," Nancy Masterson Sakamoto teaches readers about cultural differences. In an essay, explain what the author wants us to learn about the differences between Japanese and western conversational styles. Why is this information important? Use details from the essay to support your points.

Oral Response

15. Go back to question 2, 4, or 5 or to the question your teacher assigns you. Take a few minutes to expand your answer and prepare an oral response. Find additional details in "Conversational Ballgames" that support your points. If necessary, make notes to guide your oral response.

"Conversational Ballgames" by Nancy Masterson Sakamoto
Selection Test A

Critical Reading *Identify the letter of the choice that best answers the question.*

____ 1. According to "Conversational Ballgames," what happened when the author tried to take part in Japanese conversations?

    A. An argument would begin.

    B. Everyone would become angry.

    C. The conversation would stop.

    D. People would ignore her.

____ 2. To what does Sakamoto compare western-style conversation?

    A. basketball

    B. bowling

    C. tennis

    D. Ping-Pong

____ 3. What is the topic sentence of this paragraph from "Conversational Ballgames"?

    If there are more than two people in the conversation, then it is like doubles in tennis, or like volleyball. There's no waiting in line. Whoever is nearest and quickest hits the ball, and if you step back, someone else will hit it. No one stops the game to give you a turn. You're responsible for taking your own turn.

    A. If there are more than two people . . . , then it is like doubles in tennis, or like volleyball.

    B. Whoever is . . . quickest hits the ball, and if you step back, someone else will hit it.

    C. No one stops the game to give you a turn.

    D. You're responsible for taking your own turn.

____ 4. Which detail in "Conversational Ballgames" supports the main idea that Japanese-style conversations are "not at all like tennis or volleyball"?

    A. You can never argue in Japanese-style conversations.

    B. You must wait your turn in Japanese-style conversations.

    C. You may disagree in Japanese-style conversations.

    D. You may interrupt in Japanese-style conversations.

____ 5. According to "Conversational Ballgames," why is a Japanese-style conversation like a game of bowling?

    A. Each person speaks in turn, just as players take turns in a game of bowling.

    B. People form conversational leagues that are much like bowling leagues.

    C. Each person tries to better his or her last score, just as bowlers do.

    D. People stand up when they speak, just as players stand to bowl.

___ 6. According to "Conversational Ballgames," why do Japanese students have trouble speaking English?

A. They use the Japanese style of conversation.

B. They do not know enough English words.

C. They speak English too quietly.

D. They have strong accents.

___ 7. According to "Conversational Ballgames," how is Japanese-style dinner conversation different from western-style dinner conversation?

A. In the Japanese style, people talk constantly throughout the meal.

B. In the Japanese style, people eat alone or with one other person.

C. In the Japanese style, people do not engage in long conversations.

D. In the Japanese style, people talk only during the dessert course.

___ 8. According to "Conversational Ballgames," on what point do Japanese speakers and western-style speakers agree?

A. It is rude to talk with the mouth full.

B. It is rude to argue with strangers.

C. It is rude to take turns speaking.

D. It is rude to speak quickly or loudly.

___ 9. According to "Conversational Ballgames," how do westerners carry on a conversation at a meal?

A. They eat slowly.

B. They eat while others talk.

C. They interrupt one another.

D. They talk with their mouths full.

___ 10. Which of the following statements about "Conversational Ballgames" explains why it is considered an expository essay?

A. It is a short work of nonfiction that persuades readers to appreciate Japanese culture.

B. It is a short work of nonfiction that offers the author's opinion of Japanese conversation.

C. It is a short work of nonfiction that exposes the secrets of Japanese style of conversation.

D. It is a short work of nonfiction that explains Japanese and western styles of conversation.

Vocabulary and Grammar

____ 11. How might members of an audience respond to a speaker who is *murmuring*?
A. They might ask him or her to speak loudly and clearly.
B. They might agree with his or her complaints.
C. They might be frightened by his or her threats.
D. The might be satisfied with the sound of his or her voice.

____ 12. Which item is *indispensable* for survival?
A. television
B. water
C. computers
D. roads

____ 13. Which of the following sentences contains a conjunction?
A. We were unconsciously playing entirely different conversational ballgames.
B. Whether you agree or disagree, your response will return the ball to me.
C. I don't serve a new ball from my original starting line.
D. There is no rush, no excitement, no scramble for the ball.

____ 14. How many conjunctions are there in this sentence?
And the more vigorous the action, the more interesting and exciting the game.
A. 0   B. 1   C. 2   D. 3

Essay

15. In an essay, describe an advantage and a disadvantage of one of the styles of conversation described in "Conversational Ballgames." First, briefly describe the conversational style. Then, explain one advantage and one disadvantage. Use examples from the selection to support your points.

16. In an essay, describe what makes "Conversational Ballgames" an expository essay. What is the author's purpose? Is she explaining, defining, or interpreting something? Explain your response by referring to the selection.

17. **Thinking About the Big Question: What should we learn?** In an essay, explain what Nancy Masterson Sakamoto wants us to learn about the differences between Japanese and western conversational styles in "Conversational Ballgames." Why is this information important? Use details from the essay to support your points.

"Conversational Ballgames" by Nancy Masterson Sakamoto
Selection Test B

Critical Reading *Identify the letter of the choice that best completes the statement or answers the question.*

___ 1. According to "Conversational Ballgames," what happened when the author tried to take part in conversations in Japanese?
A. An argument would break out.
B. Everyone would smile politely.
C. The conversation would stop.
D. People would glare at her.

___ 2. Why did the author of "Conversational Ballgames" have difficulty conversing in Japanese?
A. She made many grammatical errors.
B. She used a foreign conversational style.
C. Women are not expected to speak when men are present.
D. Her accent made her speech very difficult to understand.

___ 3. The author of "Conversational Ballgames" compares western-style conversation to
A. basketball and soccer.
B. bowling and pool.
C. tennis and volleyball.
D. tennis and Ping-Pong.

___ 4. A Japanese-style conversation is compared to a game of bowling because
A. people scramble to talk as if they were scrambling to take a turn in a game of bowling.
B. each person speaks in turn, just as people take turns in a game of bowling.
C. each person tosses off an idea as if they were players on a bowling league.
D. people speak softly, as if they were spectators at a bowling alley.

___ 5. What is the topic sentence of this paragraph from "Conversational Ballgames"?
No wonder everyone looked startled when I took part in Japanese conversations. I paid no attention to whose turn it was, and kept snatching the ball halfway down the alley and throwing it back at the bowler. Of course the conversation died. I was playing the wrong game.

A. No wonder everyone looked startled when I took part in Japanese conversations.
B. I paid no attention . . . and kept snatching the ball . . . throwing it back at the bowler.
C. Of course the conversation died.
D. I was playing the wrong game.

___ 6. According to "Conversational Ballgames," Japanese students have trouble speaking English because they
A. continue to use the Japanese style of conversation.
B. are unable to speak with an American accent.
C. are unable to master difficult sentence structures.
D. do not know enough words to make themselves understood.

____ 7. According to "Conversational Ballgames," what is one way in which Japanese-style dinner conversation is different from western-style dinner conversation?
A. In Japan, people take turns talking at meals, just as they do at other times.
B. In Japan, people sit at long tables and talk only to the person sitting next to them.
C. In Japan, people do not engage in long conversations while they are eating.
D. In Japan, people talk only after the main course, when they are having dessert.

____ 8. According to "Conversational Ballgames," Japanese and westerners agree that
A. it is rude to talk with your mouth full.
B. it is important to discuss differences.
C. it is rude to speak out of turn.
D. it is important to be understood.

____ 9. The author of "Conversational Ballgames" says that westerners can speak and eat at the same time because
A. they eat exceptionally slowly.
B. they pause to let others respond.
C. they interrupt one another.
D. they talk with their mouths full.

____ 10. Which statement explains why "Conversational Ballgames" is an expository essay?
A. It is a short work of nonfiction that exposes the strategies of conversational styles.
B. It is a short work of nonfiction that describes the author's experiences in Japan.
C. It is a short work of nonfiction that expresses the author's opinion of Japanese culture.
D. It is a short work of nonfiction that explains Japanese and western styles of conversation.

____ 11. Which title best describes "Conversational Ballgames"?
A. "Playing Games in a New Country"
B. "How to Play Tennis"
C. "Japanese Conversations"
D. "Styles of Conversation"

Vocabulary and Grammar

____ 12. Two roads run *parallel* when they
A. extend in opposite directions and never meet.
B. curve outward, away from each other, forming perfect arcs.
C. extend in the same direction at the same distance apart, never meeting.
D. intersect at right angles and then continue in straight lines, never meeting again.

____ 13. In which sentence is the word *elaboration* used correctly?
A. The speaker used elaboration to be sure her voice would be heard in the auditorium.
B. The speaker's elaboration of the difficult concept made it understandable to everyone.
C. The elaboration between the two scientists helped them solve the mystery.
D. The audience's elaboration of the speaker was obvious from the applause.

____ 14. Which of these statements from "Conversational Ballgames" contains a conjunction?
   A. I realized that just as I kept trying to hold western-style conversations . . . , so my English students kept trying to hold Japanese-style conversations.
   B. Then, after everyone is sure that you have completely finished your turn, the next person in line steps up to the same starting line, with a different ball.
   C. It is no easier for me to "just listen" during a conversation than it is for my Japanese students to "just relax" when speaking with foreigners.
   D. If I have not yet learned to do conversational bowling in Japanese, at least I have figured out one thing that puzzled me for a long time.

____ 15. Which sentence from "Conversational Ballgames" contains three conjunctions?
   A. I carry your idea further, or answer your questions or objections, or challenge or question you.
   B. Of course, if one of us gets angry, it spoils the conversation, just as it spoils a tennis game.
   C. Whoever is nearest and quickest hits the ball, and if you step back, someone else will hit it.
   D. Everyone waits until the ball has reached the end of the alley, and watches to see if it knocks down all the pins, or only some of them, or none of them.

____ 16. Which word in this quotation from "Conversational Ballgames" is a conjunction?
   Since westerners think that conversation is an indispensable part of dining, and indeed would consider it impolite not to converse with one's dinner partner, I found this Japanese custom rather strange.

   A. an
   B. and
   C. indeed
   D. to

Essay

17. Most Americans are used to the western style of conversation described by Nancy Masterson Sakamoto in "Conversational Ballgames." Imagine a conversation in the Japanese style. How would that conversation be different from the conversations you are used to? In an essay, describe what would be different about the Japanese-style conversation. Cite details from Sakamoto's essay to support your points.

18. In "Conversational Ballgames," Nancy Masterson Sakamoto says,
   It is no easier for me to "just listen" during a conversation than it is for my Japanese students to "just relax" when speaking with foreigners.

   What does she mean by that? How does the statement reflect the subject of her essay? In an essay of your own, explain the statement and the author's meaning. Support your explanation with details from the selection.

19. **Thinking About the Big Question: What should we learn?** In discussing the differences in two conversational styles in "Conversational Ballgames," Nancy Masterson Sakamoto teaches readers about cultural differences. In an essay, explain what the author wants us to learn about the differences between Japanese and western conversational styles. Why is this information important? Use details from the essay to support your points.

Vocabulary Warm-up Word Lists

Study these words. Then, complete the activities that follow.

Word List A

abuses [uh BYOOZ iz] *v.* uses wrongly or mistreats
　　It is not fair to other people when someone <u>abuses</u> the honor system.

creation [kree AY shuhn] *n.* the universe and everything in it
　　One sunny morning, Dee looked around and marveled at all <u>creation</u>.

creative [kree AY tiv] *adj.* able to create
　　Kate felt <u>creative</u> when she sat down to play the piano.

presence [PREZ uhns] *n.* the act of existing or being present
　　Ricky's enthusiastic <u>presence</u> always brightened up a meeting.

privacy [PRY vuh see] *n.* the condition of being private or withdrawn from public view
　　Jenna loved the <u>privacy</u> of her garden, with its high shrubs.

shameful [SHAYM fuhl] *adj.* bringing or causing disgrace
　　Don felt that it was <u>shameful</u> not to honor his elders.

values [VAL yooz] *n.* the social principles that people live by and hold to be important
　　One of our most important <u>values</u> is honesty.

worthy [WER thee] *adj.* having value or merit or meriting something
　　The poem was <u>worthy</u> of publication.

Word List B

blotting [BLAHT ing] *v.* erasing or getting rid of
　　The new office building is <u>blotting</u> out our view of the river.

companionship [kuhm PAN yuhn ship] *n.* the state of having the company of others
　　The twins enjoyed each other's <u>companionship</u>.

distrust [dis TRUHST] *n.* a lack of confidence in
　　When people cannot be relied on, there is <u>distrust</u>.

genuine [JEN yoo in] *adj.* real, true, or authentic
　　Her feelings of concern for Debra are <u>genuine</u>.

promote [pruh MOHT] *v.* to help to bring about
　　Brushing you teeth will <u>promote</u> better dental health.

reassuring [ree uh SHOOR ing] *adj.* assuring again
　　Seeing her friend's <u>reassuring</u> smile made Marie feel less nervous.

sufferings [SUHF uhr ingz] *n.* pains or distresses
　　Poverty had brought many <u>sufferings</u> to the family.

welfare [WEL fer] *n.* programs concerned with giving aid to those in need
　　Is it society's responsibility to provide <u>welfare</u> to those in need?

Name _____ Date _____

Exercise A *Fill in each blank in the paragraph below with an appropriate word from Word List A. Use each word only once.*

Cindy and her friend Bob enjoy their history class. That is because of the

[1] _____ of their teacher, Mr. Ross. Mr. Ross teaches history in an

inspiring and [2] _____ way. He teaches about the past, but he also

teaches about the present, about the [3] _____ of today's society.

There is always plenty of discussion. For example, the class talked about how,

in all [4] _____, saving the environment is one of the most

[5] _____ causes. Many students believe that if someone

[6] _____ the environment by polluting it, he or she is doing a

[7] _____ thing. Another interesting discussion concerned people's right

to [8]_____. Many students believe that some things are personal and it

is important in a free society to keep them that way.

Exercise B *Find a synonym for each word in the following vocabulary list. Then, use each synonym in a sentence that makes its meaning clear. Refer to a thesaurus if you need help.*

1. blotting   **Synonym:** _____

   _____

2. companionship   **Synonym:** _____

   _____

3. distrust   **Synonym:** _____

   _____

4. genuine   **Synonym:** _____

   _____

5. promote   **Synonym:** _____

   _____

6. reassuring   **Synonym:** _____

   _____

7. sufferings   **Synonym:** _____

   _____

8. welfare   **Synonym:** _____

   _____

"I Am a Native of North America" by Chief Dan George
Reading Warm-up A

Read the following passage. Pay special attention to the underlined words. Then, read it again, and complete the activities. Use a separate sheet of paper for your written answers.

One day the seventh graders were asked to write about their heroes. There were many excited whispers as the students discussed whom they would choose. Some chose athletes; others chose actors. Some thought historic leaders were <u>worthy</u> heroes. Alan thought long and hard about who, in all <u>creation</u>, was his biggest hero. Who had taught him important principles and ideals? Suddenly, Alan knew the answer, and he wrote this essay:

"My hero is not famous. He is my uncle Brian, who came to live with my family when I was nine years old. At the time, I did not welcome his <u>presence</u> because his arrival meant that I would have to share a bedroom with my brother. It meant that I would have less <u>privacy</u>. I protested, but my parents told me that Uncle Brian needed our help. They asked me to give him a chance.

"At first, I avoided spending time with Uncle Brian, and sometimes I was rude to him. That did not stop him from being interested in me, though. He always asked me if I needed help with homework. One day as I struggled with a math problem, I accepted his help, and we solved the problem together. Uncle Brian did not just help me. I noticed that he always helped carry in groceries and did yard work. I started to realize how <u>shameful</u> and unhelpful my attitude toward him had been.

"One thing about Uncle Brian was that he spent part of his time in the cellar. I heard him hammering and sawing away. At last, I went downstairs to see what he was doing. He showed me the beautiful kitchen table he was building for us. I had not known that he was a <u>creative</u> woodworker. I asked him if I could help, and he said yes.

"I learned important <u>values</u> from my uncle, like how to get along with and respect others. I discovered that when someone <u>abuses</u> another person, it does not feel good. When people work together, however, it feels great! Thank you, Uncle Brian, for these gifts."

1. Circle the word that <u>worthy</u> describes. What does *worthy* mean?

2. Rewrite the sentence that contains <u>creation</u>, using a synonym for the word. In all *creation*, who is your biggest hero?

3. Underline the words that explain why Alan did not welcome his uncle's <u>presence</u>. Use *presence* in a sentence.

4. Circle the words that tell to whom Alan protested about having less <u>privacy</u>. What is *privacy*?

5. Underline the words that tell what Alan realized was <u>shameful</u>. What is an antonym of *shameful*?

6. Underline the sentence that tells why Alan thinks his uncle is a <u>creative</u> woodworker. What other sorts of things might be considered *creative*?

7. Underline the words that explain the <u>values</u> that Alan learned from Uncle Brian. What are *values*?

8. Underline the words that tell how someone feels if he or she <u>abuses</u> another person. Define *abuses*.

"I Am a Native of North America" by Chief Dan George
Reading Warm-up B

Read the following passage. Pay special attention to the underlined words. Then, read it again, and complete the activities. Use a separate sheet of paper for your written answers.

Vancouver's First Nations are the tribes of Native Americans who lived in what is now part of British Columbia, in Canada. The arrival of European explorers affected them, <u>blotting</u> out many of their customs. The <u>sufferings</u> of the Native Americans included dying from diseases brought by the explorers from Europe. They also included the settlers' attempt to change or do away with the Native Americans' culture. It is <u>reassuring</u> to know, however, that much of their culture has been kept alive by the Native Americans who still live in this region.

The memories of the Native Americans' culture have been handed down from generation to generation by oral tradition. *Oral tradition* means "word of mouth." Many of these stories concern nature. They explain the origins of the land and those who live on it. Supernatural animals and beings are characters in those stories. The stories <u>promote</u> the idea that the land and its bounty are gifts to be used wisely.

Another strong value among the First Nations is the importance of <u>companionship</u>. During the winter months, the people lived off the food they had prepared and preserved in other seasons. Wintertime gave them time to socialize and gather for ceremonies. Generosity was also valued. Food was provided to anyone who needed it. That custom formed a system of tribal <u>welfare</u>.

When Europeans landed on the shores of Vancouver, some Native Americans warned of the dangers brought by the new settlers. Unfortunately, their feelings of <u>distrust</u> proved to be correct. Nevertheless, some Native Americans were friendly to the explorers and settlers. One explorer wrote of the <u>genuine</u> openness of the Native Americans and how he was charmed by their liveliness.

Today's descendants of the First Nations play an important part in Vancouver's culture. Their efforts to keep their people's culture alive enable everyone to appreciate the area's past and present.

1. Underline the words that tell who caused the <u>blotting</u> out of Native American customs. What does *blotting* mean?

2. Circle the words that tell more about the <u>sufferings</u> of the Native Americans. Use *sufferings* in a sentence.

3. Circle the words that tell what is <u>reassuring</u> to know. What else might feel *reassuring*?

4. Underline the words that tell what the stories <u>promote</u>. Define *promote*.

5. During which season did the Native Americans enjoy <u>companionship</u>? When else might someone enjoy the *companionship* of others?

6. Why was the giving of food to visitors and those who needed it a form of <u>welfare</u>? Define *welfare*.

7. Underline the sentence that tells more about the feelings of <u>distrust</u> that some Native Americans had. What is *distrust*?

8. Circle the word that <u>genuine</u> describes. What is an antonym of *genuine*?

Name _____ Date _____

"**I Am a Native of North America**" by Chief Dan George
Writing About the Big Question

 What should we learn?

Big Question Vocabulary

analyze	curiosity	discover	evaluate	examine
experiment	explore	facts	information	inquire
interview	investigate	knowledge	question	understand

A. *Choose one word from the list above to fill the blanks in the sentences below. There may be more than one right answer.*

1. Many Americans wish to _____ Native American culture.

2. Like many Americans, Chief George has _____ of two cultures.

3. If you could _____ Chief George, what _____ would you ask him?

B. *Follow the directions in responding to each of the items below.*

1. List two different times that you learned something new about your own country. Write your response in complete sentences.

   _____

   _____

2. Choose one of the experiences you listed in number 1. Write two sentences describing that experience. Use at least two of the Big Question vocabulary words. You may use the words in different forms (for example you can change *analyze* to *analyzing*).

   _____

   _____

C. *Complete the sentence below. Use the completed sentence as the beginning of a short paragraph in which you discuss the big question.*

   In order for people to live together in a society, they must _____

   _____

   _____

"I Am a Native of North America" by Chief Dan George
Reading: Make Connections Between Key Points and Supporting Details to Understand the Main Idea

The **main idea** is the most important thought or concept in a work or a passage of text. Sometimes the author directly states the main idea of a work and then provides key points that support it. These key points are supported in turn by details such as examples and descriptions. Other times the main idea is unstated. The author gives you *only* the key points or supporting details that add up to a main idea. To understand the main idea, **make connections between key points and supporting details.** Notice how the writer groups details. Look for sentences that pull details together.

In this passage from "I Am a Native of North America," Chief George states key points and provides details that support the main idea of the essay:

> I am afraid my culture has little to offer yours. But my culture did prize friendship and companionship. It did not look on privacy as a thing to be clung to, for privacy builds up walls and walls promote distrust. My culture lived in big family communities, and from infancy people learned to live with others.

DIRECTIONS: *Write the main idea of Chief George's essay on the line below. Then, read each passage, and write its key point and the details that support it.*

Main idea: _____

And beyond this acceptance of one another there was a deep respect for everything in nature that surrounded them. My father loved the earth and all its creatures. The earth was his second mother. The earth and everything it contained was a gift from See-see-am . . . and the way to thank this great spirit was to use his gifts with respect.

1. **Key point:** _____

2. **Details:** _____

_____

Love is something you and I must have. We must have it because our spirit feeds upon it. We must have it because without it we become weak and faint. Without love our self-esteem weakens. Without it our courage fails. Without love we can no longer look out confidently at the world. Instead we turn inwardly and begin to feed upon our own personalities and little by little we destroy ourselves.

3. **Key point:** _____

4. **Details:** _____

_____

"I Am a Native of North America" by Chief Dan George
Literary Analysis: Reflective Essay

A **reflective essay** is a brief prose work that presents a writer's feelings and thoughts, or reflections, about an experience or idea. The purpose is to communicate these thoughts and feelings so that readers will respond with thoughts and feelings of their own. As you read a reflective essay, think about the ideas the writer is sharing. Think about whether your responses to the experience or idea are similar to or different from the writer's.

In this passage from "I Am a Native of North America," Chief George reflects on life in apartment buildings:

> I see people living in smoke houses hundreds of times bigger than the one I knew. But the people in one apartment do not even know the people in the next and care less about them.

Chief George thinks about how neighbors do not know one another and concludes that they do not care about one another.

A. DIRECTIONS: *In the second column of the chart, summarize Chief George's thoughts about each experience described in the first column. Then, in the third column, write your response. That is, describe your own thoughts on the subject.*

Experience	Author's Thoughts	My Thoughts
1. Chief George describes his grandfather's smoke house.		
2. Chief George's father finds him killing fish "for the fun of it."		
3. Chief George sees his culture disappearing.		

B. DIRECTIONS: *Write the first paragraph of a reflective essay of your own. Include a description of an experience and your thoughts about it. Write on one of these topics:*

- the role of nature in your life
- the importance of tradition in your life
- the meaning of family in your life

_____

_____

_____

_____

_____

"I Am a Native of North America" by Chief Dan George
Vocabulary Builder

Word List

communal   distinct   hoarding   integration   justifies   promote

A. DIRECTIONS: *Use the italicized word in each sentence in a sentence of your own.*

1. Chief George seeks to *promote* a greater understanding of Native American culture.

   _____

2. Chief George suggests that *communal* living teaches people to respect one another.

   _____

3. A critical situation sometimes *justifies* a drastic solution.

   _____

4. Social scientists can identify many *distinct* cultures in North America.

   _____

5. Native American culture does not prize the *hoarding* of private possessions.

   _____

6. Many peoples see *integration* into American culture as inevitable.

   _____

B. WORD STUDY: *The Latin root* -just *means "law" or "right." Read the following sentences. Use your knowledge of the Latin root* -just *to write a full sentence to answer each question.*

1. If a decision is *unjust*, is it fair?

   _____

2. If there is no *justification* for your mistake, are you free from blame?

   _____

3. Is a *justifiable* complaint one that should be taken seriously?

   _____

Name _____ Date _____

"I Am a Native of North America" by Chief Dan George
Enrichment: Promoting a Message

In his support of many Native American causes, Chief Dan George typically chose to express himself in poetic—rather than fiery—language. How might Chief George's message in "I Am a Native of North America" be translated into a different medium—say, television?

DIRECTIONS: *Imagine that you have been hired to translate the message of "I Am a Native of North America" into a thirty-second television commercial. Complete the following items in preparation for your work.*

Message: This message may not be the only words you write for your commercial, but it is the main idea. It must be conveyed in thirty seconds, so make it brief and memorable. Write it here:

_____

_____

Target audience: What age group do you wish to reach? Do you wish to narrow down your audience even further? Select one group or a combination of groups, and explain why you want to reach this group or groups:

_____

_____

Sound and style: Will you use a speaker? If so, will he or she be onscreen, or will you use a voiceover? Will you use a music soundtrack? If so, what music will you use? What images will you show?

_____

_____

_____

Other content: What besides the main message do you wish to say? How will you convey your information? Will writing appear on the screen, or will everything be spoken? (You should at least credit yourself as the sponsor of the message.) Write out the rest of the text for your commercial. If you'd like, describe the typefaces you will use for any text that appears on the screen.

_____

_____

_____

_____

_____

_____

_____

"I Am a Native of North America" by Chief Dan George
Open-Book Test

Short Answer *Write your responses to the questions in this section on the lines provided.*

1. In the first two paragraphs of "I Am a Native of North America," Chief Dan George talks about his early life and his people. He makes two main points. What are they?

   a. _____

   b. _____

2. In the beginning of "I Am a Native of North America," the author reflects on communal living. What three values does he believe communal living teaches people?

   _____

   _____

   _____

3. In "I Am a Native of North America," Chief Dan George's father was very disappointed when he saw his son gaffing for fish "just for the fun of it." What main idea does the father's disappointment support? Explain.

   _____

   _____

   _____

4. In the middle of "I Am a Native of North America," Chief Dan George writes that he sees people living in large "smoke houses" with people in apartments next to each other. What observation does the author make about the relationship of these neighbors?

   _____

   _____

   _____

5. Chief Dan George reflects on wars in America's past. What conclusion does he draw about this in the middle of "I Am a Native of North America"?

   _____

   _____

6. In the middle of "I Am a Native of North America," Chief Dan George writes that it is difficult for him to understand a culture that attacks nature. Do you think Chief Dan George believes people can change their ways? Why or why not?

   _____

   _____

   _____

7. Chief Dan George reflects on privacy toward the end of "I Am a Native of North America." How does he view privacy? What does he believe privacy leads to?

_____

_____

8. Chief George believes there are major differences between white culture and Native American culture. In the chart below, list two ways from "I Am a Native of North America" in which white culture and Native American culture are different. Then, answer the question that follows the chart.

White Culture	Indian Culture

What does Chief Dan George say is the only thing that can help both cultures?

_____

9. The main idea is the most important idea in a piece of writing. What is the main idea of "I Am a Native of North America"?

_____

_____

10. In "I Am a Native of North America," Chief Dan George writes about the distinct cultures he has lived in. What is a distinct culture? Base your answer on the meaning of *distinct*.

_____

Essay

Write an extended response to the question of your choice or to the question or questions your teacher assigns you.

11. According to "I Am a Native of North America," Chief Dan George learned important lessons in his childhood. In an essay, describe one of his childhood experiences. Then, explain the understanding of the world that Chief Dan George learned from the experience.

12. In "I Am a Native of North America," Chief Dan George talks about two major criticisms of white culture. In an essay, explain those criticisms. What problems does he see in the world today? What solutions does he offer? Use details from the essay to support your explanation.

13. In "I Am a Native of North America," Chief George expresses his views of community. In an essay, describe his views. What kind of community does he suggest is best, and why? What problems does he see in today's communities?

14. **Thinking About the Big Question: What should we learn?** Chief Dan George thinks that one of the most important things for humans to learn is how to love. In an essay, analyze Chief George's definition of love. Why does he think it is important to learn to love?

Oral Response

15. Go back to question 6, 7, or 8 or to the question your teacher assigns you. Take a few minutes to expand your answer and prepare an oral response. Find additional details in "I Am a Native of North America" that support your points. If necessary, make notes to guide your oral response.

Name _____ Date _____

Critical Reading *Identify the letter of the choice that best answers the question.*

____ 1. What did communal living teach Chief George's father?
    A. to find privacy while living with others
    B. to be quiet in noisy surroundings
    C. to love others and feel at home with them
    D. to make peace with fighting neighbors

____ 2. How does Chief George's father feel when he sees his son gaffing for fish?
    A. proud
    B. disappointed
    C. furious
    D. amused

____ 3. From his father, Chief George learns how people should treat nature. What does he learn?
    A. to treat nature with respect
    B. to treat nature with caution
    C. to treat nature with fear
    D. to treat nature with bravery

____ 4. Why does Chief George have trouble accepting the way he sees people living today?
    A. They live in houses that are far too big for them.
    B. They do not know or care about their neighbors.
    C. They do not live close to nature anymore.
    D. They prefer to live in big cities and suburbs.

____ 5. What does Chief George think of communal living?
    A. He believes it is old-fashioned.
    B. He believes it is no longer necessary.
    C. He believes it teaches companionship and love.
    D. He believes it promotes hoarding and secretiveness.

____ 6. What are Chief George's thoughts about the wars in America's past?
    A. He thinks they were regrettable but necessary.
    B. He believes they will be the downfall of the culture.
    C. He does not understand a culture that justifies them.
    D. He fears their effects on Native Americans.

____ 7. According to Chief George, why do white people harm the environment?

    A. They are selfish and greedy.

    B. They have not learned to love nature.

    C. They hate and fear nature.

    D. They do not know they are harming it.

____ 8. What does Chief George see as a major difference between white culture and Indian culture?

    A. White people do not love the things outside them.

    B. White people do not live with their families.

    C. White people do not have long-standing traditions.

    D. White people do not hoard private possessions.

____ 9. Which of these quotations from "I Am a Native of North America" supports the main idea that everyone must have love?

    A. "Already many of our young people have forgotten the old ways."

    B. "Everyone likes to give as well as receive."

    C. "The earth was his second mother."

    D. "Without it our courage fails."

____ 10. According to Chief George, why is privacy harmful?

    A. It leads to distrust.

    B. It leads to jealousy.

    C. It destroys the ability to feel love.

    D. It destroys close-knit communities.

____ 11. Which quotation from "I Am a Native of North America" supports the main idea that Indian culture is dying?

    A. "I wish you had taken something from our culture."

    B. "You and I need the strength and joy that comes from knowing that we are loved."

    C. "And many have been shamed of their Indian ways by scorn and ridicule."

    D. "I am afraid my culture has little to offer yours."

____ 12. What is the main idea of "I Am a Native of North America"?

    A. We must learn to treat the environment with respect.

    B. We must keep Indian culture from disappearing.

    C. We must learn to love each other and all of creation.

    D. We must all live together in order to find peace.

Vocabulary and Grammar

____ 13. What might you say about something that is *distinct*?
A. It is difficult to see at night.
B. It is found only in a certain place.
C. It is far away.
D. It is unlike anything else.

____ 14. What might someone do to *promote* a cause?
A. keep it small
B. criticize it
C. advertise it
D. keep it secret

____ 15. Which of these sentences about "I Am a Native of North America" contains a prepositional phrase?
A. Chief George admired his father a great deal.
B. Chief George believes people are becoming too isolated.
C. Chief George believes his culture is in danger.
D. Chief George learned to love and respect nature.

Essay

16. In the opening paragraphs of his essay, Chief Dan George makes two major points about his culture and how he grew up. What are they? In an essay, summarize those two main ideas, and cite two details that he uses to support each idea.

17. According to "I Am a Native of North America," Chief Dan George learned important lessons in his childhood. In an essay, describe one childhood experience that contributed to Chief George's understanding of the world as an adult. Cite examples from the selection to support your argument.

18. **Thinking About the Big Question: What should we learn?** Chief Dan George thinks that one of the most important things for humans to learn is how to love. In an essay, explain what Chief George means by *love*. Why does he think it is important to learn to love?

"I Am a Native of North America" by Chief Dan George
Selection Test B

Critical Reading *Identify the letter of the choice that best completes the statement or answers the question.*

_____ 1. From communal living, Chief George's father learned
A. how to enjoy privacy while living with others.
B. how to enjoy quiet in distracting surroundings.
C. how to love others and feel comfortable with them.
D. how to promote peace in a diverse community.

_____ 2. The author reflects on communal living to show that
A. it can lead to isolation and distrust.
B. it can stop conflict and war.
C. it can foster love and acceptance.
D. it can conquer loneliness.

_____ 3. What main idea does this quotation from "I Am a Native of North America" support?
And I shall never forget his disappointment when once he caught me gaffing for fish "just for the fun of it."
A. It is cruel to kill animals.
B. It is cruel to gaff for fish.
C. We must not hunt with hatred in our hearts.
D. We must show respect for all living things.

_____ 4. When Chief George was a boy, how did his father explain that he should not kill fish for fun?
A. He says that there would be no fish left if everyone killed them for fun.
B. He says that the Great Spirit would be angry if the boy killed the fish.
C. He says that the Great Spirit wants the boy to love all creatures.
D. He says that the fish are his brothers and feed him when he is hungry.

_____ 5. Chief George has trouble accepting the way he sees people living today because
A. they live in houses that are far too big and isolating.
B. they no longer know or care about their neighbors.
C. they live in cities and are not close to nature.
D. they no longer live with their families.

_____ 6. Chief George reflects on wars in America's past and concludes that
A. they were regrettable but sometimes necessary.
B. they will be the downfall of the culture.
C. he cannot understand a culture that justifies them.
D. he cannot imagine their effect on Indian culture.

_____ 7. Chief George believes that people harm the environment because
A. they are greedy and do not think of the future.
B. they have not learned to love nature.
C. they fear the power of nature.
D. they are ignorant of the rules of nature.

____ **8.** In comparing white culture and Indian culture, Chief George finds that
   A. white people do not love what is not their own.
   B. white people do not live with their families.
   C. white people do not have long-standing traditions.
   D. white people do not hoard private possessions.

____ **9.** In what ways does Chief George think humans are different from animals?
   A. They have the capacity to love.
   B. They hunt animals and eat meat.
   C. They are capable of making war.
   D. They live in large family groups.

____ **10.** What main idea does this quotation from "I Am a Native of North America" support?
   Without it [love] our courage fails.

   A. Everyone needs to feel love.
   B. Everyone must respect the earth.
   C. People must not make war.
   D. People must learn to live together.

____ **11.** Chief George believes privacy can be harmful because
   A. it leads to distrust.
   B. it promotes envy.
   C. it destroys the ability to feel love.
   D. it destroys close-knit communities.

____ **12.** What main idea does this quotation from "I Am a Native of North America" support?
   And many have been shamed of their Indian ways by scorn and ridicule.

   A. American Indian culture has little to offer white culture.
   B. American Indians can no longer love the natural world.
   C. The American Indian culture is dying out.
   D. Whites and Indians will never get along.

____ **13.** Which statement reveals one of Chief George's main points in "I Am a Native of North America"?
   A. All my grandfather's sons and their families lived in this large dwelling.
   B. It was called a smoke house, and it stood down by the beach along the inlet.
   C. It is also difficult for me to understand the deep hate that exists among people.
   D. My white brother does many things well for he is more clever than my people.

____ **14.** What makes "I Am a Native of North America" a reflective essay?
   A. The author shares his ideas about living in two cultures.
   B. The author reveals how the white culture harms the earth.
   C. The author expresses the importance of living communally.
   D. The author ends the piece with the words "I have spoken."

Vocabulary and Grammar

___ 15. Chief George speaks highly of *communal* living because
    A. it is quiet and peaceful.
    B. it is shared by everyone.
    C. it is far from the cities.
    D. it is private and secure.

___ 16. When someone *justifies* a behavior, he or she
    A. claims that it was a reasonable thing to do.
    B. claims that it was an important thing to do.
    C. punishes whoever was responsible for it.
    D. rewards whoever was responsible for it.

___ 17. Which words are prepositions in this sentence?

And I shall never forget his disappointment when once he caught me gaffing for fish "just for the fun of it."

    A. I, his, he, me
    B. for, for, of
    C. forget, caught, gaffing
    D. disappointment, fish, fun

___ 18. What are the prepositional phrases in this sentence from "I Am a Native of North America"?

It is the power to love that makes him the greatest of them all . . . for he alone of all animals is capable of love.

    A. to love, for he alone, of all animals
    B. of them all, of all animals, of love
    C. it is the power, that makes him
    D. the power, the greatest, all animals

Essay

19. In an essay, analyze Chief George's definition of love. How does his definition support an important point that he makes in "I Am a Native of North America"?

20. In "I Am a Native of North America," Chief Dan George talks about two major criticisms of white culture. In an essay, explain those criticisms. What problems does he see in the world today? What solutions does he offer? Use details from the essay to support your explanation.

21. In "I Am a Native of North America," Chief George expresses his views of community. In an essay, describe those views. What kind of community does he suggest is best? What problems does he see in today's communities?

22. **Thinking About the Big Question: What should we learn?** Chief Dan George thinks that one of the most important things for humans to learn is how to love. In an essay, analyze Chief George's definition of love. Why does he think it is important to learn to love?

Study these words from the selections. Then, complete the activities.

Word List A

clinging [KLING ing] *v.* holding on to tightly; sticking
> The kitten was <u>clinging</u> tightly to the tree, so it was hard to get her down.

dismal [DIZ muhl] *adj.* gloomy; drab; cheerless; depressing
> It was such a <u>dismal</u> day that we decided not to go for a walk after all.

ermine [UHR min] *n.* white fur with black tips; the winter coat of a small animal; a symbol of royalty or nobility
> The queen's cape was edged with <u>ermine</u>.

fantasy [FAN tuh see] *n.* an image or a dream created by the imagination
> He had a <u>fantasy</u> that he would one day play professional basketball.

interrupted [in tuh RUHP tid] *adj.* stopped; halted; broken up into parts
> The politician's speech was <u>interrupted</u> several times.

obsession [ahb SE shuhn] *n.* a thought, feeling, or interest that takes over the mind completely
> He developed such an <u>obsession</u> with video games that he never saw his friends.

patiently [PAY shuhnt lee] *adv.* without complaint
> She waited <u>patiently</u> while her friend tried on many pairs of shoes.

refuse [re FYOOS] *n.* trash; garbage; things thrown away or no longer wanted
> A lot of <u>refuse</u> spilled out of the dumpster and into the street.

Word List B

avid [AV id] *adj.* eager; enthusiastic
> She was an *avid* reader of true crime books.

consumer [kuhn SOOM uhr] *n.* a person who buys and uses things
> It is important to be an informed *consumer* and to gather information before you buy.

desire [di ZYUHR] *n.* something that you want or wish for
> Her greatest desire was to receive a puppy for her birthday.

discussing [dis KUS ing] *v.* talking about a subject with another person or other people
> My parents stayed up late at night <u>discussing</u> the possibility of moving to another city.

incongruous [in KAHN groo us] *adj.* out of place; looking as if it doesn't belong
> The new plastic furniture looked <u>incongruous</u> in the historic house.

inspired [in SPYURD] *v.* stimulated to do something; encouraged to greater effort
> He was so <u>inspired</u> by the candidate's speech that he decided to make a donation to her campaign.

recurring [ri KUHR ing] *adj.* happening over and over again; repeating
> She had a <u>recurring</u> nightmare in which she was being chased by a lion.

scattering [SKAT uhr ing] *v.* spreading around
> My little sister walked through the yard, <u>scattering</u> her toys all over the place.

Name _____ Date _____

"Volar: To Fly" by Judith Ortiz Cofer
Vocabulary Warm-up Exercises

Exercise A *Fill in the blanks, using each word from Word List A only once.*

When I was younger, my favorite activity was playing dress-up. I was an only child, so my stuffed animals were my playmates for this [1] _____. They would sit [2] _____ as I dressed them for their roles. My stuffed lion wore a cape of acrylic that looked like [3] _____, and he played the king. I, of course, was the queen. My other toys were our subjects, and they had to obey us. These make-believe activities helped me forget the dingy and [4] _____ apartment in which we lived. The stairs were often piled with [5] _____ that our neighbors left there. I hated it when my mother [6] _____ my play. I ate dinner quickly to return to my room. Soon, make-believe became an [7] _____. I wanted to do nothing else, [8] _____ to my role as a queen even when I was at school.

Exercise B *Decide whether each statement below is true or false. Explain your answers.*

1. He was an <u>avid</u> football fan, so he never missed a game.
   T/F _____

2. She walked into her room, <u>scattering</u> her books in a neat pile.
   T/F _____

3. They didn't like <u>discussing</u> things, so they talked for hours.
   T/F _____

4. The shiny plastic chairs looked <u>incongruous</u> with the old oak table inherited from her grandmother.
   T/F _____

5. <u>Recurring</u> fees are charged over and over again.
   T/F _____

6. She tries to be a good <u>consumer</u> by researching products before she buys.
   T/F _____

7. Her greatest <u>desire</u> was to see her granddaughter graduate from college.
   T/F _____

8. The author was so <u>inspired</u> by the response to his story that he never wrote another word.
   T/F _____

"Volar: To Fly" by Judith Ortiz Cofer
Reading Warm-up A

Read the following passage. Pay special attention to the underlined words. Then, read it again, and complete the activities. Use a separate sheet of paper for your written answers.

When I was young, my family moved to England for two years. I was four and my sister was two when we went. Of course, we were too young to have any say in the decision. We were so young that we were not yet in school, so our studies were not <u>interrupted</u>. On the way to London, we traveled <u>patiently</u> on the long plane ride, <u>clinging</u> to our parents when the plane ride got bumpy. My main memory of that trip is that we both got airsick.

Once we got there, I loved it! We lived near a huge park with a special space called an adventure playground. It had many wooden structures, tunnels, ropes, and bridges for kids to climb on. This was the perfect place to enact my favorite <u>fantasy</u> of being lost on a desert island and having to build a shelter and forage for food. The <u>dismal</u> weather, gray and rainy, didn't bother me at all, even when it disrupted my stay at the playground. London was a big, old, dirty city; outside the tourist areas, there was often <u>refuse</u> on the streets. This was not a problem to me; in fact, in provided food for the swarms of pigeons in the park. I loved to run toward them, getting very close before they decided to take flight. I laughed and laughed as they rose into the air.

There was much more to love. I developed an <u>obsession</u> with royalty. One day, my parents decided to give me a treat. We went to the Tower of London, where the royal jewels are on display. There we saw the rings, bracelets, and necklaces that belonged to the queens—and kings—of England. The diamonds, emeralds, rubies, and other precious jewels sparkled amazingly! The most dazzling of all was the royal crown, worn by a model of the queen, cloaked in <u>ermine</u>. It's been twenty-five years since I saw that crown, but I still remember how it made me feel. I have never been back. I'm afraid that reality wouldn't live up to my childhood memory.

1. Underline the words that explain what was not <u>interrupted</u>. Do people like being *interrupted* when they talk?

2. Is it hard to wait <u>patiently</u>? Write a word that is the opposite of *patiently*.

3. Write a sentence using the word <u>clinging</u>. What are some other words with the same meaning?

4. There are many books and games that employ <u>fantasy</u>. Tell why you think they are good or bad.

5. Name some things that can be <u>dismal</u>. Give some words that mean the opposite of *dismal*.

6. Is there a problem with <u>refuse</u> in your neighborhood? What are some other words for *refuse*?

7. Do you know anyone with an <u>obsession</u>? How is an *obsession* different from just liking something?

8. What would a cloak made of <u>ermine</u> look like? What color would it be?

"Volar: To Fly" by Judith Ortiz Cofer
Reading Warm-up B

Read the following passage. Pay special attention to the underlined words. Then, read it again, and complete the activities. Use a separate sheet of paper for your written answers.

People have always been fascinated by sleep and dreams. After all, we don't know what is happening when we sleep, and that makes us curious.

For many years, people have been <u>inspired</u> to determine the function of dreams. Numerous theories offer explanations as to why we dream. Some suggest that dreams have solely a physical function. Others, that they serve a mental and emotional purpose.

Some researchers study the body's movements and physiological changes during sleep, and others study brain waves. Scientists now divide sleep into four sections (five if you count the period when you are just falling asleep). These four stages of sleep repeat in cycles of 90 to 120 minutes from four to seven times during the night. One of these stages is known as REM sleep; REM stands for Rapid Eye Movement. A sleeper's eyes, though closed, show very rapid movement during this period, and it is the time when most dreaming occurs.

Some people remember their dreams well, and other people think that they don't dream at all, but every person dreams. Scientists have shown that people are most likely to remember those dreams that happen late in the sleep period. There is disagreement among scientists about the structure of dreams. Some believe that dreams are random images <u>scattering</u> through the mind and that people impose a structure like a story on these images because that is how they are used to thinking of things. Others believe that dream narratives offer clues to a person's waking life. Research remains inconclusive, as it is difficult to determine the answer.

A person who believes that all dreams have meaning might be an <u>avid</u> <u>consumer</u> of dream books and other guides to interpreting dreams. These people may spend time <u>discussing</u> their dreams to try to understand themselves. Some believe that <u>recurring</u> dreams offer clues to what is going on in their minds. They think that a dream may reflect a hidden <u>desire</u>, and even that those elements of dreams seeming bizarre and <u>incongruous</u> have meaning.

1. Underline the words that explain what people are <u>inspired</u> to do. Then, describe someone or something that has *inspired* you.

2. Underline what is <u>scattering</u> through the mind during sleep.

3. Give some words that mean the same thing as <u>avid</u>. Name something of which you are an *avid* fan.

4. Each of us is a <u>consumer</u> of many things. Name some items of which you are a *consumer*.

5. Underline why some people spend time <u>discussing</u> their dreams. Give some other words that mean *discussing*.

6. Have you ever had a <u>recurring</u> dream? What are some other ways of saying *recurring*?

7. What are some other words that mean the same thing as <u>desire</u>? Why might a *desire* be hidden?

8. Underline the word that gives a clue to <u>incongruous</u>. Give other words that have a meaning similar to *incongruous*.

"**Volar: To Fly**" by Judith Ortiz Cofer
Writing About the Big Question

What should we learn?

Big Question Vocabulary

analyze	curiosity	discover	evaluate	examine
experiment	explore	facts	information	inquire
interview	investigate	knowledge	question	understand

A. *Choose one word from the list above and use it to complete each sentence. There may be more than one right answer.*

1. Imagine the places you could _____ if you knew how to fly.

2. Children often like to _____ with different personalities.

3. Judith seems to _____ her parents' feelings very well.

B. *Follow the directions in responding to each of the items below.*

1. List two different times that you learned something new about your parents. Write your response in complete sentences.

_____

_____

2. Choose one of the experiences you listed in number 1. Write two or more sentences describing that experience. Use at least two of the Big Question vocabulary words. You may use the words in different forms (for example you can change *analyze* to *analyzing*).

_____

_____

C. *Complete the sentence below. Use the completed sentence as the beginning of a short paragraph in which you discuss the big question.*

Family connections are _____

_____

_____.

"**Volar: To Fly**" by Judith Ortiz Cofer

Reading: Make Connections Between Key Points and Supporting Details to Understand the Main Idea

The **main idea** is the most important thought or concept in a work or a passage of text. Sometimes, the author directly states the main idea of a work and then provides key points that support it. These key points are supported in turn by details such as examples and descriptions. Other times, the main idea is unstated. The author gives *only* the key points or supporting details that add up to a main idea. To understand the main idea, **make connections between key points and supporting details.** Notice how the writer groups details. Look for sentences that pull details together.

In this passage from "Volar: To Fly," Judith Ortiz Cofer states a key point and provides details that support the main idea of the essay:

> At twelve I was an avid consumer of comic books—*Supergirl* being my favorite. I spent my allowance of a quarter a day on two twelve-cent comic books or a double issue for twenty-five. I had a stack of *Legion of Super Heroes* and *Supergirl* comic books in my bedroom closet that was as tall as I.

DIRECTIONS: *Write the main point of Cofer's essay "Volar: To Fly" on the line below. Then, read each passage, and write its key point and the details that support it.*

Main idea: _____

From up there, over the rooftops, I could see everything, even beyond the few blocks of our barrio; with my X-ray vision I could look inside the homes of people who interested me. Once I saw our landlord, whom I knew my parents feared, sitting in a treasure-room dressed in an ermine coat and a large gold crown. He sat on the floor counting his dollar bills. I played a trick on him. Going up to his building's chimney, I blew a little puff of my super-breath into his fireplace, scattering his stacks of money so that he had to start counting all over again.

1. **Key point:** _____
2. **Details:** _____

I could more or less program my Supergirl dreams in those days by focusing on the object of my current obsession. This way I "saw" into the private lives of my teachers, and in the last days of my childish fantasy and the beginning of adolescence, into the secret room of the boys I liked.

3. **Key point:** _____
4. **Details:** _____

"**Volar: To Fly**" by Judith Ortiz Cofer
Literary Analysis: Reflective Essay

A **reflective essay** is a brief prose work that presents a writer's feelings and thoughts, or reflections, about an experience or idea. The purpose is to communicate these thoughts and feelings so that readers will respond with thoughts and feelings of their own. As you read a reflective essay, think about the ideas the writer is sharing. Think about whether your responses to the experience or idea are similar to or different from the writer's.

In this passage from "Volar: To Fly," Judith Ortiz Cofer describes the view from her kitchen window:

> The view was of a dismal alley that was littered with refuse thrown from windows. The space was too narrow for anyone larger than a skinny child to enter safely, so it was never cleaned.

A. DIRECTIONS: *In the second column of the chart, summarize Judith Ortiz Cofer's thoughts about each experience described in the first column. Then, in the third column, write your response. That is, describe your own thoughts on the subject.*

Experience	Author's Thoughts	My Thoughts
1. Reading comic books		
2. "Seeing" her neighbors and friends in dreams		
3. Overhearing her mother's desire to fly		

B. DIRECTIONS: *Write the first paragraph of a reflective essay of your own. Include a description of an experience and your thoughts about it. Write on one of these topics:*

- the role of nature in your life
- the importance of tradition in your life
- the meaning of family in your life

_____

_____

_____

_____

Name _____ Date _____

"Volar: To Fly" by Judith Ortiz Cofer
Vocabulary Builder

Word List

adolescence   avid   dismal   interrupted   obsession   refuse

A. DIRECTIONS: *Use the italicized word in each sentence in a sentence of your own.*

1. Before she reached *adolescence*, Judith Ortiz Cofer dreamed of flying.

   _____

2. Judith Ortiz Cofer was an *avid* reader of comic books.

   _____

3. The view out of the kitchen window was *dismal*.

   _____

4. As a child, Judith Ortiz Cofer never *interrupted* her parents' quiet time together.

   _____

5. Sometimes an *obsession* can affect our dreams.

   _____

6. *Refuse* littered the air shaft outside of Judith Ortiz Cofer's childhood apartment.

   _____

B. WORD STUDY: *The Latin root -rupt- means "break" or "burst." Read the following sentences. Use your knowledge of the Latin root -rupt- to write a full sentence to answer each question.*

1. Would a quiet conversation *disrupt* science class?

   _____

2. If a water main *ruptured*, would traffic be heavy?

   _____

3. Could a baby sleep through a *disruption*?

   _____

"Volar: To Fly" by Judith Ortiz Cofer
Enrichment: Popular Culture

In "Volar: To Fly," the narrator dreams of having the amazing powers of Supergirl, a comic-book superhero. Supergirl is a spinoff of the long-running Superman comic book series, which was so popular that it gained even larger audiences on television and in several movies.

Superman was the first major comic-book superhero. His popularity inspired the creation of many other such heroes.

DIRECTIONS: *Use the chart below to guide you in library and Internet research on the key facts about the superheroes listed. Use the blank row to add information about a superhero of your choice that is not listed below.*

Superhero	Superpowers	Real Name or Secret Identity	TV Versions	Movie Versions
Superman				
Spiderman				
Batman				
The Hulk				
Wonder Woman				
Green Lantern				
Captain America				

Name _____ Date _____

"I Am a Native of North America" by Chief Dan George
"Volar: To Fly" by Judith Ortiz Cofer
Integrated Language Skills: Grammar

Prepositions and Prepositional Phrases

A **preposition** relates a noun or pronoun that follows the preposition to another word in the sentence. In *The key is in the lock*, the preposition *in* relates *lock* to *key*. These are some common prepositions:

above	beyond	in	of	over	under
behind	for	inside	on	through	up
below	from	into	outside	to	with

A **prepositional phrase** begins with a preposition and ends with the noun or pronoun that follows it. In *The key is in the lock*, the prepositional phrase is *in the lock*.

A. DIRECTIONS: *The following sentences are from "I Am a Native of North America" and "Volar: To Fly." In each sentence, underline each prepositions, and circle the prepositional phrases.*

1. I blew a little puff of my super-breath into his fireplace
2. I can still see him as the sun rose above the mountaintop in the early morning.
3. There was a deep respect for everything in nature.
4. In my dream I climbed the stairs to the top of our apartment building.
5. I could look inside the homes of people who interested me.
6. In the course of my lifetime I have lived in two distinct cultures.
7. I remember, as a little boy, fishing with him up Indian River.
8. I could see everything, even beyond the few blocks of our barrio.

B. Writing Application: *Write a paragraph about an artistic talent that you or someone you know possesses. Use at least three prepositional phrases. Underline each preposition, and circle the prepositional phrases.*

_____

_____

_____

_____

_____

"I Am a Native of North America" by Chief Dan George
"Volar: To Fly" by Judith Ortiz Cofer

Integrated Language Skills: Support for Writing an Outline

To prepare to write an **outline** of "I Am a Native of North America" or "Volar: To Fly," create a word web. Write the main idea in the center circle. In each of the circles around it, write a key point. In the circles around each key point, write details that support the key point.

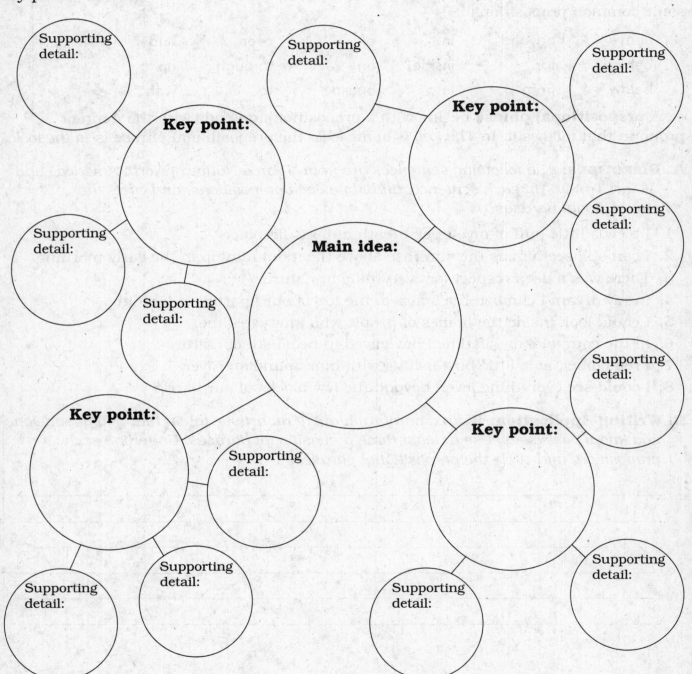

Now, use your word web to make an outline of the essay.

"**I Am a Native of North America**" by Chief Dan George
"**Volar: To Fly**" by Judith Ortiz Cofer

Integrated Language Skills: Support for Extend Your Learning

Listening and Speaking: "I Am a Native of North America"

To prepare a **response** to "I Am a Native of North America," write a one-sentence summary of the essay's message. Then, state whether you agree or disagree with the message. Finally, write two reasons that support your response.

Author's message: _____

_____

My response: _____

_____

Reason 1: _____

_____

Reason 2: _____

_____

Listening and Speaking: "Volar: To Fly"

To prepare a **response** to "Volar: To Fly," write a one-sentence summary of the essay's message. Then, state whether you agree or disagree with the message. Finally, write two reasons that support your response.

Author's message: _____

_____

My response: _____

_____

Reason 1: _____

_____

Reason 2: _____

_____

Name _____   Date _____

"Volar: To Fly" by Judith Ortiz Cofer
Open-Book Test

Short Answer *Write your responses to the questions in this section on the lines provided.*

1. Judith Ortiz Cofer, author of "Volar: To Fly," remembers that when she was 12 years old, *Supergirl* was her favorite comic book. Based on the essay, how do you think the author, now an adult, feels about the character Supergirl? Why?

   _____

   _____

   _____

2. The author of "Volar: To Fly" says that when she was 12, her stack of *Supergirl* comic books was as tall as she was. Why is this detail important?

   _____

   _____

   _____

3. One of the key points in "Volar: To Fly" is that the author longed to have a special power. In the beginning of the essay, the author tells about a recurring dream. What two details from the dream support the key point?

   _____

   _____

   _____

4. In the middle of the essay, the author of "Volar: To Fly" describes a dream in which she blows her super-breath into the landlord's chimney and scatters his money everywhere. What key point does this detail support?

   _____

   _____

   _____

5. In the middle of "Volar: To Fly," the author says that she "saw" into the private lives of her neighbors and teachers. What does she mean by this?

   _____

   _____

   _____

6. Based on details in "Volar: To Fly," describe the relationship between the author's mother and father.

   _____

   _____

   _____

7. In "Volar: To Fly," what is written on the clock over the sink? Why do you think the author includes this detail?

_____

_____

_____

8. Did the author of "Volar: To Fly" ever treat her *Supergirl* comic books as if they were refuse? Base your answer on the definition *refuse*.

_____

_____

_____

_____

9. Fill in the chart by summarizing the author's feelings about these two experiences in "Volar: To Fly." Then, answer the questions that follow the chart.

Experience	Author's Thoughts
The author spends her allowance of 25¢ a day on *Supergirl* comic books.	
The author's mother is unable to return to Puerto Rico.	

What book or story is a favorite of yours?_____

What thoughts or feelings do you have about this book or story?_____

_____

10. In "Volar: To Fly," what desire do the author and her mother have in common?

_____

_____

Essay

Write an extended response to the question of your choice or to the question or questions your teacher assigns you.

11. Judith Ortiz Cofer had a *Supergirl* comic book collection as a child. This collection plays an important role in her reflective essay, "Volar: To Fly." In an essay, talk about how buying and keeping the comic books must have made the young Cofer feel. Then, point out the similarities between the comic book character and Cofer's recurring dream.

12. How does the author of "Volar: To Fly" feel about her old *Supergirl* comic books? What main idea does the example of the comic books help Judith Ortiz Cofer express in her essay? Answer these questions in an essay of your own. Be sure to use examples from the Judith Ortiz Cofer's essay to support your answers.

13. In an essay, discuss the title of Judith Ortiz Cofer's essay, "Volar: To Fly." Consider these questions: What does the title tell you about the essay's main idea? In what way does it suggest that the text is a reflective essay? Support your points with three references to the selection.

14. **Thinking About the Big Question: What should we learn?** Based on "Volar: To Fly," what does Judith Ortiz Cofer want us to learn about super powers? Where might she say the true super powers are to be found?

Oral Response

15. Go back to question 1, 5, or 7 or to the question your teacher assigns you. Take a few minutes to expand your answer and prepare an oral response. Find additional details in the essay to support your points. If necessary, make notes to guide your oral response.

Name _____ Date _____

"Volar: To Fly" by Judith Ortiz Cofer

Selection Test A

Critical Reading *Identify the letter of the choice that best answers the question.*

____ 1. As a child, Judith Ortiz Cofer dreams of flying. What habit does she have that may encourage her dreams?
   A. She reads comic books.
   B. She lies in bed awake.
   C. She listens to her parents talking in the kitchen.
   D. She watches birds from her window.

____ 2. Where does this story take place?
   A. in Puerto Rico
   B. in Mexico
   C. in a large American city
   D. in the country

____ 3. Why does the writer wait in bed until her mother comes to wake her?
   A. Her mother enjoys waking her.
   B. She likes to think about her dreams.
   C. Her mother has a rule that she can't wake up early.
   D. She doesn't want to interrupt her parents' time together.

____ 4. What does the writer's mother wish to do?
   A. visit her family
   B. join the circus
   C. be patient and full of grace
   D. sleep later in the morning

____ 5. Why can't the writer's family visit Puerto Rico?
   A. The beach is closed.
   B. The trip is too expensive.
   C. Her father is afraid of flying.
   D. The children have school.

____ 6. Why does the writer wish to fly?
   A. to see into the private lives of people who interested her
   B. to fight crime
   C. to tease her landlord
   D. to strengthen her skinny arms and legs

____ 7. Why do you think the title of this essay is in both Spanish and English?
   A. to appeal to Spanish teachers
   B. because the writer is both Puerto Rican and American
   C. to please the writer's mother
   D. to show off

____ 8. How does the writer feel about her white "princess" furniture?

A. It doesn't belong in her bedroom.   C. It's beautiful.

B. It gets dirty too easily.   D. It gives her strange dreams.

____ 9. How would you describe the atmosphere in the kitchen when the writer's parents were together?

A. angry   C. tense

B. happy   D. full of longing

____ 10. Which of these quotations from "Volar: To Fly" expresses Judith Ortiz Cofer's feelings about flying?

A. *I spent my allowance of a quarter a day on two twelve-cent comic books*

B. *my arms would harden into steel*

C. *From up there, over the rooftops, I could see everything, even beyond the few blocks of our barrio*

D. *my tight curls still clinging to my head, skinny arms and legs*

____ 11. Which sentence best describes one of the *main ideas* of "Volar: To Fly"?

A. Some people wish to fly away from their lives, even if temporarily.

B. Mothers and daughters have the same dreams.

C. Anyone can be a superhero.

D. You shouldn't think about the past.

____ 12. Which of the following quotations supports the idea that Judith Ortiz Cofer wasn't seeing reality in her dreams?

A. *Once I saw our landlord . . . sitting in a treasure-room dressed in an ermine coat and a large gold crown.*

B. *my parents safely asleep in their beds*

C. *I'd wake up in my tiny bedroom*

D. *We could rent a car, go to the beach*

____ 13. What conclusion can you draw about a person who dreams of flying?

A. She is happy with her life.   C. She likes the nighttime.

B. She wants to escape.   D. She is far from home.

Vocabulary and Grammar

____ 14. How much interest do people pay to an *obsession*?

A. a great deal   C. a little

B. some   D. none

____ 15. What might you say about a room that is *dismal*?

A. It is too bright.   C. It is gloomy.

B. It is just bright enough.   D. It is gray.

____ 16. Where is a good place to put *refuse*?

A. in the ocean   C. in your hair

B. in the garbage can   D. in space

____ 17. When does someone experience *adolescence*?

A. as a baby   C. during their teenaged years

B. as a small child   D. as a senior citizen

____ 18. How would you describe something that has been *interrupted*?

A. disturbed   C. remarked

B. soothed   D. sad

____ 19. Which of these sentences contains a **prepositional phrase**?

A. The writer's mother longed to see her family.

B. The writer loved her dreams.

C. The writer's mother and father were thoughtful people.

D. Puerto Rico is a sunny island.

____ 20. What is the **preposition** in the following sentence: *The writer was full of sad memories.*

A. of   C. was

B. The   D. full

Essay

21. In "Volar: To Fly" the author and her mother want to fly. In a brief essay, explain whether their reasons for wanting to fly are the same or different. Support your answer with details from the reading.

22. What is the main idea of "Volar: To Fly"? Support your answer with at least two details from her writing.

23. Does Judith Ortiz Cofer feel sorry for her mother? Write an essay in which you describe how the author might feel about her mother. Support your answer with details from "Volar: To Fly."

24. **Thinking About the Big Question: What should we learn?** The narrator of "Volar: To Fly" dreams every night that she is Supergirl. What does Judith Ortiz Cofer want us to learn about superpowers? Where might she say the true superpowers are to be found?

Name _____ Date _____

"**Volar: To Fly**" by Judith Ortiz Cofer
Selection Test B

Critical Reading *Identify the letter of the choice that best answers the question.*

_____ 1. In "Volar: To Fly," the narrator's youthful daydreams about flying represent her desire to
A. become an actress who portrays a superhero.
B. seek a better life.
C. return to her homeland of Puerto Rico.
D. show her parents how powerful she really is.

_____ 2. Which is a detail of "Volar: To Fly" that supports the idea that the narrator loves to read comic books?
A. She spends her entire allowance on comic books.
B. She dresses up in a Supergirl costume every night.
C. She subscribes to several different superhero comics.
D. She has watched every episode of *Supergirl* on television.

_____ 3. In "Volar: To Fly," the narrator's fantasy of having long straight blond hair reveals what key aspect of her personality?
A. She tends to neglect her schoolwork.
B. She is unrealistic about what she can expect of life.
C. She has good taste in role models.
D. She is insecure about her personal appearance.

_____ 4. In "Volar: To Fly," the narrator's fantasy about the landlord's fancy clothes shows that she views him as
A. fashionable   B. handsome   C. greedy   D. cruel

_____ 5. In "Volar: To Fly," the narrator makes use of which of her imagined superpowers?
A. X-ray vision   B. flight   C. super-breath   D. super-strength

_____ 6. As used by the narrator and her mother, the idea of flying—*volar*—represents which aspect of their personalities?
A. a thirst for excitement
B. a love of romantic heroes
C. the ambition for wealth and power
D. the expression of unfulfilled longings

_____ 7. According to the narrator of "Volar: To Fly," which of her current interests is most typical of "the beginning of adolescence"?
A. looking into the lives of her neighbors
B. prying into the private lives of her teachers
C. looking into the secret rooms of boy she likes
D. disrupting their landlord's counting of his money

_____ 8. Which of the following best captures the narrator's feeling about finding herself back in her bedroom after a night of dreaming about being Supergirl?
A. security
B. warmth
C. disappointment
D. anger

___ 9. Which detail from "Volar: To Fly" most clearly supports the main idea that the narrator grew up in a family of modest means?
A. "I could see everything".
B. "tiny apartment"
C. "white 'princess' furniture"
D. "cafe con leche"

___ 10. What idea does the narrator convey by putting the phrase "wake me" in quotation marks in the following sentence from "Volar: To Fly"?

She would "wake me" exactly forty-five minutes after they had gotten up.

A. She remains asleep even after her mother tries to awaken her.
B. Her mother often forgets to come in and wake her up.
C. Her mother wakes her up too harshly.
D. She is already awake.

___ 11. In "Volar: To Fly," what aspect of the narrator's personality is revealed by her unwillingness to intrude on her parents' private time in the morning by waking up earlier?
A. She is lazy.   C. She is jealous.
B. She is fearful.   D. She is considerate.

___ 12. In the morning, while lying in bed, the narrator of "Volar: To Fly" spends most of her time
A. thinking about what to wear to school that day.
B. daydreaming about the boy she likes.
C. listening to her parents' conversation in the kitchen.
D. trying to come up with an excuse to stay home from school that day.

___ 13. From the parents' conversation in the kitchen in "Volar: To Fly," the reader learns which of the following about the father's personality?
A. He is more of a dreamer than his wife.
B. He is more practical-minded than his wife.
C. He is not a good listener.
D. He is easily intimidated by his wife.

___ 14. From the parents' kitchen conversation in "Volar: To Fly," the reader can tell that the narrator and her mother share which of the following personality traits?
A. They are both dreamers.
B. They are both happy with their lives.
C. They are both afraid of the father.
D. They are both proud of their Puerto Rican heritage.

___ 15. In "Volar: To Fly," which of the following best describes the mother's attitude at the end of the story, after her husband tells her that it is not possible for the family to go to Puerto Rico?
A. despairing   B. wishful   C. joyful   D. angry

Vocabulary and Grammar

___ 16. If you had an *obsession* about something, would you likely
A. have no interest in it.
B. never talk about it.
C. think about it constantly.
D. seldom think about it.

____ **17.** If a pianist gave a *dismal* performance at a piano recital, the tone of the reviews in the next day's newspapers would most likely be
    A. highly critical.
    B. politely respectful.
    C. wildly enthusiastic.
    D. partially favorable.

____ **18.** A collection of *refuse* would most likely contain which of the following?
    A. discarded junk
    B. valuable jewelry
    C. sports memorabilia
    D. fossils of prehistoric animals

____ **19.** Which word in this sentence from "Volar: To Fly" is a conjunction?

I could more or less program my Supergirl dreams in those days by focusing on the object of my current obsession.

    A. more   **B.** or   **C.** in   **D.** my

____ **20.** Which sentence from "Volar: To Fly" contains a conjunction?
    A. At twelve I was an avid consumer of comic books. . . .
    B. In the morning I'd wake up in my tiny bedroom. . . .
    C. In the kitchen my mother and father would be talking softly over cafe con leche.
    D. Actually, he would be carrying that part of the conversation.

Essay

21. In "Volar: To Fly," the narrator identifies closely with Supergirl. With which character from fiction, movies, comic books, or TV do you identify most closely? Why? In an essay, identify the characteristics of the character that you admire most, and explain why those characteristics are important to you.

22. In "Volar: To Fly," the narrator makes rich use of her imagination to spin a fantasy about how she would use superpowers. Do you think that the narrator makes good use of her imagined superpowers? Why or why not? What other uses of those superpowers can you imagine? In an essay, discuss at least two other ideas for using superpowers, and why you think they are better than the ones chosen by the narrator.

23. In "Volar: To Fly," both the narrator and her mother express the wish that they could fly. In an essay, compare and contrast the narrator's and the mother's reasons for wishing they could fly. Support your answer with specific examples from the text of the selection.

24. Thinking About the Big Question: What should we learn? Based on "Volar: To Fly," what does Judith Ortiz Cofer want us to learn about super powers? Where might she say the true super powers are to be found?

Vocabulary Warm-up Word Lists

Study these words from the selection. Then, complete the activities.

Word List A

absorbed [uhb ZAWRBD] *v.* captured or occupied a person's full attention
That story so <u>absorbed</u> me that I could not put the book down until I finished the last page.

advise [ad VYZ] *v.* to offer an opinion in an effort to be helpful
I <u>advise</u> you to turn left at the next traffic light if you want to arrive more quickly.

buyer [BY uhr] *n.* person or group who purchases something
I am thrilled that I found a <u>buyer</u> for my old bicycle.

delayed [di LAYD] *v.* put off doing something until sometime later
He <u>delayed</u> telling them the good news until the whole family was together.

dreaded [DRED id] *v.* feared very strongly
We <u>dreaded</u> the sound of the high winds, for it meant that the hurricane was drawing near.

eventually [ei VEN choo uh lee] *adv.* finally; in the end; after some time has passed
We wandered around the amusement park and *eventually* decided to stop for pizza.

solution [suh LOO shun] *n.* an answer to a problem or a mystery
If your dog runs away when you let him out, the <u>solution</u> might be to put up a fence.

worthwhile [wuhrth HWYL] *adj.* worth the time or effort spent
It is a <u>worthwhile</u> activity to work in a food bank.

Word List B

accomplishment [uh KAHM plish ment] *n.* achievement; successful completion
He recited the Declaration of Independence from memory—quite an <u>accomplishment</u>.

despite [di SPYT] *prep.* in spite of; even though
<u>Despite</u> her smile as she congratulated the winner, she was disappointed about losing.

fascinated [FA suh nay tid] *v.* extremely interested in; enchanted by
He was so <u>fascinated</u> by the large green bug with blue dots and brown furry legs that he spent hours trying to identify it.

image [I mij] *n.* a visual representation, copy, or picture of a person, place, or thing
You look like the <u>image</u> of your grandfather; your face is just like his when he was young.

indicated [IN di kay tid] *v.* announced; signaled
The traffic light turned green, which <u>indicated</u> that we could go.

regularly [REG yuh luhr lee] *adv.* repeatedly; normally
Can you believe that he eats green eggs and ham <u>regularly</u> for breakfast?

superior [soo PEER ee uhr] *adj.* better than; higher; higher up in rank or quality
After tasting the vanilla cake and the carrot cake, he said the carrot cake was <u>superior</u>.

quest [KWEST] *n.* search; hunt; journey with an important goal
At the mall, I went on a <u>quest</u> to find the perfect shoes to wear to my cousin's party.

Name _____ Date _____

"The Legacy of 'Snowflake' Bentley" by Barbara Eaglesham
"No Gumption" by Russell Baker
Vocabulary Warm-up Exercises

Exercise A *Fill in the blanks, using each word from Word List A only once.*

Abby and Ken [1] _____ the job of cleaning out the cellar. There was so much
stuff to sort through. They [2] _____ doing the unwelcome chore until a friend
suggested that they have a garage sale. She began to [3] _____ them on how to
sell things they no longer wanted. "It can be very [4] _____ to spend even a little
time organizing things you no longer want. You can get rid of stuff and make money,
too." After that, Abby and Ken got so [5] _____ in the task of finding items for
the garage sale that they did not mind cleaning out the cellar after all. On the day of the
garage sale, there seemed to be a [6] _____ for each item. Business was brisk,
and [7] _____ most of the things were sold. Abby and Ken agreed that the
garage sale had been a good [8] _____ to the problem of a cluttered cellar.

Exercise B *Decide whether each statement is true or false. Circle T or F. Then, explain your
answer.*

1. Someone who achieves a goal <u>despite</u> many obstacles has succeeded.
   T / F _____

2. If we <u>regularly</u> take a walk every day, we do not normally take a walk.
   T / F_____

3. "<u>Superior</u>" workmanship means high-quality work.
   T / F_____

4. When the woman <u>indicated</u> which scarf she wanted to buy, we did not know which
   one she wanted.
   T / F_____

5. A football team that wins every game all season can say that its winning record is
   an <u>accomplishment</u>.
   T / F _____

6. If a man took a tour of a new city and found himself bored by everything he saw,
   you could say he was <u>fascinated</u> by the sights of the city.
   T / F_____

7. An ocean explorer who searches all over the world for sunken treasure is on a <u>quest</u>.
   T / F_____

8. A school yearbook usually contains an <u>image</u> of each student and teacher at a school.
   T / F _____

"The Legacy of 'Snowflake' Bentley" by Barbara Eaglesham
"No Gumption" by Russell Baker
Reading Warm-up A

Read the following passage. Pay special attention to the underlined words. Then, read it again, and complete the activities. Use a separate sheet of paper for your written answers.

The Great Depression began in the United States at the end of 1929 and lasted into the 1940s. The Depression was the longest, most severe economic collapse in American history. The stock market fell, unemployment was very high, and people could not afford simple things like food and clothing.

Serious flaws in the economy had developed in the 1920s. On the surface, the twenties looked prosperous. The economy seemed to be doing well. The reality was that the rich got richer, but the income of the common people did not rise. At the same time, new fads and inventions absorbed people's imagination. Manufacturers pushed each new product. Advertisers who worked for the manufacturers convinced people they could buy things on credit. Buying on credit meant that the buyer of an item delayed payment. The item would be paid for later. Unfortunately, as the economy worsened, people lost their jobs. They were not able to pay for things they had bought on credit. As a result, their lost their homes and possessions.

The crisis was made worse by the crash of the stock market in October 1929. Stocks lost $10 billion to $15 billion in value. President Herbert Hoover tried to advise Americans about the economy by saying it was stable, but they dreaded the thought of losing their money. They started to withdraw their savings from banks. The banks did not have enough money to cover all the withdrawals. People lost their life savings.

Eventually, the situation improved after Franklin Delano Roosevelt was elected president in 1932. His policies restored confidence in the economy. Part of his solution was to direct large amounts of government money and effort into public works. He created many worthwhile projects that built roads and buildings. Other big programs were for the media and arts. Together, these projects provided jobs for thousands of unemployed people. The government also took more responsibility for supplying food and other help to people in need.

1. Underline the words that tell what absorbed people's imagination. Name a few items or ideas that have *absorbed* your own imagination.

2. Underline the sentence that tells what happens when a buyer purchases something on credit. What is a *buyer*?

3. Circle the word that tells what is delayed in a purchase on credit. Use *delayed* in a sentence.

4. Underline the words that tell how Hoover tried to advise the people about the economy. Define *advise*.

5. Circle the words that tell what people dreaded. What is a synonym for *dreaded*?

6. Underline the words that tell when it was that the situation eventually improved. Define *eventually*.

7. Underline words that explain some things Roosevelt did to find a solution to the crisis in the economy. Use *solution* in a sentence.

8. Underline the words that tell some of the reasons that Roosevelt's projects were worthwhile. Write a sentence telling about something *worthwhile* that you have done.

"The Legacy of 'Snowflake' Bentley" by Barbara Eaglesham
"No Gumption" by Russell Baker
Reading Warm-up B

Read the following passage. Pay special attention to the underlined words. Then, read it again, and complete the activities. Use a separate sheet of paper for your written answers.

The word "photography" comes from two Greek words that translate roughly to mean "drawing with light." Photography is a method for recording a still <u>image</u> of the world onto a flat surface. This type of picture has a long history.

As far back as the fifth century B.C., people used a device known as a *camera obscura*. This was a box with a pinhole opening on one end. A bit of the outside world shone in through the hole and was projected on the opposite end of the box. This invention especially <u>fascinated</u> artists interested to see how three-dimensional objects appeared on a flat surface. Artists had to trace these pictures to save them.

What we think of today as "photography" started in the early 1800s, when people discovered how to save pictures onto metal plates treated with chemicals. Perhaps the most famous method was the *daguerreotype (duh* GE *roh typ)*. Each plate had to be exposed a long time to light, so a person had to sit still about 20 minutes per picture. This invention was considered a huge <u>accomplishment</u>; people did not have to hire a painter to record what a loved one looked like.

<u>Despite</u> its popularity, this process was soon replaced by <u>superior</u> methods that worked faster, easier, and resulted in pictures printed on paper. By the late 1800s, people were using small portable cameras that contained film.

Photos regularly appeared in magazines, newspapers, and books. The spread of photography <u>indicated</u> how important these images were becoming all over the world.

In the early twentieth century, color film became available. Throughout that century, cameras contained film, and pictures were printed on all kinds of paper.

The <u>quest</u> to bring photography into the computer age resulted in the invention of digital cameras for home use in 1995. Pictures, captured on electronic sensors instead of on film, could be transferred to a computer and, in an instant, sent around the world.

1. Circle a nearby word that has a meaning similar to <u>image</u>. Write a list of places where you might see a photographic *image* everyday.

2. Underline the word that has a meaning similar to <u>fascinated</u>. What new inventions have *fascinated* you?

3. Circle the name of an <u>accomplishment</u> in photography in the 1800s. Give a synonym for *accomplishment*.

4. A common method of photography was replaced <u>despite</u> its popularity. What does that mean? Why was it replaced?

5. Underline the word that <u>superior</u> describes. Define *superior*.

6. Underline where you could <u>regularly</u> find photos. What is the opposite of *regularly*?

7. Circle the words that tell what was <u>indicated</u> by the spreading popularity of photography. Use *indicated* in a sentence.

8. Underline the words that tell the outcome of the <u>quest</u> to bring photography into the computer age. Define *quest*.

Name _____ Date _____

Writing About the Big Question

What should we learn?

Big Question Vocabulary

analyze	curiosity	discover	evaluate	examine
experiment	explore	facts	information	inquire
interview	investigate	knowledge	question	understand

A. *Choose one word from the list above to complete each sentence. There may be more than one right answer.*

1. "Snowflake" Bentley liked to _____ with snow crystals.

2. It can be difficult to _____ a career that suits your personality.

3. Authors who write about themselves never need to conduct an

_____ .

B. *Follow the directions in responding to each of the items below.*

1. List two different times that you learned you had a talent for something. It can be something important or something silly. Write your response in complete sentences.

_____

_____

2. Choose one of the experiences you listed in number 1. Write two sentences describing that experience. Use at least two of the Big Question vocabulary words. You may use the words in different forms (for example you can change *analyze* to *analyzing*).

_____

_____

C. *Complete the sentence below. Use the completed sentence as the beginning of a short paragraph in which you discuss the big question.*

When you discover something you love to do, you should _____

_____

_____ .

"A Special Gift: The Legacy of 'Snowflake' Bentley" by Barbara Eaglesham
"No Gumption" by Russell Baker

Literary Analysis: Comparing Biography and Autobiography

In an **autobiography**, a person tells his or her own life story. Writers may write about their own experiences to explain their actions, to provide insight into their choices, or to show the personal side of an event.

In contrast, in a **biography**, a writer tells the life story of another person. Writers of biographies often write to analyze a person's experiences and actions. Biographies often present their subject as an example from which readers can learn a lesson.

Some biographies and autobiographies are short essays that focus on a particular episode in the subject's life.

Both biography and autobiography focus on actual events and offer insight to explain a person's actions or ideas. However, the forms have these important differences:

Biography
- More objective
- Based on research

Autobiography
- More personal
- Based on memory and emotion

A. Read the following sentences. Determine whether they belong to an autobiography or a biography. Use the line provided to explain your answer.

1. I was born in Detroit during the Depression.

    _____ **autobiography/biography Explanation:** _____
    _____

2. As children, my brother and I often whispered secrets late into the night.

    _____ **autobiography/biography Explanation:** _____
    _____

3. Historians agree that Jimmy Carter has been very productive since he left the presidency.

    _____ **autobiography/biography Explanation:** _____
    _____

B. Complete the following sentences:

1. Autobiographies are _____, _____, _____.
   One thing I like about autobiographies is _____.
2. Biographies are _____, _____, _____. I
   would like to read a biography of the following people: _____.

"A Special Gift: The Legacy of 'Snowflake' Bentley" by Barbara Eaglesham
"No Gumption" by Russell Baker
Vocabulary Builder

Word List

aptitude   crucial   evaporated   gumption
hexagons   microscope   negatives   paupers

A. DIRECTIONS: *Use the italicized word in each sentence in a sentence of your own.*

1. Russell Baker had an *aptitude* for writing.

_____

2. Baker's mother thinks gumption is *crucial* to success in life.

_____

3. The snow crystals *evaporated* quickly.

_____

4. *Gumption* may be something you are born with.

_____

5. Honeycombs are a grid of *hexagons*.

_____

6. Ordinary objects look different under the *microscope*.

_____

7. *Negatives* must not get wet.

_____

8. He achieved great success, even though his father and grandfather were *paupers*.

_____

B. DIRECTIONS: *Write the letter of the word that is most similar in meaning to the word from the Word List.*

____ 1. aptitude
     A. talent   B. desire   C. joy   D. luck
____ 2. crucial
     A. dull   B. ugly   C. minor   D. important
____ 3. evaporated
     A. vanished   B. melted   C. dried up   D. disappeared
____ 4. gumption
     A. talent   B. drive   C. personality   D. good looks
____ 5. hexagons
     A. six-sided figures   B. shapes   C. curses   D. seven-sided figures
____ 6. paupers
     A. poor people   B. dancers   C. thieves   D. leaders

Name _____ Date _____

"A Special Gift: The Legacy of 'Snowflake' Bentley" by Barbara Eaglesham
"No Gumption" by Russell Baker
Writing Support for Comparing Literary Works

	(Biography) "Snowflake" Bentley	(Autobiography) Russell Baker
How was each character influenced by his parents?		
What is your overall impression of the person?		
What kind of information helped you form your opinion?		
Which person do you feel you understand better?		

Now, use your notes to write an essay in which you compare and contrast what you learned about "Snowflake" Bentley with what you learned about Russell Baker.

"The Legacy of 'Snowflake' Bentley" by Barbara Eaglesham and
"No Gumption" by Russell Baker
Open-Book Test

Short Answer *Write your responses to the questions in this section on the lines provided.*

1. Toward the end of "The Legacy of 'Snowflake' Bentley," author Barbara Eaglesham writes that photographing snowflakes was "a labor of love" for Wilson Bentley. What does this phrase mean? What does it tell you about Bentley?

_____

_____

_____

2. In the last paragraph of "The Legacy of 'Snowflake' Bentley," the reader learns that Bentley was also a musician and scientist. What did he do as a musician? What did he do as a scientist?

Musician: _____

Scientist: _____

3. Did Wilson Bentley create any photographs of snow crystals that had evaporated? Base your response on the meaning of the word *evaporated*.

_____

_____

_____

4. What does Russell Baker's mother mean when she says in the beginning of "No Gumption," "You've got no more gumption than a bump on a log"?

_____

_____

_____

5. Early in "No Gumption," Russell Baker includes details about his sister, Doris. What do these details tell you about Doris? What do they tell you about young Russell?

_____

_____

_____

6. Near the end of "No Gumption," Baker's mother suggests that maybe Russell could be a writer. What does this comment show about his mother?

_____

_____

7. Reread the first sentences of "The Legacy of 'Snowflake' Bentley" and "No Gumption." Which story is based on research? Which is based on personal memory?

_____

_____

_____

8. How are young Wilson Bentley in "The Legacy of 'Snowflake' Bentley" and young Russell Baker in "No Gumption" different? How are they similar? Give an example of each.

_____

_____

_____

9. How are Wilson Bentley's mother in "The Legacy of 'Snowflake' Bentley" and Russell Baker's mother in "No Gumption" alike?

_____

_____

10. Use the following words to complete this Venn diagram: *autobiography, biography, tell about someone's life*. Then, following the diagram, explain how autobiography and biography are different.

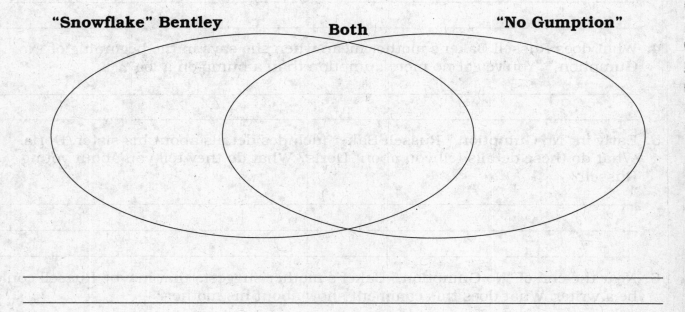

"Snowflake" Bentley   Both   "No Gumption"

_____

_____

Name _____ Date _____

Essay

Write an extended response to the question of your choice or to the question or questions your teacher assigns you.

11. In "No Gumption," Russell Baker's mother accuses him of lacking "gumption." What might Baker's mother say about Wilson Bentley? Would she enjoy having him as a son? Why or why not? Answer these questions in a short essay.

12. Imagine that "The Legacy of 'Snowflake' Bentley" is an autobiography, and "No Gumption" is a biography. How would each story be different? What information might be deleted from each story? What information might each story gain? Answer these questions in an essay. Support your ideas with references to each text.

13. Both "The Legacy of 'Snowflake' Bentley" and "No Gumption" reveal their subjects' values, or what the main characters consider most important in life. Sometimes these values are directly stated. Other times values are only hinted at. In an essay, identify and discuss what Bentley and Baker seem to value most. Include details or quotations from each story to illustrate your ideas.

14. **Thinking About the Big Question: What should we learn?** Imagine you are interviewing Wilson Bentley of "The Legacy of 'Snowflake' Bentley" and Russell Baker of "No Gumption." In an essay, tell how you think the two men would answer this question: *What should we learn, and why?*

Oral Response

15. Go back to question 7, 8, or 9 or to the question your teacher assigns you. Take a few minutes to expand your answer and prepare an oral response. Find additional details in "The Legacy of 'Snowflake' Bentley" and/or "No Gumption" that support your points. If necessary, make notes to guide your oral response.

"A Special Gift: The Legacy of 'Snowflake' Bentley" by Barbara Eaglesham
"No Gumption" by Russell Baker
Selection Test A

Critical Reading *Identify the letter of the choice that best answers the question.*

____ 1. What gift does "Snowflake" Bentley get on his fifteenth birthday?
    A. an old microscope   **C.** socks
    B. a popgun   **D.** new skis

____ 2. What does "Snowflake" Bentley finally manage to do when he is nineteen years old?
    A. publish a book   **C.** stop a snow crystal from melting
    B. go to college   **D.** photograph a snow crystal

____ 3. What does Russell Baker's mother despise?
    A. comic books   **C.** inactivity
    B. dirty dishes   **D.** *The Saturday Evening Post*

____ 4. What is Russell Baker's first job?
    A. collecting garbage   **C.** writing
    B. selling newspapers   **D.** baby-sitting

____ 5. How did "Snowflake" Bentley contribute to science?
    A. by cataloging more than two thousand examples of snow crystals
    B. by cataloging more than a million examples of snow crystals
    C. by purchasing expensive photographic equipment
    D. He didn't make any contribution to science.

____ 6. Which adjective best describes "Snowflake" Bentley?
    A. curious   **C.** business-minded
    B. flaky   **D.** spoiled

____ 7. What prevents Russell Baker from succeeding as a salesman?
    A. He can't speak English.
    B. He doesn't enjoy selling things.
    C. He spends the nickles he earns on candy.
    D. His mother doesn't teach him how to sell.

____ 8. Which adjective best describes Russell Baker?
    A. shy   **C.** ambitious
    B. enterprising   **D.** crafty

_____ 9. What is the meaning of the maxim: "The early bird gets the worm"?

   A. People who wake up early are more likely to succeed.

   B. Fisherman should get started early.

   C. Birds wake up hungry.

   D. It can be healthy to sleep in.

_____ 10. Which excerpt from "A Special Gift: The Legacy of 'Snowflake' Bentley" suggests why the author may have considered "Snowflake" Bentley a subject worthy of this short biography?

   A. *And nothing fascinated him more than snowflakes.*

   B. *Then, holding his breath, he would observe the crystal.*

   C. *He . . . would finally be able to share the beauty of his snow crystals with the world.*

   D. *He is remembered as the not-so-flaky-after-all "Snowflake" Bentley.*

_____ 11. Which excerpt from "No Gumption" would you <u>not</u> find in a biography?

   A. *The flaw . . . she had already spotted was lack of gumption.*

   B. *The most desirable job on earth sprang instantly to mind.*

   C. *Uncle Allen had made something of himself by 1932.*

   D. *There were two filling stations at the intersection with Union Avenue. . . .*

_____ 12. What is Russell Baker's tone in *No Gumption*?

   A. sad   C. funny

   B. angry   D. serious

_____ 13. Why do you think Russell Baker chose to write about his first job?

   A. to make fun at his sister

   B. because it explains why he became a writer

   C. to come to grips with a painful memory

   D. to make readers feel sorry for him

_____ 14. What main idea do "A Special Gift: The Legacy of 'Snowflake' Bentley" and "No Gumption" share?

   A. Boys are lazy.

   B. Boys will be boys.

   C. It's important to find work that you love.

   D. As a child, you should do what your parents want you to do.

Name _____ Date _____

Vocabulary and Grammar

___ **15.** What would be a good profession for someone with an *aptitude* for math?
A. mathematician
B. cook
C. garbage man
D. poet

___ **16.** What is the purpose of a *microscope*?
A. to make things look larger
B. to make things like smaller
C. to freeze snow
D. to take pictures

___ **17.** How many sides does a *hexagon* have?
A. 2
B. 4
C. 6
D. 8

___ **18.** Which of the following items cannot *evaporate*?
A. water
B. sweat
C. snow crystals
D. sand

___ **19.** Which of the following is something a *pauper* lacks?
A. money
B. drive
C. friends
D. dreams

___ **20.** How important is a *crucial* decision?
A. very
B. somewhat
C. not very
D. not at all

Essay

21. Write an essay in which you answer one of the following questions:
A. How are "Snowflake" Bentley goals different from his father's goals?
B. How are Russell Baker's goals different from his mother's goals?

22. In an essay, compare and contrast Russell Baker's humorous writing with Barbara Eaglesham's more serious style. Use at least three details to back up your main idea. Which writer do you like more? Why?

23. Which character is more vivid to you: "Snowflake Bentley" or Russell Baker? Do you think the difference can be explained by the fact that one selection is a biography and the other one is an autobiography? If so, why does that make a difference?

24. **Thinking About the Big Question: What should we learn?** Wilson Bentley and Russell Baker have different views of what we should learn in life. Imagine you are interviewing Wilson Bentley of "The Legacy of 'Snowflake' Bentley" and Russell Baker of "No Gumption." In an essay, tell how you think the two men would answer this question: What should we learn, and why?

Unit 3 Resources: Types of Nonfiction
© Pearson Education, Inc. All rights reserved.
114

"A Special Gift: The Legacy of 'Snowflake' Bentley" by Barbara Eaglesham
"No Gumption" by Russell Baker
Selection Test B

Critical Reading *Identify the letter of the choice that best answers the question.*

1. What gift does "Snowflake" Bentley receive on his fifteenth birthday?
   A. an old microscope   C. a sling-shot
   B. a popgun   D. new skis

____ 2. What did "Snowflake" Bentley finally manage to do when he was nineteen years old?
   A. publish a book
   B. draw a snow crystal
   C. find two identical snow crystals
   D. photograph a snow crystal

____ 3. What does Russell Baker's mother despise?
   A. comic books
   B. dirty dishes
   C. inactivity
   D. *The Saturday Evening Post*

____ 4. What is Russell Baker's first job?
   A. collecting garbage
   B. selling newspapers
   C. reporting stories
   D. baby-sitting

____ 5. How did "Snowflake" Bentley contribute to science?
   A. by cataloging more than two thousand examples of snow crystals
   B. by inspiring artists
   C. by purchasing expensive photographic equipment
   D. He didn't make any contribution to science.

____ 6. Which adjective best describes "Snowflake" Bentley?
   A. curious
   B. flaky
   C. business-minded
   D. spoiled

____ 7. What prevents Russell Baker from succeeding as a salesman?
   A. poor language skills
   B. lack of drive
   C. dishonesty
   D. a disinterested mother

_____ 8. Why do you think the executive at the Curtis Publishing Company asks Russell Baker so many questions about his desire to succeed?
A. to make sure he will work hard
B. to "sell" Russell Baker the job
C. because he wants to meet Russell's Uncle Allen
D. because he likes to talk

_____ 9. What is the meaning of the maxim: "The early bird gets the worm"?
A. People who wake up early are more likely to succeed.
B. Fisherman should get started early.
C. Birds wake up hungry.
D. It can be healthy to sleep in.

_____ 10. Which excerpt from "A Special Gift: The Legacy of 'Snowflake' Bentley" suggests why the author may have considered Snowflake Bentley a subject worthy of this short biography?
A. *And nothing fascinated him more than snowflakes.*
B. *Then, holding his breath, he would observe the crystal and hurry to draw what he saw before it evaporated into thin air.*
C. *He never made more than a few thousand dollars from his work, but it had been a labor of love and he was satisfied to know that he would finally be able to share the beauty of his snow crystals with the world.*
D. *To the people of Jericho, he is remembered as the not-so-flaky-after-all "Snow-flake" Bentley.*

_____ 11. Which excerpt from "No Gumption" would you <u>not</u> find in a biography?
A. *The flaw in my character which she had already spotted was lack of gumption.*
B. *The most desirable job on earth sprang instantly to mind.*
C. *Uncle Allen had made something of himself by 1932.*
D. *There were two filling stations at the intersection with Union Avenue. . . .*

_____ 12. What is Russell Baker's tone in "No Gumption"?
A. melancholy   C. humorous
B. angry   D. serious

_____ 13. Why do you think Russell Baker chose to write about his first job?
A. to poke fun at his sister
B. because it explains why he became a writer
C. to come to grips with a painful memory
D. to gain readers, sympathy

_____ 14. What main theme do "A Special Gift: The Legacy of 'Snowflake' Bentley" and "No Gump-tion" share?
A. Boys must be taught how to work.
B. Country life is healthier for growing boys.
C. It's important to find work that you love.
D. As a child, you should do what your parents want you to do.

Vocabulary and Grammar

____ 15. What would be a good profession for someone with an *aptitude* for math?
   A. mathematician
   B. cook
   C. garbage man
   D. poet

____ 16. What is the purpose of a *microscope*?
   A. to make things look larger
   B. to make things look smaller
   C. to freeze snow crystals
   D. to photograph small particles

____ 17. How many sides does a *hexagon* have?
   A. 2
   B. 4
   C. 6
   D. 8

____ 18. Which of the following items cannot *evaporate*?
   A. water
   B. sweat
   C. snow crystals
   D. sand

____ 19. Which of the following is something a *pauper* lacks?
   A. money
   B. drive
   C. friends
   D. dreams

____ 20. How would you rate the importance of a *crucial* decision?
   A. very highly
   B. somewhat highly
   C. low
   D. very low

Essay

21. Write an essay in which you compare and contrast "Snowflake" Bentley's goals with those of his father *or* Russell Baker's goals with those of his mother. Explain why parents and children often have different ideas about how they should spend their time.

22. In an essay, compare and contrast Russell Baker's style of writing with Barbara Eaglesham's style. Which writer do you find more compelling? Why?

23. In an essay, compare and contrast how well you feel you know "Snowflake" Bentley and Russell Baker. How do the rules of biography and autobiography affect what you learned?

24. **Thinking About the Big Question: What should we learn?** Imagine you are interviewing Wilson Bentley of "The Legacy of 'Snowflake' Bentley" and Russell Baker of "No Gumption." In an essay, tell how you think the two men would answer the question: *What should we learn, and why*?

Name _____ Date _____

Exposition: How-to Essay

Prewriting: Gathering Details

Use the following chart to make a simple list of the materials or steps of a process you know well in the first column. Then, in the second column, add specific details for each area that you can include in your essay.

Simple List of Materials or Steps:	Additional Specific Details to Include in My Essay:

Drafting: Organizing Directions

Use the following graphic organizer to create a chain of events by writing the steps in your process in the order in which they occur.

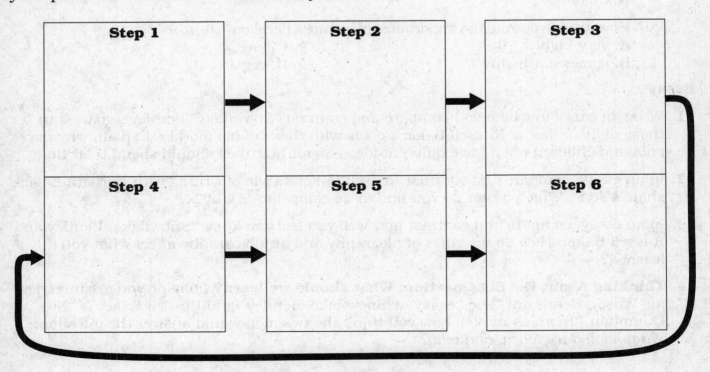

Name _____ Date _____

How-to Essay: Integrating Grammar Skills

Revising to Combine Sentences Using Conjunctions

A series of short sentences can sound choppy. In addition, the relationship between those sentences will often be unclear. You can solve both problems by using conjunctions to combine sentences with related ideas. Study this chart to choose conjunctions that make the relationship clear.

Type of Conjunction	Conjunctions	What They Show
coordinating	*and, or, nor*	equal relationship
coordinating	*but, yet*	contrasting relationship
subordinating	*although, though, even though, while*	contrasting relationship
subordinating	*because, since, so that*	cause-and-effect relationship
subordinating	*after, as soon as, when, until*	time relationships
subordinating	*where, wherever*	spatial relationships
subordinating	*if, unless*	conditional relationships

Identifying Conjunctions to Combine Choppy Sentences

A. DIRECTIONS: *Circle the conjunction that combines the two clauses into one sentence by best expressing the relationship between the clauses.*

1. Melons taste good, (and, but) most types are very healthy.
2. Bananas are more fattening than other fruits, (or, but) they are also more filling.
3. You can eat apples raw, (or, since) you can bake them.
4. You can lose weight (if, until) you eat low-calorie fruits and vegetables.

Fixing Choppy Sentences

B. DIRECTIONS: *For each item, combine the two choppy sentences into a single sentence that shows the relationship in parentheses. Write your new sentence on the line provided.*

1. (cause-and-effect) Many dieters eat vegetables. They are low in fat.

_____

2. (contrast) Raw carrots are rich in vitamin A. Cooking them loses some vitamins.

_____

3. (equal) You can eat spinach raw. You can cook it in a little olive oil.

_____

4. (time) You must wash spinach thoroughly. You add it to salad.

_____

Unit 3: Types of Nonfiction
Benchmark Test 5

MULTIPLE CHOICE

Reading Skill: Main Idea

1. What is the main idea of a selection?
   A. the topic of the selection
   B. the first sentence of the selection
   C. the details of the selection
   D. the central message of the selection

2. Which strategy would help a reader find the main idea?
   A. outlining
   B. summarizing
   C. skimming
   D. scanning

3. Which strategy would help a reader find supporting details?
   A. outlining
   B. summarizing
   C. skimming
   D. scanning

4. What is the most effective way to figure out an unstated main idea?
   A. Make connections between key points and supporting details.
   B. Figure out which of the details are supporting details.
   C. Read closely and reread if necessary to locate the main idea.
   D. Skim (look over the text quickly) or scan (run your eyes over the text).

Read the selection. Then, answer the questions that follow.

(1) The most catastrophic weather disaster in the United States was a Category 4, or extreme, hurricane that struck Galveston, Texas, on September 8, 1900. (2) A 15-foot storm surge killed more than 8,000 people on the low-lying island. (3) In an effort to prevent a similar disaster in the future, the island's elevation was raised above sea level. (4) Workers also constructed a sea wall to try to protect the city.

5. Which sentence gives the main idea of the selection?
   A. sentence one
   B. sentence two
   C. sentence three
   D. sentence four

6. Which sentence gives the most important supporting details?
   A. sentence one
   B. sentence two
   C. sentence three
   D. sentence four

Reading Skill: Analyze Author's Argument

Read the selection. Then, answer the questions that follow.

A killer is spreading poison across the earth. Rain polluted by the gases given off by factories and motor vehicles is being turned into acid. This "acid rain" is slowly destroying our environment. Acid rain has already damaged millions of acres of forests. It runs off into waterways, polluting drinking water and killing plant and animal life. Acid rain also has a harmful effect on the human body, causing lung disease and other health problems. Even our structures are affected, as the caustic rain eats away at buildings and monuments.

Acid rain has proved to be difficult to control, so government officials have hesitated to do anything about it. This cannot go on. We must urge our representatives to pass stronger antipollution laws with stiff punishment if they are not obeyed. We must act now before it is too late.

7. Which is a statement of the author's main point of view?
   A. Millions of acres of forests have been damaged by acid rain.
   B. Acid rain has a harmful effect on the human body.
   C. The government has done little about acid rain because it is difficult to control.
   D. Acid rain is a danger to the environment and must be stopped.

8. What is the primary intent of this selection?
   A. to inform lawmakers about acid rain
   B. to persuade readers to take action against acid rain
   C. to explain where acid rain comes from
   D. to describe the effects of acid rain on the human body

9. Which of the following actions would the author find most effective?
   A. Doctors meet to discuss treatments for lung diseases caused by acid rain.
   B. The government sets aside money to repair buildings damaged by acid rain.
   C. Lime is dropped in waterways to counter the effects of pollutants.
   D. Laws are passed to strictly control exhaust fumes from vehicles.

Literary Analysis: Essays

10. What is an expository essay?
    A. an essay that describes someone or something
    B. an essay that explains, defines, or interprets
    C. an essay that tells about someone's life
    D. an essay that presents the author's feelings or thoughts

11. What is the main focus of a reflective essay?
    A. an essay that tells a narrative, or story
    B. an essay that explains, defines, or interprets
    C. an essay that tells about a person's life
    D. an essay that presents the author's feelings or thoughts

Read the selection. Then, answer the questions that follow.

The Enlightenment and the Scientific Revolution were twin explosions in thinking that made the 17th and 18th centuries one of the most exciting and dynamic eras in European history. People came to believe in the power of human reason apart from the guidance of religion. Astronomers concluded that the sun rather than the Earth was the center of the universe, philosophers questioned kings' divine right to rule, and explorers brought back new ideas from the Middle and Far East. Modern thought stems from the Enlightenment, and contemporary science is a result of the Scientific Revolution.

12. What kind of essay is the selection?
   A. persuasive
   B. reflective
   C. expository
   D. descriptive

13. What is the main purpose of the selection?
   A. to persuade
   B. to present feelings and thoughts
   C. to describe
   D. to explain

14. What change in thinking occurred during the Enlightenment and the Scientific Revolution?
   A. People looked to the Bible for answers to all questions.
   B. People believed what their rulers told them to.
   C. People accepted what their teachers taught them.
   D. People relied on their abilities to reason.

Read the selection. Then, answer the questions that follow.

My closest friend's name is Miss Ruth—at least that is what I call her. She is seventy years old. My unexpected friendship with Miss Ruth began when I was thirteen. I wanted to earn money by doing yard work. My friends would never have approached the grand old lady of Elm Street, but I just marched up the steps and knocked on her front door. Miss Ruth, who took pride in her good judgment of people, looked me up and down, and then gave me a job.

15. What kind of essay is the selection?
   A. persuasive
   B. reflective
   C. expository
   D. descriptive

16. What is the main purpose of the selection?
   A. to present feelings or thoughts
   B. to describe
   C. to explain
   D. to persuade

17. What is a likely secondary purpose?
   A. to persuade kids to get an after-school job
   B. to explain the importance of friendship
   C. to describe an unusual friendship
   D. to persuade kids to befriend the elderly

Literary Analysis: Biography and Autobiography

18. The following sentence most likely came from which type of writing?

I reached tentatively for the tiny, pink piglet.

A. reflective essay
B. expository essay
C. biography
D. autobiography

19. In what way are biography and autobiography alike?

A. They are both imaginative fiction.
B. They both describe interesting events.
C. They both tell someone's life story.
D. They both tell about the writer's life.

20. What is the most significant difference between biography and autobiography?

A. Biography tells what someone does, and autobiography tells what someone thinks.
B. Biography describes someone else's life, and autobiography describes the writer's life.
C. Biography is accurate, and autobiography is inventive.
D. Biography tells about someone's entire life, and autobiography tells about incidents in someone's life.

Vocabulary: Suffixes and Roots

21. What is the meaning of the word formed by adding the suffix *-able* to the end of the word *notice*?

A. capable of being seen
B. able to see in advance
C. tending to see things
D. not worthy of being seen

22. Using your knowledge of the suffix *-ness*, what is the meaning of the word *awkwardness* in the following sentence?

We noticed his awkwardness on the dance floor, but his partner did not seem to mind.

A. act causing embarrassment
B. characterized by being difficult to manage
C. condition of being clumsy
D. relating to a lack of skill

23. What does the suffix *-able* mean in the word *disposable*?

A. lacking in
B. tending to
C. full of
D. capable of being

24. Using your knowledge of the root *-rupt-*, what is the meaning of *interrupt* in the following sentence?

"I hate to interrupt your conversation," but I really need to talk to you now," John said to his mother and father.

A. add to
B. break into
C. blend into
D. subtract from

25. Using your knowledge of the root *-just-*, what is the best definition of *justifies* as it is used in the following sentence?

The actor's award justifies the director's decision to cast him in the role.

A. provides an excuse for   C. shows to be right

B. goes against   D. does not explain

26. How does the word *erupts* reflect the meaning of the root *-rupt-*?

A. If something *erupts*, it bursts or breaks out.   C. If something *erupts* it captures something else.

B. If something *erupts*, it spills.   D. If something *erupts*, it goes underground.

Grammar: Coordinating Conjunctions

27. Which word in the following sentence is a conjunction?

Slowly but surely Dan's dog learned to respond to hand signals.

A. but   C. began

B. dog   D. to

28. How are coordinating conjunctions normally used?

A. to connect subordinating to main clauses   C. to connect the same type of sentence elements

B. to connect three items in a series   D. to connect sentences

29. Which of the following sentences contains a coordinating conjunction?

A. These days, Keegan is either crabby or melancholy.   C. Pack your lunch before you forget.

B. I was late for school because I ignored the alarm.   D. Harvey would be a great cat if he didn't shed so much.

30. Which conjunction would best combine the following sentences?

You can't borrow the car. I need it to drive to work.

A. and   C. because

B. or   D. unless

31. Which conjunction would best combine the following sentences?

I love to write. I am less enthusiastic about editing.

A. and   C. yet

B. but   D. when

Grammar: Prepositions

32. What is the function of a preposition in a sentence?
    A. to express action
    B. to show the subject of the sentence
    C. to tell more about the subject
    D. to connect a noun or pronoun to another word

33. Which word in the following sentence is a preposition?

    Hannah sat down and wrote a long e-mail to her father.

    A. and
    B. a
    C. to
    D. her

34. With what type of word does a prepositional phrase end?
    A. a preposition
    B. a verb or adverb
    C. an article or adjective
    D. a noun or pronoun

ESSAY

Writing

35. Which do you think is better, being the oldest child in a family or being the youngest? Write a compare-and-contrast essay in which you assess the advantages and disadvantages of both birth positions. Cite at least two advantages and two disadvantages.

36. Plan an essay describing your favorite sport or game to a foreign visitor who has no idea what it is or how it is played. Outline your essay in a three-level outline using Roman numerals to identify key points and capital letters to identify supporting details. Be sure to indent.

37. Everyone is an expert—at something! Pick something you know how to make or do well: a craft project, a food dish, or another skill at which you shine. Then, write a how-to essay that lists the steps necessary to accomplish the project. Be sure to include all the necessary materials and list the steps in sequential order.

Unit 3: Types of Nonfiction   Skills Concept Map—2
What should we learn?

Words you can use to discuss the Big Question

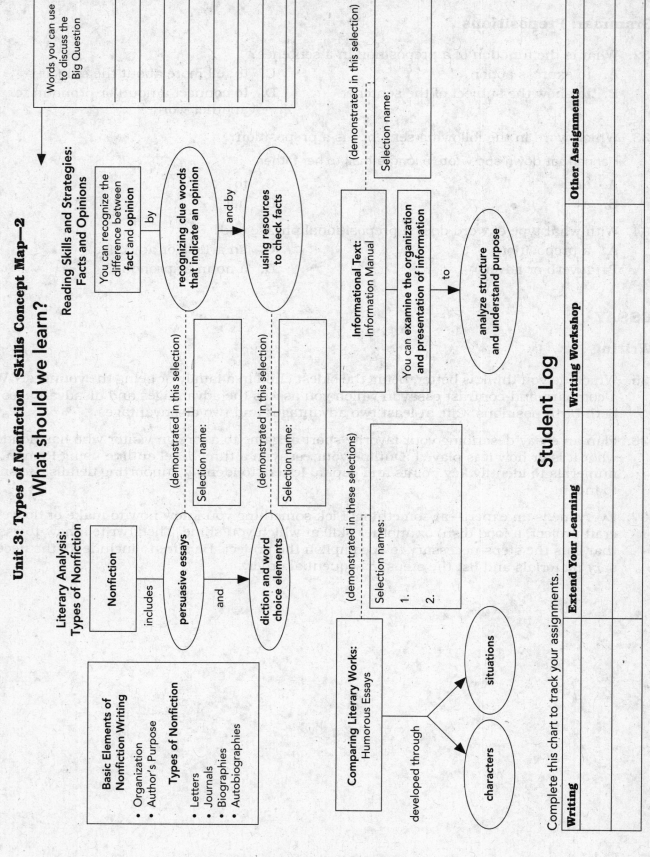

Reading Skills and Strategies: Facts and Opinions

You can recognize the difference between fact and opinion

by

recognizing clue words that indicate an opinion

and by

using resources to check facts

(demonstrated in this selection)

Selection name: _____

Literary Analysis: Types of Nonfiction

Nonfiction

includes

persuasive essays

and

diction and word choice elements

(demonstrated in this selection)

Selection name: _____

(demonstrated in this selection)

Selection name: _____

Basic Elements of Nonfiction Writing
- Organization
- Author's Purpose

Types of Nonfiction
- Letters
- Journals
- Biographies
- Autobiographies

Informational Text: Information Manual

You can examine the organization and presentation of information

to

analyze structure and understand purpose

(demonstrated in this selection)

Selection name: _____

Comparing Literary Works: Humorous Essays

developed through

situations

characters

(demonstrated in these selections)

Selection names:

1. _____
2. _____

Student Log

Complete this chart to track your assignments.

Writing	Extend Your Learning	Writing Workshop	Other Assignments

"The Eternal Frontier" by Louis L'Amour
Vocabulary Warm-up Word Lists

Study these words. Then, complete the activities that follow.

Word List A

achieve [uh CHEEV] *v.* to succeed in doing; accomplish
Stuart is confident of his ability to <u>achieve</u> good grades.

automobile [aw tuh moh BEEL] *n.* a passenger car
Dina's first <u>automobile</u> was a red sedan.

considered [kuhn SID uhrd] *v.* regarded as; thought to be
Madison was <u>considered</u> talented by those who knew her.

enable [en AY buhl] *v.* to give the means, opportunity, or ability to
These shoes <u>enable</u> me to walk long distances without tiring.

outer [OW tuhr] *adj.* relatively far out or far removed
Humans have always been fascinated by <u>outer</u> space.

scarcely [SKAYRS lee] *adv.* only just; barely
Because she had not studied much, Hannah <u>scarcely</u> passed the test.

system [SIS tuhm] *n.* a group of things or parts that work together as a whole
The brain and spinal cord are the center of the nervous <u>system</u>.

vehicle [VEE uh kuhl] *n.* any device used to carry something
Barry's primary <u>vehicle</u> is a ten-speed bicycle.

Word List B

asteroids [AS tuhr oydz] *n.* large objects made of rock moving around in space
Do you think <u>asteroids</u> resulted from an exploded planet?

atmospheric [at muhs FIR ik] *adj.* having to do with the gases surrounding Earth
<u>Atmospheric</u> pressure is less on a mountaintop than at sea level.

destiny [DES tuh nee] *n.* the outcome or fate that is bound to come
Amy is sure that free will can change one's <u>destiny</u>.

development [di VEL uhp muhnt] *n.* an instance of growing larger or better
Yvonne's stage of physical <u>development</u> is typical for her age.

obvious [AHB vee uhs] *adj.* easy to see or understand; plain
It was <u>obvious</u> that Steven was getting ready to cry.

origin [AWR uh jin] *n.* that in which something has its beginning; a source
What is the <u>origin</u> of the word *photograph*?

paved [PAYVD] *adj.* covered with concrete, asphalt, or brick
Simon's <u>paved</u> driveway is starting to crack.

solar [SOH luhr] *adj.* of or having to do with the sun
There may be more than nine planets in our <u>solar</u> system.

"The Eternal Frontier" by Louis L'Amour
Vocabulary Warm-up Exercises

Exercise A *Fill in each blank in the paragraph below with an appropriate word from Word List A. Use each word only once.*

For the past six months, Daniel had [1] _____ buying a new car. The old one was [2] _____ able to get up the hill to his house. He needed a [3] _____ that could [4] _____ a speed of at least sixty-five miles per hour on the freeway. The [5] _____ he had been driving for the past ten years needed a complete overhaul of the [6] _____. The only good thing about the old car was its [7] _____ appearance, for Daniel always kept it waxed. A recent pay raise at his job would finally [8] _____ him to replace the old car.

Exercise B *Answer the questions with complete explanations.*

1. Can lights that run on <u>solar</u> power be recharged at night?
_____

2. What are three things a baby learns in the first year of <u>development</u>?
_____

3. If it appeared that your <u>destiny</u> was to be unfit, what could you do to change it?
_____

4. What is your favorite <u>atmospheric</u> condition?
_____

5. What would be the greatest danger for a spaceship traveling through the orbit of <u>asteroids</u>?
_____

6. Would you rather drive on <u>paved</u> roads or unpaved roads?
_____

7. What is one common word you can name whose <u>origin</u> is a foreign language?
_____

8. What would be some <u>obvious</u> signs that someone has a cold?
_____

"The Eternal Frontier" by Louis L'Amour
Reading Warm-up A

Read the following passage. Pay special attention to the underlined words. Then, read it again, and complete the activities. Use a separate sheet of paper for your written answers.

A Model T <u>automobile</u> came "in any color you choose, so long as it's black." That is probably Henry Ford's most famous statement about his most famous car. It is not, however, the most important. The nature of Ford's gift to the world is revealed in another statement. When the Model T was first made, in October 1908, he said, "I will build a motor car for the great multitude." That is just what the Model T became. Before the Model T, only the well-to-do could buy a motor <u>vehicle</u>. Henry Ford made it possible for ordinary workers to buy one, too.

How did Ford <u>achieve</u> that? The answer lies in his <u>system</u> of producing cars. He was not the first person to use the assembly line to produce a car. He did, however, push the idea to its <u>outer</u> limits.

In 1906, Ford began working on a secret plan to develop the Model T. It took him two years. He finally presented an affordable car for $825. By 1912, he had improved the assembly line. He was able to reduce the price to $575. For the first time, a car cost less than the average annual wage in the United States.

In 1914, Henry Ford made a startling move. He raised his workers' pay. Most workers then earned $2.38 for a nine-hour day. He said he would pay $5 for an eight-hour day. Many businessmen <u>considered</u> Ford's move reckless. Most people could <u>scarcely</u> believe it when the company's profits doubled over the next two years. The raise would <u>enable</u> workers earning $5 a day to buy cars of their own. Thus, some of the money was returned to Ford's company. Raising his workers' salaries "was one of the finest cost-cutting moves we ever made," he said later.

1. Circle the name of the <u>automobile</u> that is being discussed. Use *automobile* in a sentence.

2. Underline the word that describes the word <u>vehicle</u>. What does *vehicle* mean?

3. What was Henry Ford able to <u>achieve</u>? What is another word for *achieve*?

4. Underline the words that tell what Henry Ford's <u>system</u> was for. Describe a *system* you use to get something done.

5. Circle the word that <u>outer</u> describes. Use the phrase *outer limits* in a sentence.

6. Underline the word that tells what many businessmen <u>considered</u> Ford's plan to be. What does *considered* mean?

7. Circle the words that are modified by the adverb <u>scarcely</u>. Use *scarcely* in a sentence.

8. Underline the words that tell what the raise would <u>enable</u> workers earning $5 a day to do. What else might a raise in pay *enable* someone to do?

Name _____ Date _____

"The Eternal Frontier" by Louis L'Amour
Reading Warm-up B

Read the following passage. Pay special attention to the underlined words. Then, read it again, and complete the activities. Use a separate sheet of paper for your written answers.

The history of space exploration began with Galileo's invention of the telescope in the early part of the seventeenth century. The first telescopes were not strong, but they improved in time. Their <u>development</u> continued over the next three hundred years. The telescope has become our primary tool for observing the stars and planets.

Today our telescopes are large and powerful. The Hubble space telescope, for example, orbits above Earth's atmosphere. It allows us to see far into space. Yet the planets and <u>asteroids</u> of our <u>solar</u> system still hold many mysteries. The first planetary missions of the National Aeronautics and Space Administration (NASA) were "fly-bys." The spacecraft simply zoomed by a planet. As they did, they took pictures. They also gathered <u>atmospheric</u> data. Then they continued on—out into deep space. Their <u>destiny</u> is unknown. It is true that those spacecraft are no longer useful to scientists. However, they <u>paved</u> the way for later space probes that were able to orbit the planets.

We can learn a great deal more about a planet by orbiting it. Planets in the inner solar system were studied by the *Viking* orbiters at Mars and the *Magellan* orbiter at Venus. *Galileo* was launched in 1989 and reached Jupiter in 1995. It was the first spacecraft to orbit Jupiter in the outer solar system.

Why should we explore Jupiter? Jupiter holds clues that may help us understand the <u>origin</u> of our solar system. Those clues might tell us how it has developed for the past four and a half billion years. One of Jupiter's moons has active volcanoes. Others consist of strange, icy land. We wonder how they compare with Earth. Can we find evidence of life elsewhere in our solar system? What can the other planets teach us about Earth? It is <u>obvious</u> that the answers will not be known soon. Through space probes like *Galileo*, however, scientists are getting a greater understanding of the solar system.

1. Underline the words that tell what invention underwent <u>development</u>. Use *development* in a sentence.

2. Circle the word that names other bodies in the solar system besides <u>asteroids</u>. What are *asteroids*?

3. Underline the word that the adjective <u>solar</u> modifies. Name three objects in our *solar* system.

4. Circle the word that tells what the spacecraft did with the <u>atmospheric</u> data. Use *atmospheric* in a sentence.

5. Underline the word that tells about the <u>destiny</u> of the spacecraft. What might someone believe about his or her own *destiny*?

6. Circle the words that tell what the "fly-bys" paved the way for. Tell how the expression <u>paved</u> *the way* relates to the word *paved*.

7. Underline the word that tells what may help us understand our solar system's <u>origin</u>. Use *origin* in a sentence.

8. Circle the words that explain what is <u>obvious</u>. Write one truth about the solar system that is *obvious*.

"The Eternal Frontier" by Louis L'Amour
Writing About the Big Question

What should we learn?

Big Question Vocabulary

analyze	curiosity	discover	evaluate	examine
experiment	explore	facts	information	inquire
interview	investigate	knowledge	question	understand

A. *Choose one word from the list above to complete each sentence. There may be more than one right answer.*

1. Do you believe the desire to _____ is part of human nature?

2. Astronauts need the traits of bravery and _____.

3. I read an interesting _____ with a space shuttle astronaut.

B. *Follow the directions in responding to each of the items below.*

1. What do you think can be learned from space travel? Write at least two complete sentences, using one or more of the Big Question vocabulary words. You may use the words in different forms (for example you can change *analyze* to *analyzing*).

   _____

   _____

2. What do you think can be learned from traveling to another city, state or country? Write at least two complete sentences, using one or more of the Big Question vocabulary words. You may use the words in different forms (for example you can change *experiment* to *experiments*).

   _____

   _____

C. *Complete the sentence below. Use the completed sentence as the beginning of a short paragraph in which you discuss the big question.*

When we stop asking questions about the unknown _____

   _____

   _____

Name _____ Date _____

"The Eternal Frontier" by Louis L'Amour
Reading: Fact and Opinion

When you read nonfiction, it is important to be able to distinguish between fact and opinion. A **fact** is something that can be proved true. An **opinion** is a person's judgment or belief. It may be supported by factual evidence, but it cannot be proven.

As you read, **recognize clue words that indicate an opinion,** as in the phrases "I believe" and "in my opinion." Also look for words such as *always, never, must, cannot, best, worst,* and *all,* which may indicate a broad statement that reveals a personal judgment. Emotional statements are also often clues to opinion.

You can tell that the statement below from "The Eternal Frontier" is an opinion because it cannot be proven. Another hint is that it contains the word *must.*

What is needed now is leaders with perspective; we need leadership on a thousand fronts, but they must be men and women who can take the long view and help to shape the outlines of our future.

DIRECTIONS: *Identify each of the following quotations from "The Eternal Frontier" as a* fact *or an* opinion. *Then, briefly explain your answer. For quotations identified as opinions, point out any words or phrases that indicate it is an opinion.*

1. "All that has gone before is preliminary."

   Fact / Opinion: _____ **Explanation:** _____

   _____

2. "In 1900 there were 144 miles of surfaced road in the United States. Now there are over 3,000,000."

   Fact / Opinion: _____ **Explanation:** _____

   _____

3. "There will always be the nay-sayers, those who cling to our lovely green planet as a baby clings to its mother."

   Fact / Opinion: _____ **Explanation:** _____

   _____

4. "We have a driving need to see what lies beyond [the frontier] . . ."

   Fact / Opinion: _____ **Explanation:** _____

   _____

5. "We landed men on the moon; we sent a vehicle beyond the limits of the solar system, a vehicle still moving farther and farther into that limitless distance."

   Fact / Opinion: _____ **Explanation:** _____

   _____

6. "Nor is the mind of man bound by any limits at all."

   Fact / Opinion: _____ **Explanation:** _____

   _____

"The Eternal Frontier" by Louis L'Amour
Literary Analysis: Persuasive Essay

A **persuasive essay** is a piece of nonfiction that presents a series of arguments to convince readers that they should believe or act in a certain way. Below are some techniques that are often used in persuasive essays. When you read a persuasive essay, be aware of these techniques; you will need to decide whether they are powerful enough to persuade you to accept the author's ideas.

- **Appeals to authority:** using the opinions of experts and well-known people
- **Appeals to emotion:** using words that convey strong feeling
- **Appeals to reason:** using logical arguments backed by statistics and facts

DIRECTIONS: *In the left-hand column of the following chart, copy down statements from "The Eternal Frontier" that include appeals to emotion. In the right-hand column, copy down statements that include appeals to reason. Find at least two examples of each kind of appeal. (The essay does not make any appeals to authority.)*

Appeals to Emotion	Appeals to Reason

Name _____ Date _____

"**The Eternal Frontier**" by Louis L'Amour
Vocabulary Builder

Word List

antidote   atmospheric   destiny   frontier   impetus   preliminary

A. DIRECTIONS: *Answer each question in a complete sentence. In your answer, use one of the Word List words in place of the italicized word or phrase.*

1. What *unexplored region* might you want to learn more about?

_____

2. Can you recommend a *cure* for an hour spent working in the hot sun?

_____

3. What is the *driving force* behind studying for a test?

_____

4. What kind of examination might be given *before* a major examination?

_____

5. What is one important use of the gases *surrounding Earth*?

_____

6. Do you believe humankind will find its *future* in space?

_____

B. WORD STUDY: *The Latin root -peti- means "to ask for," "to request," or "to strive after." Read the following sentences. Use your knowledge of the Latin root -peti- to write a full sentence to answer each question. Include the italicized word in your answer.*

1. When you *petition* your principal, are you hoping for a response?

_____

2. Can *competition* motivate a person to improve her skills?

_____

3. Does *repetition* help you learn new words?

_____

"The Eternal Frontier" by Louis L'Amour
Enrichment: Space Exploration

Scientists have explored many parts of our solar system already, using manned and unmanned spacecraft. Use reference books, the Internet (for example, nasa.gov), or both to find out what has been learned from the space missions listed below. Then, write a brief description in the right-hand column of the chart.

Spacecraft	What It Did
Apollo 11	
Venera 7	
Mariner 9	
Pioneer 10	
Mariner 10	
Ulysses	
Galileo	

"The Eternal Frontier" by Louis L'Amour
Open-Book Test

Short Answer *Write your responses to the questions in this section on the lines provided.*

1. Author Louis L'Amour writes in "The Eternal Frontier" about the exploration of space. He says that "all that has gone before was preliminary." What does he mean? Base your answer on the meaning of *preliminary*.

   _____

   _____

2. The author of "The Eternal Frontier" mentions the automobile, radio, television, and flight. What is his purpose in talking about these inventions?

   _____

   _____

   _____

3. A fact is a statement that can be proved. An opinion is a belief or judgment that cannot be proved. In "The Eternal Frontier," L'Amour says that there were 144 miles of roads in the United States in 1900. Is this a fact or an opinion? How do you know?

   _____

   _____

   _____

4. L'Amour refers to the nay-sayers in "The Eternal Frontier." Whom does he mean? What does he think of them?

   _____

   _____

   _____

5. In "The Eternal Frontier," what does Louis L'Amour mean when he says that if we had focused only on the earth, "we would still be hunters and gatherers"? Explain.

   _____

   _____

   _____

6. In "The Eternal Frontier," L'Amour writes that "the space effort gave great impetus to the development of computing devices." What might have happened without that impetus? Base your answer on the meaning of *impetus*.

   _____

   _____

   _____

7. Does this statement near the end of "The Eternal Frontier" appeal to reason or to emotion? Explain your answer.

   Transistors, chips, integrated circuits, Teflon, new medicines, new ways of treating diseases, new ways of performing operations, . . . are linked to the space effort.

   _____

   _____

   _____

   _____

8. In "The Eternal Frontier," the author appeals both to reason and to emotion. When he writes at the end of his essay, "If we are content to live in the past, we have no future," to which is he appealing? Explain.

   _____

   _____

   _____

9. The author of "The Eternal Frontier" uses both facts and opinions to make his points. In the chart below, list three facts and three opinions from "The Eternal Frontier." Then, answer the question that follows the chart.

Facts	Opinions

   Which do you find more persuasive in this essay, facts or opinions? Why?

   _____

   _____

10. "The Eternal Frontier" is a persuasive essay. What is Louis L'Amour trying to persuade us to do? How do you know?

   _____

   _____

   _____

   _____

Essay

Write an extended response to the question of your choice or to the question or questions your teacher assigns you.

11. In "The Eternal Frontier," Louis L'Amour tries to persuade his readers that his opinions are reasonable. He uses appeals to emotion and to reason. In an essay, discuss L'Amour's use of either emotion or reason in his persuasive essay. Tell how he uses facts and opinions to persuade the reader. Give examples from the selection to illustrate your points.

12. In "The Eternal Frontier," Louis L'Amour attempts to persuade his readers that they should support the exploration of outer space. In an essay, summarize L'Amour's argument. Tell why he believes that space exploration is important. Then, state your own opinion. Do you agree or disagree? Why? Refer to L'Amour's arguments to defend your position.

13. In "The Eternal Frontier," Louis L'Amour writes, "If we are content to live in the past, we have no future." In an essay, tell whether or not you agree with this statement and explain your position. Support your points with references to the selection.

14. **Thinking About the Big Question: What should we learn?** In "The Eternal Frontier," Louis L'Amour discusses the past when explaining what we should do in the future. In an essay, tell what he thinks we should learn from the past. How does it help us plan for the future? Refer to examples in the essay to support your points.

Oral Response

15. Go back to question 2, 5, or 9 or to the question your teacher assigns you. Take a few minutes to expand your answer and prepare an oral response. Find additional details in "The Eternal Frontier" that support your points. If necessary, make notes to guide your oral response.

"The Eternal Frontier" by Louis L'Amour
Selection Test A

Critical Reading *Identify the letter of the choice that best answers the question.*

____ 1. Which word or phrase in this statement from "The Eternal Frontier" indicates that the author is expressing an opinion?

    All that has gone before is preliminary.

    A. All
    B. has gone
    C. before
    D. preliminary

____ 2. According to Louis L'Amour, what might stand in the way of progress?
    A. a devastating war
    B. a negative attitude
    C. a lack of money
    D. a terrible disease

____ 3. Why does the author of "The Eternal Frontier" mention the car, radio, television, and flight?
    A. to show that progress is occurring quickly
    B. to prove we have gone as far as we can
    C. to remind us that change takes time
    D. to urge us to stop wasting our potential

____ 4. How can you tell that this statement from "The Eternal Frontier" is a fact?

    In 1900 there were 144 miles of surfaced road in the United States.

    A. It contains a statistic.
    B. It can be proved true.
    C. It cannot be proved true.
    D. It comes from a reference book.

____ 5. Where does Louis L'Amour think we should travel?
    A. to the planets
    B. to the moon
    C. to the asteroids
    D. to outer space

_____ 6. How can you tell that this statement from "The Eternal Frontier" is an opinion?

Mankind is not bound by its atmospheric envelope or by its gravitational field, nor is the mind of man bound by any limits at all.

A. It contains a statistic.

B. It can be proved true.

C. It cannot be proved true.

D. It is an expert's idea.

_____ 7. According to Louis L'Amour, what should our leaders do?

A. They should pass laws to make space exploration easier.

B. They should raise the money needed for space travel.

C. They should show us what the future can hold for us.

D. They should volunteer to travel on a space mission.

_____ 8. What does Louis L'Amour say about the vehicle we sent beyond the solar system?

A. It is an example of the kind of vehicle we should send into space.

B. It is an example of the difficulty of sending people into space.

C. It proves that we have the technology to attempt space travel.

D. It can prove to someone that we made the effort to go into space.

_____ 9. How does this statement from "The Eternal Frontier" appeal to emotion?

If we are content to live in the past, we have no future.

A. It contains an expert's opinion.

B. It presents a logical argument.

C. It conveys strong feelings.

D. It reveals the author's opinion.

_____ 10. What is Louis L'Amour trying to persuade us to do in "The Eternal Frontier"?

A. give money to the space program

B. show interest in space exploration

C. understand history better

D. train to become astronauts

Vocabulary and Grammar

_____ 11. What might be an *antidote* to a crowded city street?

A. a quiet country road

B. an incurable disease

C. a well-attended concert

D. a popular restaurant

___ **12.** In which sentence is the word *frontier* used logically?

    A. The people waiting to see the space show moved to the *frontier* of the line.

    B. Houses were built on the crowded *frontier*, well away from the wilderness.

    C. Space is the next *frontier* because most places on Earth have been explored.

    D. The visitors to the space show left their hats and coats in the spacious *frontier*.

___ **13.** What part of this sentence from "The Eternal Frontier" does the underlined word represent?

    Our frontier <u>lies</u> in outer space.

    A. subject

    B. simple subject

    C. predicate

    D. simple predicate

___ **14.** What part of this sentence about "The Eternal Frontier" does the underlined word represent?

    The <u>author</u> of the essay talks about progress and the future.

    A. subject

    B. simple subject

    C. predicate

    D. simple predicate

Essay

15. In an essay, describe Louis L'Amour's purpose in "The Eternal Frontier." Answer this question: What is he trying to get his readers to do or believe? Give examples to support your point.

16. In "The Eternal Frontier," Louis L'Amour tries to persuade his readers that his opinions are reasonable. He uses appeals to emotion and appeals to reason. In an essay, discuss L'Amour's use of one of these methods of persuasion. Give examples from the selection to illustrate your points.

17. Thinking About the Big Question: What should we learn? In "The Eternal Frontier," Louis L'Amour discusses the past when he explains what we should do in the future. In an essay, tell what he thinks we should learn from the past. How does it help us plan for the future? Refer to examples in the essay to support your points.

"The Eternal Frontier" by Louis L'Amour
Selection Test B

Critical Reading *Identify the letter of the choice that best completes the statement or answers the question.*

____ 1. Why does Louis L'Amour refer to the moon and planets as "mere stepping stones"?
A. We can use them to move spacecraft toward outer space.
B. Their gravitational forces can push us into outer space.
C. They have the same qualities as outer space.
D. They will teach us what we need to know to reach outer space.

____ 2. Why does Louis L'Amour think we can move into space quickly?
A. We are facing a devastating war.
B. The space program has unlimited funds.
C. We have made rapid progress in the past.
D. Many people support the space program.

____ 3. In "The Eternal Frontier," Louis L'Amour mentions cars, television, and flight to show that
A. human beings can rapidly progress toward exploration of space.
B. technologically, human beings have progressed as far as possible.
C. massive change occurs only in spurts and over long periods of time.
D. if they are to survive, human beings must stop wasting their potential.

____ 4. Which of these statements from "The Eternal Frontier" is a fact?
A. In 1900 there were 144 miles of surfaced road in the United States.
B. What is needed now is leaders with perspective.
C. We are a people born to the frontier.
D. It is our destiny to move out, to accept the challenge, to dare the unknown.

____ 5. According to Louis L'Amour, we need leaders who will
A. pass laws making space exploration mandatory.
B. raise the funds necessary for space exploration.
C. show society what the future might be.
D. volunteer to travel on space missions.

____ 6. Whom does L'Amour refer to as "the nay-sayers" in "The Last Frontier"?
A. those who do not support technological development
B. those who do not believe we should explore outer space
C. those who do not want to become astronauts
D. those who do not believe the Earth can be saved

____ 7. According to "The Eternal Frontier," what role has history played in humanity's movement toward the goal of exploring space?
A. It shows that humankind has already turned away from exploration.
B. It shows that humankind has always sought the frontier.
C. It shows that the exploration of frontiers can be dangerous.
D. It shows that humankind has much to do on Earth before exploring space.

____ 8. Which of these statements from "The Eternal Frontier" is an opinion?
   A. The question I am most often asked is, "Where is the frontier now?"
   B. In the past seventy years we have developed the automobile, radio, television, transcontinental and transoceanic flight, and the electrification of the country.
   C. The frontier is the line that separates the known from the unknown.
   D. Mankind is not bound by its atmospheric envelope or by its gravitational field, nor is the mind of mankind bound by any limits at all.

____ 9. Which of these statements from "The Eternal Frontier" is a fact?
   A. The moon, the asteroids, the planets, these are mere stepping stones.
   B. Wherever it [the frontier] may be, and we have a driving need to see what lies beyond.
   C. We landed men on the moon; we sent a vehicle beyond the limits of the solar system.
   D. It is our destiny to move out, to accept the challenge, to dare the unknown.

____ 10. Which of the following statements relating to "The Eternal Frontier" appeals to reason?
   A. People should explore space because they have prepared themselves mentally to do so.
   B. Americans must explore space because the frontier has always been part of their culture.
   C. The space industry is important because other life forms must know we once existed.
   D. The space industry has been beneficial in giving impetus to much new technology.

____ 11. Which of these statements from "The Eternal Frontier" reveals that the essay is intended to persuade?
   A. In 1900 there were 144 miles of surfaced road in the United States.
   B. There will always be the nay-sayers, those who cling to our lovely green planet.
   C. We landed men on the moon; we sent a vehicle beyond the limits of the solar system.
   D. It is our destiny to move out, to accept the challenge, to dare the unknown.

____ 12. Which of these statements from "The Eternal Frontier" appeals to emotion?
   A. Paved roads and the development of the automobile have gone hand in hand.
   B. A few years ago we moved into outer space.
   C. The computer age has arisen in part from the space effort.
   D. If we are content to live in the past, we have no future.

Vocabulary and Grammar

____ 13. In "The Last Frontier," what does L'Amour mean when he says that "the space effort gave great *impetus* to the development of computing devices"?
   A. It was a driving force in the development of computers.
   B. It kept us from developing the fastest computers.
   C. It provided the funds for the development of computers.
   D. It created hindrances to the development of computers.

____ **14.** When L'Amour writes that "all that has gone before was *preliminary*," he means that everything that has gone before the exploration of space
   A. has meant very little.
   B. has been important.
   C. has led to the main event.
   D. has been specially planned.

____ **15.** Which word in this sentence from "The Eternal Frontier" is the simple subject?
   The computer age has arisen in part from the space effort.

   A. computer
   B. age
   C. part
   D. effort

____ **16.** What is the simple subject of this sentence from "The Eternal Frontier"?
   Where is the frontier now?

   A. Where
   B. is
   C. frontier
   D. now

____ **17.** What is the simple predicate in this sentence from "The Eternal Frontier"?
   Most of these developments have been . . . incorporated into our day-to-day life.

   A. have
   B. have been
   C. have been incorporated
   D. incorporated

Essay

18. In "The Eternal Frontier," Louis L'Amour tries to persuade his readers that they should support the exploration of outer space. In an essay, summarize L'Amour's argument. That is, tell why he believes that space exploration is important. Then, state your opinion—tell whether you agree or disagree with him. Refer to L'Amour's arguments to defend your position.

19. In "The Eternal Frontier," Louis L'Amour writes, "If we are content to live in the past, we have no future." In an essay, tell whether or not you agree with this statement, and explain why. Support your points with two references to the selection.

20. **Thinking About the Big Question: What should we learn?** In "The Eternal Frontier," Louis L'Amour discusses the past when explaining what we should do in the future. In an essay, tell what he thinks we should learn from the past. How does it help us plan for the future? Refer to examples in the essay to support your points.

Name _____ Date _____

Study these words. Then, complete the activities that follow.

Word List A

century [SEN chuh ree] *n.* any period of 100 years
   Amy's grandmother was born in the first half of the twentieth <u>century</u>.

civil [SIV uhl] *adj.* of or having to do with citizens or citizenship
   The suspect's <u>civil</u> rights were violated when his car was searched.

community [kuh MYOO nuh tee] *n.* a group of people living or working together
   Our <u>community</u> got together to raise money for the school.

concerned [kuhn SERND] *adj.* involved or interested in
   Timothy was <u>concerned</u> about the grade he was getting in science.

create [kree AYT] *v.* to cause to come into existence
   Jack's goal was to <u>create</u> a different and exciting type of art.

equality [ee KWAHL uh tee] *n.* the state of having the same rights and privileges
   Our country is founded on the principle of <u>equality</u> for all.

relations [ri LAY shuhnz] *n.* connections between people, groups, or nations
   <u>Relations</u> between England and the United States are strong.

society [suh SY uh tee] *n.* all of the people living at any one time
   <u>Society</u> benefits when the children are educated.

Word List B

backgrounds [BAK growndz] *n.* people's education and experience
   People of all <u>backgrounds</u> participated in the demonstration.

ethnic [ETH nik] *adj.* relating to a particular race, nation, or tribe
   Sunita's <u>ethnic</u> heritage includes a spicy cuisine.

fundamental [fun duh MEN tuhl] *adj.* essential; basic
   Marsha and Jan share a <u>fundamental</u> belief in the value of sharing.

issues [ISH ooz] *n.* topics or problems under discussion
   The candidates debated important economic <u>issues</u>.

positive [PAHZ uh tiv] *adj.* making a definite contribution; constructive
   Hal's <u>positive</u> attitude encouraged Sally to keep on hoping.

prejudices [PREJ uh dis iz] *n.* judgments formed before the facts are known
   <u>Prejudices</u> against other races harm everyone.

segregation [seg ruh GAY shuhn] *n.* separating racial or religious groups from each other
   School <u>segregation</u> based on race is against the law.

tolerance [TAHL uhr uhns] *n.* willingness to allow people to do, say, and believe what they want
   <u>Tolerance</u> is necessary if we are to get along.

Unit 3 Resources: Types of Nonfiction
145

"All Together Now" by Barbara Jordan
Vocabulary Warm-up Exercises

Exercise A *Fill in each blank in the paragraph below with an appropriate word from Word List A. Use each word only once.*

Social [1] _____ among the residents of our neighborhood have not been good lately. Now is the time to exercise our [2] _____ right to the pursuit of happiness! In order to [3] _____ a better sense of [4] _____ on our block and show that we truly share common interests, we will meet at Bill's house on Friday. Anyone who is [5] _____ about the condition of the playground should attend. That playground was built many, many years ago, in the last [6] _____, in fact, and it needs updating. To show that we believe firmly in [7] _____ of opportunity, everyone is invited to attend. We hope that everyone will participate. After all, we know that all of [8] _____ benefits when its children are happy and thriving.

Exercise B *Answer the questions with complete explanations.*

1. If you get annoyed when someone expresses an opinion you disagree with, are you showing <u>tolerance</u>?
   _____

2. Are people of all <u>backgrounds</u> welcome in every country throughout the world?
   _____

3. Would keeping a five-year-old from attending high school be considered an act of <u>segregation</u>?
   _____

4. Are <u>issues</u> of national importance likely to be found on the sports pages of a newspaper?
   _____

5. How does having a <u>positive</u> attitude help people to achieve their goals?
   _____

6. By definition, are people's <u>prejudices</u> ever fair? Explain.
   _____

7. Would a group of ninth graders be considered an <u>ethnic</u> group?
   _____

8. What is one <u>fundamental</u> belief that an athlete should have when playing sports? Explain.
   _____

"All Together Now" by Barbara Jordan
Reading Warm-up A

Read the following passage. Pay special attention to the underlined words. Then, read it again, and complete the activities. Use a separate sheet of paper for your written answers.

W. E. B. Du Bois was born in 1868 in Massachusetts. He died at the age of ninety-five in Ghana, Africa. During the first half of the twentieth century, he was the most important African American protest leader. He helped create the National Association for the Advancement of Colored People (NAACP) in 1909.

At first, Du Bois believed that social science could solve the race problem in America. Later, as he observed racism, he came to a different conclusion. He decided that changes in society could come about only through protest and change.

In this view, he disagreed with Booker T. Washington. At the time, Washington was the most influential leader in the African American community. Washington was telling blacks to accept discrimination for the time being. He said they should improve themselves through hard work and economic gain. He believed that in this way, African Americans would earn the respect of white Americans. Soon, their civil rights would be guaranteed. Du Bois held a completely opposite view.

In his 1903 book, *The Souls of Black Folk,* Du Bois attacked Booker T. Washington. He said that Washington's plan would not help black people. Instead, he was concerned that Washington's plan would only worsen race relations.

Two years later, Du Bois founded the Niagara movement. The main purpose of the group was to attack Booker T. Washington's ideas. It lasted only about four years, but it inspired the creation of the NAACP. Du Bois stayed with the NAACP until 1934. He was the editor of its magazine, *The Crisis.* As editor, he encouraged the development of black literature and art. He also encouraged a policy of pan-Africanism. Pan-Africanism is the belief that all people of African descent have common interests. Therefore, they should work together in the struggle for freedom and equality.

1. Circle the words that give specific information about the century. Use *century* in a sentence.

2. Underline the words that tell what Du Bois helped create. What does *create* mean?

3. Circle the words that tell how Du Bois believed society could be changed. Define *society*.

4. Underline the words that describe the community in which Washington was influential. Describe the *community* in which you live.

5. Circle the word that civil describes. Use *civil* in a sentence.

6. Underline the words that tell what Du Bois was concerned about. What does *concerned* mean?

7. Circle the word that modifies relations. Use *relations* in a sentence.

8. Underline the word that tells what, in addition to equality, the people were struggling for. Name another figure in the struggle for *equality* for African Americans.

"**All Together Now**" by Barbara Jordan
Reading Warm-up B

Read the following passage. Pay special attention to the underlined words. Then, read it again, and complete the activities. Use a separate sheet of paper for your written answers.

In 1963, President John F. Kennedy could see that America needed a strong civil rights bill. Only such a bill could secure equal protection of the laws for African Americans. On June 11, he presented such a bill to Congress. He asked for legislation for "the kind of equality of treatment which we would want for ourselves." Southern representatives blocked the bill in Congress. Civil rights leaders began to look for a way to build public support for the issues in the measure.

Up stepped A. Philip Randolph. A labor leader, Randolph was also a longtime civil rights activist. He called for a massive march on Washington. He wanted white groups as well as black groups to participate. He hoped the march would lead to a spirit of tolerance and the passage of the civil rights bill. Many groups agreed to participate—groups that had been wary of one another in the past. The leaders worked closely with the Kennedy administration. All hoped for fundamental changes in the United States. They looked forward to a country free of segregation and the prejudices that divided the country.

On August 28, 1963, more than 250,000 people marched on Washington. They gathered near the Lincoln Memorial under a nearly cloudless sky. They were there for the most positive reasons—to rally for "jobs and freedom." The list of speakers included people from nearly every segment of society. There were labor leaders, clergymen, film stars, and singers. Each speaker was given fifteen minutes.

When it was the turn of Martin Luther King, Jr., King gave a short speech about the sufferings of African Americans. He was about to sit down when the gospel singer Mahalia Jackson stopped him. She called out, "Tell them about your dream, Martin! Tell them about the dream!" That was when King made the famous speech that every schoolchild now knows. He spoke of his dream that people of all ethnic groups, colors, and backgrounds would share in an America marked by freedom and democracy.

1. Underline the words that tell what was needed to build support for the issues in the civil rights bill. Use *issues* in a sentence.

2. In what way might a person demonstrate a spirit of tolerance?

3. Underline the word that fundamental modifies. What is one of your own *fundamental* beliefs?

4. Why would civil rights leaders want an America free of segregation?

5. How can prejudices divide a country?

6. Circle the word that positive modifies. What does *positive* mean?

7. Underline the word that ethnic modifies. Use *ethnic* in a sentence.

8. Name one thing that is different about the backgrounds of people from England and people from Argentina.

Name _____ Date _____

"All Together Now" by Barbara Jordan
Writing About the Big Question

What should we learn?

Big Question Vocabulary

analyze	curiosity	discover	evaluate	examine
experiment	explore	facts	information	inquire
interview	investigate	knowledge	question	understand

A. *Replace the italicized word in the sentence below with one of the vocabulary words above. The meaning of the sentence should stay the same. There may be more than one right answer.*

1. The *details* Barbara Jordan shared in her essay changed the way I saw race relations _____.

2. Barbara Jordan wants us to *study* our own circle of friends _____.

3. It is interesting to *think about* what makes people prejudice _____.

B. *Follow the directions in responding to each of the items below.*

1. Describe one person you have met who was very different from you. Write your response in complete sentences. Use at least one of the Big Question vocabulary words. You may use the words in different forms (for example you can change *explore* to *exploration*).

_____

_____

2. Write two sentences describing what you learned from the person described in question
1. Use at least one of the Big Question vocabulary words. You may use the words in different forms (for example you can change *analyze* to *analyzing*).

_____

_____

C. *Complete the sentence below. Use the completed sentence as the beginning of a short paragraph in which you discuss the big question.*

Asking questions can help _____

_____

_____

"All Together Now" by Barbara Jordan
Reading: Fact and Opinion

When you read nonfiction, it is important to be able to distinguish between fact and opinion. A **fact** is something that can be proven true. An **opinion** is a person's judgment or belief. It may be supported by factual evidence, but it cannot be proven.

As you read, **recognize clue words that indicate an opinion,** as in the phrases "I believe" and "In my opinion." Also look for words such as *always, never, must, cannot, best, worst,* and *all,* which may indicate a broad statement that reveals a personal judgment. Emotional statements are also often clues to opinion.

You can tell that this statement from "All Together Now" is an opinion because it cannot be proven. Another hint is that it contains the phrase "I don't believe":

> Frankly, I don't believe that the task of bringing us all together can be accomplished by government.

DIRECTIONS: *Identify each of the following quotations from "All Together Now" as a fact or an opinion. Then, briefly explain your answer. For quotations identified as opinions, point out any words or phrases that indicate it is an opinion.*

1. President Lyndon B. Johnson pushed through the Civil Rights Act of 1964, which remains the fundamental piece of civil rights legislation in this century.

   Fact / Opinion: _____   **Explanation:** _____

   _____

2. One thing is clear to me: We, as human beings, must be willing to accept people who are different from ourselves.

   Fact / Opinion: _____   **Explanation:** _____

   _____

3. Children learn ideas and attitudes from the adults who nurture them.

   Fact / Opinion: _____   **Explanation:** _____

   _____

4. I absolutely believe that children do not adopt prejudices unless they absorb them from their parents or teachers.

   Fact / Opinion: _____   **Explanation:** _____

   _____

5. It is possible for all of us to work on this at home, in our schools, at our jobs.

   Fact / Opinion: _____   **Explanation:** _____

   _____

Name _____ Date _____

"**All Together Now**" by Barbara Jordan
Literary Analysis: Persuasive Essay

A **persuasive essay** is a piece of nonfiction that presents a series of arguments to convince readers that they should believe or act in a certain way. Below are some techniques that are often used in persuasive essays. When you read a persuasive essay, be aware of these techniques; you will need to decide whether they are powerful enough to persuade you to accept the author's ideas.

- **Appeals to authority:** using the opinions of experts and well-known people
- **Appeals to emotion:** using words that convey strong feeling
- **Appeals to reason:** using logical arguments backed by statistics and facts

DIRECTIONS: *In the first column of the following chart, copy statements from "All Together Now" that include appeals to authority. In the second column, copy statements that include appeals to emotion. In the third column, copy statements that include appeals to reason. Find at least one example of each kind of appeal.*

Appeals to Authority	Appeals to Emotion	Appeals to Reason

Name _____ Date _____

Vocabulary Builder

Word List

culminated   equality   fundamental   legislation   optimist   tolerant

A. DIRECTIONS: *Answer each question in a complete sentence. In your answer, use one of the Word List words in place of the italicized word or phrase.*

1. In what way have civil rights *laws* changed this country?

   _____

2. What is the *basic* rule for getting along with others?

   _____

3. What happens when people are not *accepting* of others' differences?

   _____

4. Are you *someone who takes the most hopeful view of matters*?

   _____

5. Barbara Jordan's career *reached its highest point* when she was elected to the United States House of Representatives.

   _____

6. This country was founded on the idea that everyone should enjoy *the same rights*.

   _____

B. WORD STUDY: *The Latin root -leg- means "law." Use your knowledge of the Latin root -leg- to write a full sentence to answer each question. Include the italicized word in your answer.*

1. Is a thief likely to give a *legitimate* account of his actions?

   _____

2. Would you expect an honest person to do something *illegal*?

   _____

3. Is it *legal* to cross the street when the sign reads DON'T WALK?

   _____

Name _____ Date _____

"All Together Now" by Barbara Jordan
Enrichment: Advances in Civil Rights

There have been many advances in civil rights that have helped to bring equality to all citizens of the United States. Using reference books or the Internet, find out how each of the landmarks listed on this chart advanced civil rights. In the right-hand column, describe the effects of each event.

Landmark	What It Did
Thirteenth Amendment	
Fourteenth Amendment	
Fifteenth Amendment	
Nineteenth Amendment	
Brown v. Board of Education	
Montgomery bus boycott	
Civil Rights Act of 1960	
Twenty-fourth Amendment	
Civil Rights Act of 1964	
Voting Rights Act of 1965	
Civil Rights Act of 1968	

"The Eternal Frontier" by Louis L'Amour
"All Together Now" by Barbara Jordan
Integrated Language Skills: Grammar

Subjects and Predicates

Every sentence has two parts: the **subject** and the **predicate.** The **subject** describes whom or what the sentence is about. The **simple subject** is the noun or pronoun that states exactly whom or what the sentence is about. The **complete subject** includes the simple subject and all of its modifiers.

The **predicate** is a verb that tells what the subject does, what is done to the subject, or what the condition of the subject is. The **simple predicate** is the verb or verb phrase that tells what the subject of the sentence does or is. It includes the simple predicate and any modifiers or complements.

In the following example, the simple subject and the simple predicate are in bold type. The complete subject is underlined once, and the complete predicate is underlined twice.

Louis L'Amour, a writer of novels about the American West, **has written** a persuasive essay about the importance of space exploration.

A. PRACTICE: *In each sentence, underline the simple subject once and the simple predicate twice.*

1. Louis L'Amour writes about the importance of space travel.

2. In L'Amour's view, outer space is the next frontier.

3. All of humankind longs for exploration and discovery.

4. According to Barbara Jordan, we can win the fight against prejudice.

5. Little children do not hate other people.

6. People learn to hate from parents and teachers.

B. WRITING APPLICATION: *In a paragraph of at least four sentences, describe a place you would like to explore. Underline each simple subject once and each simple predicate twice.*

_____

_____

_____

_____

_____

_____

_____

Name _____ Date _____

"The Eternal Frontier" by Louis L'Amour
"All Together Now" by Barbara Jordan
Integrated Language Skills:
Support for Writing a Persuasive Essay

Prepare to write a brief **persuasive essay** on one of the following topics:

- A letter to community leaders telling them how people in the community can promote tolerance
- A letter to government leaders advising them about space travel.

Organize your thoughts by completing the chart below. In the left-hand column, write down the goals you would like to see achieved by government or your community. In this column, explain any challenges elected officials or community members might face in trying to achieve the goal.

In the right-hand column, describe the persuasive technique you will use to make each point. Your choices are to:

- **Appeal to authority** by using opinions or experts and well-known people

- **Appeal to reason** by using logical arguments backed by facts.

- **Appeal to emotion** by using words that convey strong feelings

Points	Persuasive Techniques

Now, Use the ideas you have gathered to write your persuasive letter.

"The Eternal Frontier" by Louis L'Amour
"All Together Now" by Barbara Jordan
Integrated Language Skills:
Support for Extend Your Learning

Listening and Speaking: "The Eternal Frontier"

Use the following prompts as you work with members of your group to prepare a **public-service announcement** encouraging space travel.

The message, in brief: _____

_____

Appeal to authority: _____

_____

Appeal to emotion: _____

_____

Appeal to reason: _____

_____

Listening and Speaking: "All Together Now"

Use the following prompts as you work with members of your group to prepare a **public-service announcement** encouraging fair treatment of all people.

The message, in brief: _____

_____

Appeal to authority: _____

_____

Appeal to emotion: _____

_____

Appeal to reason: _____

_____

Name _____ Date _____

"All Together Now" by Barbara Jordan
Open-Book Test

Short Answer *Write your response to the questions in this section on the lines provided.*

1. In the beginning of "All Together Now," Barbara Jordan says that "we have the legislation we need." What does she refer to? Base your answer on the meaning of *legislation.*

   _____

2. In the beginning of "All Together Now," what does Barbara Jordan say the role of the government in promoting tolerance should be? Why?

   _____

   _____

   _____

3. In "All Together Now," Barbara Jordan appeals to authority, to reason, and to emotions to make her point. What kind of appeal does she make by referring to Martin Luther King Jr. and former president Lyndon Johnson near the beginning of her speech?

   _____

   _____

4. According to Barbara Jordan in the middle of "All Together Now," why is the Civil Rights Act of 1964 "the fundamental piece of civil rights legislation in this century"? Base your answer on the meaning of *fundamental.*

   _____

   _____

5. A fact is a statement that can be proved. An opinion states a belief or a feeling. In the middle of "All Together Now," Barbara Jordan says that the Voting Rights Act of 1965 made it possible for everyone to vote. Is this a fact or an opinion? How can you tell?

   _____

   _____

6. Does this passage from "All Together Now" appeal to reason, authority, or emotion? How can you tell?

   The Voting Rights Act of 1965 ensured that everyone in our country could vote. At last, black people and white people seemed ready to live together in peace.

   But that is not what happened . . .

   _____

   _____

7. In the middle of her speech, "All Together Now," Barbara Jordan mentions the conflict in Bosnia. Why does she mention this?

_____

_____

8. In the middle of "All Together Now," Barbara Jordan says that we, "as human beings, must be willing to accept people who are different from ourselves." How can you tell this is an appeal to emotion?

_____

_____

9. In "All Together Now," Barbara Jordan talks about creating a harmonious society. How does she think this should be done?

_____

_____

_____

10. Barbara Jordan uses both facts and opinions to make her point in "All Together Now." In the chart below, list three facts and three opinions from the essay. Then, answer the question that follows.

Facts	Opinions

Which do you find more persuasive in this speech, the facts or the opinions? Explain why. _____

_____

_____

Essay

Write an extended response to the question of your choice or to the question or questions your teacher assigns you.

11. In "All Together Now," Barbara Jordan tries to persuade her readers that there are things everyone can do to improve relations between groups of people. In an essay, describe what Jordan thinks everyone should do. Then, consider Jordan's idea that widescale change can occur if every single person makes an effort. Do you agree or disagree with this idea? Explain your answer.

12. Do you, like Barbara Jordan in "All Together Now," "believe that children do not adopt prejudices unless they absorb them from their parents or teachers"? In an essay, discuss this statement. Use examples from history, current events, or the lives of people you know to support your opinion.

13. "All Together Now" is a persuasive essay. What is Barbara Jordan trying to persuade her readers to think or do? In an essay of your own, summarize Jordan's purpose. Explain whether or not you believe she achieves that purpose. Include examples of persuasion found in the essay, and tell whether you think they are effective.

14. **Thinking About the Big Question: What should we learn?** In "All Together Now," Barbara Jordan believes that children learn "ideas and attitudes" from "the adults who nurture them." In an essay, explain what Jordan believes children should learn from their parents and teachers in order to create a harmonious society. Do you agree with her? Are there other lessons and qualities that you think children should learn from adults? How would these lessons help create a harmonious society?

Oral Response

15. Go back to question 2, 3, or 9 or to the question your teacher assigns you. Take a few minutes to expand your answer and prepare an oral response. Find additional details in "All Together Now" that support your points. If necessary, make notes to guide your oral response.

"All Together Now" by Barbara Jordan
Selection Test A

Critical Reading *Identify the letter of the choice that best answers the question.*

____ 1. According to "All Together Now," who does Barbara Jordan think should work on race relations?
  A. elected officials
  B. children
  C. parents
  D. Bosnians

____ 2. How does Barbara Jordan appeal to authority in "All Together Now"?
  A. She says that we should appeal to elected officials to solve the problem of race relations.
  B. She mentions Martin Luther King, Jr., and former President Lyndon Johnson.
  C. She says that Americans should be the authorities on race relations.
  D. She talks about the situation in Bosnia in the 1990s.

____ 3. In "All Together Now," why does Barbara Jordan mention the conflict in Bosnia?
  A. It shows that people of different ethnic backgrounds can live in peace.
  B. It shows that people of different ethnic backgrounds are not getting along.
  C. It shows that other countries have a history much like ours.
  D. It shows what happens in a place with strong civil rights laws.

____ 4. According to "All Together Now," what might happen if we do not pay attention to civil rights?
  A. We might end up like Bosnia.
  B. We will have to pass more laws.
  C. We will have to march in protest.
  D. We will end up with unhappy children.

____ 5. How can you tell that this statement from "All Together Now" is an opinion?
  I must be willing to accept people who don't look as I do and don't talk as I do.
  A. It appeals to reason.
  B. It can be proved true.
  C. It cannot be proved true.
  D. It is the opinion of an expert.

_____ 6. According to Barbara Jordan in "All Together Now," why should we put our faith in young people?

    A. They learn quickly and easily.

    B. They are born without prejudice.

    C. They want everyone to live in peace.

    D. They are kinder than adults.

_____ 7. How can you tell that this statement from "All Together Now" is an appeal to emotion?

    One thing is clear to me: We, as human beings, must be willing to accept people who are different from ourselves.

    A. It contains the opinion of an expert.

    B. It contains a logical argument.

    C. It conveys strong feelings.

    D. It reveals the author's opinion.

_____ 8. Why does Barbara Jordan care about other people?

    A. She has been taught to do so.

    B. She is following her children's example.

    C. They are her fellow human beings.

    D. It is part of her job.

_____ 9. What does Jordan want to persuade her readers to do in "All Together Now"?

    A. work to improve human relationhips

    B. follow the example set by their children

    C. support laws that promote tolerance

    D. organize marches in support of civil rights

_____ 10. What can you tell about Barbara Jordan from reading "All Together Now"?

    A. She was impatient and impractical.

    B. She was a brilliant speaker.

    C. She was tired and hopeless.

    D. She was thoughtful and caring.

Vocabulary and Grammar

_____ 11. When Jordan says that "we have the *legislation* we need" what does she mean?

    A. We have the laws we need.

    B. We have the lawyers we need.

    C. We have the rights we need.

    D. We have the government we need.

____ 12. Which statement about "All Together Now" shows that Jordan was an *optimist*?

    A. Jordan believes that improving relationships is not a job for government.

    B. Jordan says that the history of race relations in the United States has been "very rocky."

    C. Jordan suggests that bad things will happen if we do not learn to get along.

    D. Jordan believes that it is possible for everyone to work on getting along.

____ 13. What part of this sentence do the underlined words represent?

    I <u>have yet to find a racist baby</u>.

    A. subject

    B. simple subject

    C. predicate

    D. simple predicate

____ 14. What part of this sentence does the underlined word represent?

    The <u>movement</u> culminated in 1963 with the March on Washington.

    A. subject

    B. simple subject

    C. predicate

    D. simple predicate

Essay

15. In "All Together Now," Barbara Jordan tries to persuade her readers that there are things everyone can do to improve relations between groups of people. In an essay, describe what Jordan thinks everyone should do. Then, consider Jordan's notion that widescale change can occur if every single person makes an effort. Do you agree or disagree with this notion? Explain your answer.

16. In "All Together Now," Barbara Jordan uses appeals to emotion and appeals to reason to try to persuade her readers that her views are important. In an essay, cite one example of each kind of appeal. Then, explain why you do or do not find Jordan's appeals convincing.

17. **Thinking About the Big Question: What should we learn?** In "All Together Now," Barbara Jordan believes that children learn "ideas and attitudes" from "the adults who nurture them." In an essay, explain what Jordan believes children should learn from their parents and teachers. Do you agree with her? Why or why not?

Name _____ Date _____

"**All Together Now**" by Barbara Jordan
Selection Test B

Critical Reading *Identify the letter of the choice that best completes the statement or answers the question.*

_____ 1. Which of the following statements describes Barbara Jordan's view of the role of government in promoting tolerance?
   A. The government has failed to promote tolerance.
   B. The government should pass laws promoting tolerance.
   C. The government cannot do the job of promoting tolerance.
   D. The government should encourage teachers to promote tolerance.

_____ 2. How does Barbara Jordan define the term "soul force" in "All Together Now"?
   A. people working on a small scale to create a tolerant society
   B. people getting together to pray for tolerance and harmony
   C. people working together to build homes for the poor
   D. people volunteering to do all kinds of charity work

_____ 3. In "All Together Now," Barbara Jordan's main purpose is to
   A. persuade readers that a tolerant society is best created by working on a small scale.
   B. inform readers of the recent history of the civil rights movement in the United States.
   C. praise the work of the leaders of the civil rights movement of the 1960s.
   D. persuade readers that babies are born without a tendency to show prejudice.

_____ 4. According to "All Together Now," who does Barbara Jordan think can do a great deal to create tolerance in our society?
   A. elected officials
   B. young adults
   C. parents
   D. teachers

_____ 5. In "All Together Now," Barbara Jordan suggests that since the 1960s,
   A. people have no longer needed civil rights.
   B. people have learned to live harmoniously.
   C. the government has made too many laws.
   D. the momentum of that era has been lost.

_____ 6. How can you tell that the following passage from "All Together Now" appeals to reason?
   The Voting Rights Act of 1965 ensured that everyone in our country could vote. At last, black people and white people seemed ready to live together in peace.
   But that is not what happened. . . . Today the nation seems to be suffering from compassion fatigue.

   A. It is based on the opinions of authorities.
   B. It refers to well-known historical facts.
   C. It uses words that convey strong feelings.
   D. It uses logic argument backed by facts.

____ 7. In "All Together Now," Jordan mentions Bosnia in order to illustrate
A. a place where ethnic groups live together in peace.
B. a place where ethnic conflict threatens society.
C. a place where the history of race relations is like ours.
D. a place where the civil rights laws are as effective as ours.

____ 8. According to "All Together Now," how can people create a harmonious society?
A. by studying the situation in Bosnia in the 1990s
B. by tolerating people of all races and backgrounds
C. by studying the history of the civil rights movement
D. by supporting the passage of civil rights legislation

____ 9. Which of these statements from "All Together Now" is an opinion?
A. When I look at race relations today I can see . . . some positive changes.
B. President Lyndon B. Johnson pushed through the Civil Rights Act of 1964.
C. The Voting Rights Act of 1965 ensured that everyone in our country could vote.
D. I must be willing to accept people who don't look as I do and don't talk as I do.

____ 10. Which word in this sentence from "All Together Now" suggests that the statement is an opinion?

I absolutely believe that children do not adopt prejudices unless they absorb them from their parents or teachers.

A. believe
B. adopt
C. prejudices
D. absorb

____ 11. Barbara Jordan believes that we must put our faith in children because
A. they learn quickly and easily.
B. they are born without prejudice.
C. they want everyone to live in peace.
D. they are more compassionate than adults.

____ 12. Which of these statements from "All Together Now" is an appeal to emotion?
A. The movement culminated in 1963 with the March on Washington.
B. The Voting Rights Act of 1965 ensured that everyone in our country could vote.
C. One thing is clear to me: We, as human beings, must be willing to accept people who are different from ourselves.
D. Parents can actively encourage their children to be in the company of people who are of other racial and ethnic backgrounds.

____ 13. Which of these statements from "All Together Now" is a fact?
A. I don't believe that the task of bringing us all together can be accomplished by government.
B. President Lyndon B. Johnson pushed through the Civil Rights Act of 1964.
C. The best way to get this country faithful to the American dream of tolerance and equality is to start small.
D. I'm an incurable optimist.

Vocabulary and Grammar

____ 14. When Barbara Jordan refers to "the *fundamental* piece of civil rights legislation in this century," she means that
   A. it was especially easy to pass.
   B. it was based on religious beliefs.
   C. it received strong support in Congress.
   D. it served as the basis for other legislation.

____ 15. Which behavior might be displayed by someone who is *tolerant*?
   A. joining a group of people who hold opinions similar to yours
   B. listening to a variety of opinions on a controversial topic
   C. traveling to little-known places in search of adventure
   D. speaking out in support of someone who has been wronged

____ 16. What is the simple subject in this sentence from "All Together Now"?
   We can put our faith in young people as a positive force.
   A. We
   B. can
   C. can put
   D. faith

____ 17. What is the simple predicate in this sentence from "All Together Now"?
   The movement culminated in 1963 with the March on Washington.
   A. movement
   B. culminated
   C. with
   D. March

Essay

18. Do you, like Barbara Jordan, "believe that children do not adopt prejudices unless they absorb them from their parents or teachers"? In an essay, discuss this statement. Use examples from history or current events or from your own life or the lives of people you know to support your opinion.

19. "All Together Now" is a persuasive essay. What is Barbara Jordan trying to persuade her readers to think or do? In an essay of your own, summarize Jordan's purpose, and explain whether or not you believe she achieves that purpose.

20. **Thinking About the Big Question: What should we learn?** In "All Together Now," Barbara Jordan believes that children learn "ideas and attitudes" from "the adults who nurture them." In an essay, explain what Jordan believes children should learn from their parents and teachers in order to create a harmonious society. Do you agree with her? Are there other lessons and qualities that you think children should learn from adults? How would these lessons help to create a harmonious society?

Study these words. Then, complete the activities that follow.

Word List A

alarming [uh LAHRM ing] *v.* frightening or disturbing
  The noise from the leaf blower was <u>alarming</u> the ducks.

claim [KLAYM] *n.* a piece of land that someone takes legal possession of
  The gold miner worked on his <u>claim</u> along the riverbank.

experienced [ek SPEER ee enst] *adj.* having a certain knowledge or skill
  Maggie is an <u>experienced</u> pastry chef and prepares elaborate desserts.

rarely [RAYR lee] *adj.* not often
  Andy always gets up early, so he is <u>rarely</u> late for school.

regardless [ri GAHRD luhs] *prep.* in spite of or ignoring something
  Sam drives slowly in the rain, <u>regardless</u> of how late it will make him.

series [SEER eez] *n.* a number of related things that follow in order
  Julie crossed a <u>series</u> of bridges to get to the cabin.

settlement [SET uhl muhnt] *n.* a place recently populated with permanent residents
  Neighbors on the frontier <u>settlement</u> helped to build one another's barns.

territory [TER uh tawr ee] *n.* a large area of land; a region
  Much of the Alaskan <u>territory</u> remains unexplored.

Word List B

destination [des tuh NAY shuhn] *n.* the place to which someone is going
  It took the spacecraft five years to reach its <u>destination</u> near Pluto.

discipline [DIS uh plin] *n.* control over the way you or others behave
  Athletes must have the <u>discipline</u> to eat healthily and exercise every day.

domestic [duh MES tik] *adj.* tame; part of everyday life
  <u>Domestic</u> animals are used for work, for food, or as pets.

enforce [en FAWRS] *v.* to put a rule or law into effect to make sure it is obeyed
  Police officers are paid to <u>enforce</u> the law.

fringe [FRINJ] *n.* a border or edge
  We stopped on the <u>fringe</u> of the desert to check our water supply.

guilty [GIL tee] *adj.* responsible for doing something wrong
  The jury found the man <u>guilty</u> of committing a crime.

hostility [hahs TIL uh tee] *n.* a strong hatred or dislike
  The <u>hostility</u> between the enemy nations finally led to war.

livestock [LYV stahk] *n.* animals raised on a farm or ranch
  Each evening, Samuel put the cows and other <u>livestock</u> inside the barn.

"The Real Story of a Cowboy's Life" by Geoffrey C. Ward
Vocabulary Warm-up Exercises

Exercise A *Fill in each blank in the paragraph below with an appropriate word from Word List A. Use each word only once.*

Hannah had cooked in a [1] _____ of restaurants before she left New York in 1867. Being an [2] _____ chef, she planned to open a restaurant in San Francisco, where the miners spent their gold. [3] _____ of the dangers and hardships, Hannah was determined to travel alone. She entered the California [4] _____ by late autumn. During the winter, she stayed in a mining [5] _____. There, a company of prospectors had staked a [6] _____. At first she found the men's rough ways [7] _____ and feared for her safety. However, since the men were [8] _____ rude, she realized they meant no harm. Besides, they loved her pancakes!

Exercise B *Find a synonym for each word in the following list. Then, use each synonym in a sentence that makes its meaning clear. Refer to a thesaurus if you need help finding a synonym.*

1. discipline   **Synonym:** _____
   _____

2. enforce   **Synonym:** _____
   _____

3. hostility   **Synonym:** _____
   _____

4. livestock   **Synonym:** _____
   _____

5. destination   **Synonym:** _____
   _____

6. domestic   **Synonym:** _____
   _____

7. fringe   **Synonym:** _____
   _____

8. guilty   **Synonym:** _____
   _____

Name _____ Date _____

"The Real Story of a Cowboy's Life" by Geoffrey C. Ward
Reading Warm-up A

Read the following passage. Pay special attention to the underlined words. Then, read it again, and complete the activities. Use a separate sheet of paper for your written answers.

From the mid-1860s to the mid-1880s the "long drive" was a part of life for the cattle rancher. Experienced cowboys, who had learned to understand the behavior of cattle, drove over 10 million cows from Texas to cattle stations as far away as Wyoming. At first, the cattle trails were wide and open. The cows could roam and graze at will. They rarely went without water because rivers, streams, and other watering places were plentiful.

Then a series of events changed everything. First wagon trains and then railroad lines brought more people to the open country. Most of the newcomers staked a claim to land and built homes. Others set up businesses. Often, after farmers and shopkeepers established a settlement, the place grew into a town. Over time, hundreds of settlements were scattered across the prairies.

Then came the fences. These were not ordinary fences made of wood or stone. They were made from a new invention called *barbed wire*. Barbed wire is made of pointed bits of wire locked into a length of double-strand wire. Cattle on long drives soon learned to keep a distance from the barbed wire and its painful jabs.

Hundreds of barbed fences soon barricaded the land. Cattle could no longer roam freely. That meant they had less land on which to graze. Even more alarming, the fences kept cattle away from sources of water. Without places to graze and water to drink, the cattle suffered severe hardship on the long drive. Many died along the way. The ones who made it were often lean and parched. They had to be sold at a low price, and profits therefore fell.

Cattle ranchers fought back. They argued that the western territory should provide free grazing and water for all animals. They even tried to cut down the fences. Regardless of their protests, the fences stayed, and the days of the long drive came to an end.

1. Underline the words that tell what the cowboys were *experienced* in. Write about something in which you are *experienced*.

2. Underline the words that tell why the cattle *rarely* went without water. Give a synonym for *rarely*.

3. Circle the words that tell what kind of *series* changed everything. Write the meaning of *series*.

4. Circle the words that tell what kind of *claim* people made. Write a sentence using a phrase that means the same as "to stake a *claim*."

5. Circle the word that means nearly the same thing as *settlement*. Write a sentence using the word *settlement*.

6. Underline the words that tell what was *alarming*. Describe something you find *alarming*.

7. Circle the word that tells which *territory* ranchers argued should provide free grazing. Then, rewrite the sentence using a synonym for *territory*.

8. Underline the words that tell what happened *regardless* of protests. Write the meaning of *regardless*.

"The Real Story of a Cowboy's Life" by Geoffrey C. Ward
Reading Warm-up B

Read the following passage. Pay special attention to the underlined words. Then, read it again, and complete the activities. Use a separate sheet of paper for your written answers.

It was nearing sunset when Justice Matthews heard the sounds, the cry of the cows and the call of the cowboys. It was a cattle long drive just beyond the <u>fringe</u> of the pasture, he reckoned, and a big one, too.

Justice ran to the edge of the pasture. On the way he looked for his father but did not see him. That was good. His father disliked cattle drives, and his <u>hostility</u> could turn into something frightening. "They trample the fields and muddy the water," his father complained. "I want them to stay away from my land!" His father had tried to <u>enforce</u> his no-trespassing policy by putting up barbed-wire fences. The fences kept the open-range cattle out and the <u>domestic</u> cattle in. Sometimes, though, cows, goats, and other <u>livestock</u> would escape through breaks in the fence. His father would blame that on the cattle drives, too.

Justice climbed a low hill and gazed down into a shallow valley where hundreds of longhorns were passing through, stirring up the dust. Justice admired the cowboys' <u>discipline</u>, the way they worked together on horseback, turning and tightening the herd into a single moving mass. He knew they had come all the way from Texas and had been on the trail for a month: a whole month of hot, dusty, tiring work. Their <u>destination</u>, Wichita, Kansas, was 300 miles away. Justice had great admiration for cowboys, but knowing how his father disliked them, he felt <u>guilty</u> about it. All the same, Justice was sure he wanted to be a cowboy. He promised himself that someday he, too, would work the long drive from Dallas to Wichita.

1. Circle the words that tell what the <u>fringe</u> was part of. Rewrite the phrase, using a synonym for *fringe*.

2. Underline the words that explain the father's <u>hostility</u>. Write a sentence using the word *hostility*.

3. Underline the words that tell how the father tried to <u>enforce</u> his no-trespassing policy. What rule would you like to *enforce*?

4. Circle the words describing animals that are not <u>domestic</u>. Write about a *domestic* animal you are familiar with.

5. Circle the words that describe <u>livestock</u>. Rewrite the sentence using a synonym for *livestock*.

6. Underline the words that describe the cowboys' <u>discipline</u>. Define *discipline* as it is used in the sentence.

7. Circle the name of the cowboys' <u>destination</u>. Write a sentence using the word *destination*.

8. Underline the words that tell why Justice felt <u>guilty</u> about admiring cowboys. Write a sentence using an antonym of *guilty*.

"The Real Story of a Cowboy's Life" by Geoffrey C. Ward
Writing About the Big Question

What should we learn?

Big Question Vocabulary

analyze	curiosity	discover	evaluate	examine
experiment	explore	facts	information	inquire
interview	investigate	knowledge	question	understand

A. *Replace the italicized word in the sentence below with one of the vocabulary words above. The meaning of the sentence should stay the same. There may be more than one right answer.*

1. It was a good idea to *ask* cowboys about what their lives were really like
   _____.

2. It is difficult to *estimate* how many cattle were on the range at once
   _____.

3. This essay helped me *find out about* another way of life
   _____.

B. *Follow the directions in responding to each of the items below.*

1. Write about a job that you'd like to know more about and explain why. Write your response in complete sentences. Use at least one of the Big Question vocabulary words. You may change the form of the word (for example, you can change *information* to *inform.*)

   _____

   _____

2. Write about a job that you'd never want to do and explain why. Write your response in complete sentences. Use at least one of the Big Question vocabulary words. You may change the form of the word (for example, you can change *discover* to *discovery.*)

   _____

   _____

C. *Complete the sentence below. Use the completed sentence as the beginning of a short paragraph in which you discuss the big question.*

   Talking to people who participated in an event can _____

   _____

   _____

Unit 3 Resources: Types of Nonfiction
170

"The Real Story of a Cowboy's Life" by Geoffrey C. Ward
Reading: Use Resources to Check Facts

A **fact** is information you can prove. An **opinion** is a judgment.

Fact: The big herds . . . carried with them a disease . . . that devastated domestic livestock.

Opinion: The settlers' hostility was entirely understandable.

Be aware that some writers present opinions or beliefs as facts. To get to the truth, **use resources to check facts.**

Resource	Characteristics
almanac	a collection of facts and statistics on the climate, planets, stars, people, places, events, and so on, updated yearly
atlas	a collection of maps
biographical dictionary	an alphabetical listing of famous or historically significant persons with identifying information and dates of birth and death
dictionary	an alphabetical listing of words with their pronunciation and definition
encyclopedia	an alphabetically organized collection of articles on a broad range of subjects
reliable Web sites	Internet pages and articles on an extremely wide variety of topics, sponsored by individuals, companies, governments, and organizations

DIRECTIONS: *Read these passages from "The Real Story of a Cowboy's Life." Then, identify each one as a* fact *or an* opinion. *If the statement is a fact, indicate the best resource for checking it.*

1. Most Texas herds numbered about 2,000 head with a trail boss and about a dozen men in charge though herds as large as 15,000 were also driven north with far larger escorts.

   Fact/opinion: _____ **Resource:** _____

2. Regardless of its ultimate destination, every herd had to ford a series of rivers—the Nueces, the Guadalupe, the Brazos, the Wichita, the Red.

   Fact/opinion: _____ **Resource:** _____

3. After you crossed the Red River and got out on the open plains . . . it was sure a pretty sight to see them strung out for almost a mile, the sun shining on their horns.

   Fact/opinion: _____ **Resource:** _____

4. Initially, the land immediately north of the Red River was Indian territory, and some tribes charged tolls for herds crossing their land payable in money or beef.

   Fact/opinion: _____ **Resource:** _____

"The Real Story of a Cowboy's Life" by Geoffrey C. Ward
Literary Analysis: Word Choice and Diction

A writer's **word choice** and **diction** are important elements of his or her writing. The specific words a writer uses can make writing difficult or easy to read, formal or informal. Diction includes not only the vocabulary the writer uses but also the way in which the sentences are put together. Here are some questions writers consider when deciding which words to use:

- What does the audience already know about the topic? If an audience is unfamiliar with a topic, the writer will have to define technical vocabulary or use simpler language.
- What feeling will this work convey? Word choice can make a work serious or funny, academic or personal. The length and style of the sentences can make a work simple or complex.

In this passage from "The Real Story of a Cowboy's Life," notice that the author uses both technical vocabulary (*point, swing, drag*) and informal language ("eating dust"):

The most experienced men rode "point" and "swing," at the head and sides of the long herd; the least experienced brought up the rear, riding "drag" and eating dust.

DIRECTIONS: *Read each passage. Then, on the lines that follow, write down examples of technical vocabulary, formal language, and informal language. If there are no examples of a particular kind of language, write* none.

1. If . . . the cattle started running you'd hear that low rumbling noise along the ground and the men on herd wouldn't need to come in and tell you, you'd know—then you'd jump for your horse and get out there in the lead, trying to head them and get them into a mill before they scattered. It was riding at a dead run in the dark, with duct banks and prairie dog holes all around you, not knowing if the next jump would land you in a shallow grave.

Technical vocabulary: _____

Informal language: _____

Formal language: _____

2. The big herds ruined their crops, and they carried with them a disease, spread by ticks and called "Texas fever," that devastated domestic livestock. Kansas and other territories along the route soon established quarantine lines, called "deadlines," at the western fringe of settlement, and insisted that trail drives not cross them.

Technical vocabulary: _____

Informal language: _____

Formal language: _____

Name _____ Date _____

"The Real Story of a Cowboy's Life" by Geoffrey C. Ward
Vocabulary Builder

Word List

discipline   diversions   emphatic   gauge   longhorns   ultimate

A. DIRECTIONS: *Write the correct word from the Word List on each line.*

1. The teammates want to win the next match, but their _____ goal is to win the championship.

2. The fair offered games, rides, and a few other _____.

3. The cowboys tried to _____ the mood of the cattle by the way the animals moved and the cries they uttered.

4. Bosses like Charles Goodnight needed to impose _____ along the trail.

5. Settlers had an _____ message for cowboys: STAY OUT!

6. _____ are a type of cattle popular in Texas.

B. WORD STUDY: *The Latin root -vers- means "to turn." Use your knowledge of the Latin root -vers- to write a full sentence to answer each question. Include the italicized word in your answer.*

1. If you *reverse* direction do you go the opposite way?

   _____

2. If you behave in a *subversive* manner are you being supportive?

   _____

3. Can a *versatile* employee handle many different responsibilities?

   _____

Name _____   Date _____

"The Real Story of a Cowboy's Life" by Geoffrey C. Ward
Enrichment: Cowboy Songs

In "The Real Story of a Cowboy's Life," one of the cowboys talks about the songs the men would sing at night to calm the cattle. Many of those songs reflect the difficulties of the cowboy's life. Following are some of the verses to "Bury Me Not on the Lone Prairie," the song mentioned in the selection.

"Bury Me Not on the Lone Prairie"

"O bury me not on the lone prairie,"
These words came low and mournfully
From the pallid lips of the youth who lay
On his dying bed at the close of day.

"It makes no difference, so I've been told
Where the body lies when life grows cold
But grant, I pray, one wish to me
O bury me not on the lone prairie."

"I've often wished to be laid when I die
By the little church on the green hillside
By my father's grave, there let mine be
O bury me not on the lone prairie."

The cowboys gathered all around the bed
To hear the last word that their comrade said
"O partners all, take a warning from me
Never leave your homes for the lone prairie."

"O bury me not," but his voice failed there
But we paid no heed to his dying prayer
In a narrow grave, just six by three
We buried him there on the lone prairie.

We buried him there on the lone prairie
Where the buzzards fly and the wind blows free
Where rattlesnakes rattle, and the tumbleweeds
Blow across his grave on the lone prairie.

And the cowboys now as they cross the plains
Have marked the spot where his bones are lain
Fling a handful of roses on his grave
And pray to the Lord that his soul is saved.

In a narrow grave, just six by three
We buried him there on the lone prairie.

DIRECTIONS: *Answer these questions.*

1. Why does the dying youth not want to be buried on the prairie?

   _____

   _____

2. What does the youth warn the other cowboys about? Why might he give this warning?

   _____

   _____

3. How does the youth feel about his home? How does he feel about the prairie? Do you think the other cowboys share his feelings? Why or why not?

   _____

   _____

Name _____ Date _____

"The Real Story of a Cowboy's Life" by Geoffrey C. Ward
Open-Book Test

Short Answer *Write your responses to the questions in this section on the lines provided.*

1. Writers use resources such as almanacs, atlases, encyclopedias, and dictionaries to find and check their facts. At the beginning of "The Real Story of a Cowboy's Life," Geoffrey C. Ward states that most Texas herds numbered about 2,000 head of cattle. What resource would you most likely use to confirm this fact? Explain.

   _____

   _____

   _____

2. In the first paragraph of "The Real Story of a Cowboy's Life," Geoffrey C. Ward uses the words "point" and "swing." What are these words specific to? What explanation does the author give for these terms?

   _____

   _____

   _____

3. An author chooses words that can create a formal, an informal, a technical, or an academic feeling. The author writes in the beginning of "The Real Story of a Cowboy's Life" that a cowboy "had to know how to gauge the temperament of his cattle." Which two words tell you this is formal language?

   _____

   _____

   _____

4. In the beginning of "The Real Story of a Cowboy's Life," the reader is told that a cowboy had to gauge the temperament of his cattle. What would happen if he didn't gauge their temperament? Base your answer on the meaning of *gauge*.

   _____

   _____

   _____

   _____

5. What does "The Real Story of a Cowboy's Life" suggest about the behavior of cattle on the trail? What details in the essay tell you this?

   _____

   _____

   _____

   _____

6. In which resource would you most likely look to locate the rivers Nueces, Guadalupe, Brazos, Wichita, and Red mentioned in "The Real Story of a Cowboy's Life"? Explain.

   _____

   _____

   _____

7. What feeling does the word choice convey in this passage from the middle of "The Real Story of a Cowboy's Life"? Explain.

   And the cattle had been coming through there when they were still raising punkins in Illinois.

   _____

   _____

   _____

8. In the middle of "The Real Story of a Cowboy's Life," the author relates that a cowboy "slid his shotgun across the saddle in front of him and we did the same with our Winchesters." What does this tell the reader about life on the trail? Explain.

   _____

   _____

   _____

9. In the middle of "The Real Story of a Cowboy's Life," the reader learns that there were few diversions on the trail. Why might trail bosses have banned diversions? Base your answer on the meaning of *diversions*.

   _____

   _____

   _____

10. In "The Real Story of a Cowboy's Life," Geoffrey C. Ward describes the traits a cowboy needs to succeed and the traits a trail boss needs to succeed. In the chart below, list the necessary traits for each job. Then, answer the two questions that follow.

Traits a Cowboy Needs	Traits a Trail Boss Needs

Which man is most likely to ride at the head of the herd? _____

What information in the essay helps you answer this? _____

_____

Unit 3 Resources: Types of Nonfiction

Essay

Write an extended response to the question of your choice or to the question or questions your teacher assigns you.

11. In "The Real Story of a Cowboy's Life," Geoffrey C. Ward uses many instances of informal language. In an essay, explain the effect of Ward's word choice and diction. When does he use informal language? How does it contribute to the overall feeling of the selection?

12. In "The Real Story of a Cowboy's Life," Geoffrey C. Ward tells about Charles Goodnight's "article of agreement." It stated that "if one shot another he was to be tried by the outfit and hanged on the spot, if found guilty." In an essay, explain what this agreement shows about a cowboy's life. Describe the effect it might have had on the rides Goodnight led. Cite examples from the essay to support your conclusions.

13. In "The Real Story of a Cowboy's Life," Geoffrey C. Ward provides information about the cattle drives of the 1800s. In an essay, discuss whether you think Ward provides a complete picture of the drives. If he does, explain why. If you believe information is missing, tell what should be included to create a more complete picture. Back up your points with references to the essay.

14. **Thinking About the Big Question: What should we learn?** In "The Real Story of a Cowboy's Life," Geoffrey C. Ward describes what it was like to be a cowboy. In an essay, explain why it is important to learn what these men's lives were like. What impact did cowboys have on the history of our country? How do people think about cowboys and their role in American history?

Oral Response

15. Go back to question 4, 5, or 10 or to the question your teacher assigns you. Take a few minutes to expand your answer and prepare an oral response. Find additional details in "The Real Story of a Cowboy's Life" that support your points. If necessary, make notes to guide your oral response.

"The Real Story of a Cowboy's Life" by Geoffrey C. Ward
Selection Test A

Critical Reading *Identify the letter of the choice that best answers the question.*

____ 1. What feeling does the word choice in this passage from "The Real Story of a Cowboy's Life" convey?

> The most experienced men rode "point" and "swing," at the head and sides of the long herd.

    A. formal

    B. difficult

    C. technical

    D. humorous

____ 2. According to "The Real Story of a Cowboy's Life," what is a cowboy's most prized possession?

    A. his cattle

    B. his saddle

    C. his horse

    D. his gun

____ 3. According to "The Real Story of a Cowboy's Life," what was the most feared occurrence on the cattle trail?

    A. nighttime stampedes

    B. bad weather

    C. "jay-hawkers"

    D. cattle thieves

____ 4. What was the purpose of Charles Goodnight's "article of agreement," according to "The Real Story of a Cowboy's Life"?

    A. It kept the cowboys from stealing cattle.

    B. It kept the cowboys from shooting each other.

    C. It made sure that the cowboys got paid.

    D. It made sure that the cowboys finished the drive.

____ 5. In which resource would you most likely look to locate the rivers mentioned in "The Real Story of a Cowboy's Life"?

    A. an almanac

    B. an atlas

    C. an encyclopedia

    D. a dictionary

____ 6. What feeling does the word choice in this passage from "The Real Story of a Cowboy's Life" convey?

> And the cattle had been coming through there when they were still raising punkins in Illinois.

    A. formal

    B. informal

    C. technical

    D. academic

____ 7. According to "The Real Story of a Cowboy's Life," what caused the hostility between the settlers and the cowboys?

    A. The cowboys made too much noise in town.

    B. The cowboys stole the settlers' chickens.

    C. The herds ruined crops and spread disease.

    D. The herds raised a great deal of dust.

____ 8. According to "The Real Story of a Cowboy's Life," what did most trail bosses prohibit on the trail?

    A. gambling

    B. drinking

    C. singing

    D. fighting

____ 9. Which statement best summarizes what Teddy Blue says about cowboy songs?

    A. The cowboys sang "Bury Me Not on the Lone Prairie."

    B. The cowboys sang to keep the cattle calm.

    C. The cowboys took turns singing verses.

    D. The cowboys enjoyed singing on quiet, clear nights.

____ 10. Where would you most likely look to find the words to the song mentioned in "The Real Story of a Cowboy's Life"?

    A. a geographical dictionary

    B. an encyclopedia

    C. a biographical dictionary

    D. a reliable Web site

____ 11. According to "The Real Story of a Cowboy's Life," what does a cowboy need?

    A. courage and a love of conflict

    B. a sense of direction and the desire for wealth

    C. a love of animals and a love of family

    D. a love of danger and the ability to work hard

Vocabulary and Grammar

_____ 12. What do cowboys do when they *gauge* the mood of cattle?
   A. They round up the cattle.
   B. They judge the cattle.
   C. They steer the cattle.
   D. They soothe the cattle.

_____ 13. What was the cowboys' *ultimate* destination?
   A. the final stop on the trail
   B. the midpoint on the trail
   C. the first stop on the trail
   D. the highest point on the trail

_____ 14. Which of these sentences contains a compound subject?
   A. The cattle settled down for the night.
   B. The cowboys and their herds traveled every day.
   C. The cowboys ate and sang in the evenings.
   D. A cowboy cherished his saddle and his horse.

_____ 15. Which of these sentences about "The Real Story of a Cowboy's Life" contains a compound predicate?
   A. Cowboys ate biscuits and beef stew.
   B. "Jay-hawkers" and Indians disrupted the cattle drives.
   C. Homesteaders threatened the cowboys and tried to stop them.
   D. The cowboys faced danger and hardship on the trail.

Essay

16. In "The Real Story of a Cowboy's Life," Geoffrey Ward describes the cattle drives of the 1800s. In an essay of your own based on Ward's essay, describe the qualities and skills that would have made a good trail boss. Consider, for example, how Charles Goodnight showed those traits.

17. In "The Real Story of a Cowboy's Life," Geoffrey Ward uses many instances of informal language. In an essay, explain the effect of Ward's word choice and diction. When does he use informal language? How does it contribute to the overall feeling of the selection?

18. **Thinking About the Big Question: What should we learn?** In "The Real Story of a Cowboy's Life," Geoffrey C. Ward describes what it was like to be a cowboy. In an essay, explain why it is important to learn what these men's lives were like. Support your answer with specific details from the selection.

"The Real Story of a Cowboy's Life" by Geoffrey C. Ward
Selection Test B

Critical Reading *Identify the letter of the choice that best completes the statement or answers the question.*

_____ 1. In which resource would you most likely check to confirm the fact that most Texas herds numbered about 2,000 head of cattle?
   A. an almanac
   B. an atlas
   C. an encyclopedia
   D. a biographical dictionary

_____ 2. According to "The Real Story of a Cowboy's Life," a cowboy's most prized possession was
   A. his honor.
   B. his saddle.
   C. his horse.
   D. his gun.

_____ 3. According to "The Real Story of a Cowboy's Life," why did cowboys fear nighttime stampedes?
   A. The cattle were much fiercer at night.
   B. Indians or settlers were likely to attack at night.
   C. They could hardly afford to have their sleep disturbed.
   D. They were more likely to be dragged to death at night.

_____ 4. What does "The Real Story of a Cowboy's Life" suggest about cattle?
   A. They are jittery.
   B. They like to swim across rivers.
   C. They will not travel more than fifteen miles a day.
   D. They do not like to hear the same songs sung again and again.

_____ 5. Charles Goodnight's need for an "article of agreement" suggests that cowboys were generally
   A. honorable and trustworthy.
   B. likely to get into violent fights.
   C. unable to read or write.
   D. inclined to steal cattle.

_____ 6. Which resource would you most likely check to learn the location of the Nueces, the Guadalupe, the Brazos, the Wichita, and the Red rivers?
   A. an almanac
   B. an atlas
   C. a biographical dictionary
   D. a dictionary

____ 7. Which of these statements is an example of informal language?
    A. A cowboy had to know how to gauge the temperament of his cattle.
    B. The settlers' hostility was entirely understandable.
    C. I've monkeyed as long as I want to with you.
    D. Most trail bosses banned liquor. Goodnight prohibited gambling, too.

____ 8. According to "The Real Story of a Cowboy's Life," how was the cowboys' singing related to their job?
    A. It helped to keep the cattle calm.
    B. It kept the cowboys from gambling.
    C. It prevented fighting among the cowboys.
    D. It made the settlers friendlier to the cowboys.

____ 9. Which of these lines from "The Real Story of a Cowboy's Life" is an example of formal language?
    A. A cowboy had to know how to gauge the temperament of his cattle.
    B. And the cattle had been coming through there when they were still raising punkins in Illinois.
    C. I've monkeyed as long as I want to with you.
    D. "Bury Me Not on the Lone Prairie" was a great song for awhile, but . . . they sung it to death.

____ 10. Which of these statements from "The Real Story of a Cowboy's Life" contains technical language?
    A. The most experienced men rode "point" and "swing" at the head and sides of the long herd.
    B. A cowboy had to know how to gauge the temperament of his cattle.
    C. The settlers' hostility was entirely understandable.
    D. "Bury Me Not on the Lone Prairie" was a great song for awhile, but . . . they sung it to death.

____ 11. What does this sentence from "The Real Story of a Cowboy's Life" tell the reader about life on the trail?

    He slid his shotgun across the saddle in front of him and we did the same with our Winchesters.

    A. A cowboy's job could be dangerous.
    B. Cowboys took good care of their guns.
    C. Cowboys were most threatened by settlers.
    D. A cowboy had to have a gun to survive on the trail.

Vocabulary and Grammar

____ 12. In "The Real Story of a Cowboy's Life," Geoffrey Ward states that "there were few *diversions* on the trail." In other words,
    A. there was not much time to sleep.   C. there were few amusements.
    B. there were few people around.   D. there was not much food.

____ 13. Which word means almost the same as the underlined word in this sentence?
Regardless of its <u>ultimate</u> destination, every herd had to ford a series of rivers.

A. early
B. difficult

C. final
D. timely

____ 14. If a cowboy plans to *investigate* a campsite, he will
A. look at its location on a map.
B. call in help from other cowboys.

C. examine it to gain information.
D. describe it to other cowboys.

____ 15. What is the compound predicate in this sentence about "The Real Story of a Cowboy's Life"?
In a stampede, the cattle turn and run blindly.

A. the cattle
B. cattle turn

C. turn and run
D. run blindly

____ 16. Which words in the following sentence form a compound predicate?
The cowboys rode all day and sang for half the night.

A. cowboys, rode
B. rode, sang

C. all, half
D. day, night

____ 17. Which words in this sentence form a compound subject?
Charles Goodnight and his men brought their herd safely along the trail.

A. his, their
B. herd, trail

C. brought, along
D. Charles Goodnight, men

Essay

18. In "The Real Story of a Cowboy's Life," Geoffrey Ward tells about Charles Goodnight's "article of agreement." It stated that "if one shot another he was to be tried by the outfit and hanged on the spot, if found guilty." In an essay, explain what this agreement shows about a cowboy's life, and describe the effect it might have had on the rides Goodnight led. Cite examples from the selection to support your conclusions.

19. In "The Real Story of a Cowboy's Life," Geoffrey Ward provides a great deal of information about the cattle drives of the 1800s. In an essay, discuss whether you think Ward succeeds in providing a complete picture of the drives. If he does succeed, explain why. If you believe information is missing, describe what would make for a more complete picture. Back up your points with references to the selection.

20. **Thinking About the Big Question: What should we learn?** In "The Real Story of a Cowboy's Life," Geoffrey C. Ward describes what it was like to be a cowboy. In an essay, explain why it is important to learn what these men's lives were like. What impact did cowboys have on the history of our country? How do people think about cowboys and their role in American history?

Vocabulary Warm-up Word Lists

Study these words. Then, complete the activities that follow.

Word List A

blunt [BLUHNT] *adj.* not sharp
  Maxine used a <u>blunt</u> knife to scrape paint off the wall.

boldness [BOHLD nes] *n.* fearlessness and great confidence
  The raccoon entered the house with surprising <u>boldness</u>.

casually [KAZH wuh lee] *adv.* doing something without planning or by chance
  Ryan <u>casually</u> brushed the fly away from his sandwich.

clammy [KLAM ee] *adj.* unpleasantly damp
  The floor of the shower room felt <u>clammy</u> under David's feet.

defense [dee FENS] *n.* a method for protecting something
  Taking vitamin C provides a good <u>defense</u> against catching a cold.

horizon [huh RY zuhn] *n.* the line where land or sea seems to meet the sky
  The sun slipped slowly beneath the faraway <u>horizon</u>.

marsh [MAHRSH] *n.* area of low, waterlogged land
  Many kinds of waterfowl live in the <u>marsh</u>.

region [REE juhn] *n.* a large land area
  The Great Plains <u>region</u> covers hundreds of square miles.

Word List B

aggressors [uh GRES uhrz] *n.* persons or animals that attack without being provoked
  When <u>aggressors</u> attack an anthill, fighter ants defend the colony.

camouflaged [KAM uh flahzhd] *adj.* having coloring or covering that allows animals or humans to look like their surroundings
  The camp, <u>camouflaged</u> with branches and leaves, was nearly invisible.

desirable [di ZYR uh buhl] *adj.* worth having or doing
  Pauline thinks that train travel is more <u>desirable</u> than flying.

reptiles [REP tylz] *n.* coldblooded animals
  Snakes and other <u>reptiles</u> come out during the day to warm in the sun.

scientific [sy uhn TIF ik] *adj.* relating to the principles of science
  The <u>scientific</u> explanation of flight is complex.

varying [VAYR ee ing] *adj.* differing qualities in things of the same type
  Candies of <u>varying</u> flavors, size, and color were displayed in the shop window.

vegetation [vej uh TAY shuhn] *n.* plants that cover an area
  The floor of the jungle is covered with thick <u>vegetation</u>.

wilds [WYLDZ] *n.* areas that have been left in their natural state
  Members of the environmentalist group camped out in the <u>wilds</u> of Alaska.

Name _____ Date _____

"Rattlesnake Hunt" by Marjorie Kinnan Rawlings
Vocabulary Warm-up Exercises

Exercise A *Fill in each blank in the paragraph below with an appropriate word from Word List A. Use each word only once.*

Carter watched the storm clouds moving heavily along the [1] _____ like dark castles floating on the sea. The dampness made his skin feel [2] _____ and his clothes stick to his body. Carter studied the area around him: the soggy [3] _____ on his left and the empty shoreline on his right. If the storm turned into a hurricane, the [4] _____ along the coast will have no [5] _____ against the high surf. A seagull landed near Carter's boot and [6] _____ began to hunt for food. The [7] _____ end of its beak made little craters in the sand. The gull's [8] _____ in landing so near surprised Carter, then made him smile. The presence of the gull was a sign that the storm would stay far out at sea.

Exercise B *Answer the questions with complete explanations.*

1. Is having good health more <u>desirable</u> than having a lot of money?
_____

2. Is a <u>scientific</u> principle usually accepted as a fact?
_____

3. Is a <u>camouflaged</u> animal easy to find in the forest?
_____

4. Do <u>reptiles</u> prefer colder climates?
_____

5. Do hats of <u>varying</u> styles all look alike?
_____

6. Can <u>aggressors</u> be trusted to leave weaker creatures alone?
_____

7. When you travel into the <u>wilds</u>, should you pack everything you need to survive?
_____

8. If a yard is covered in <u>vegetation</u>, is it full of greenery?
_____

"Rattlesnake Hunt" by Marjorie Kinnan Rawlings
Reading Warm-up A

Read the following passage. Pay special attention to the underlined words. Then, read it again, and complete the activities. Use a separate sheet of paper for your written answers.

"They say that if you are lost in the Everglades, you die. That is, of course, if you have no food, no shelter, and no survival skills," Alicia said as she stared at the sawgrass prairie stretching before her. Her gaze swept along the distant horizon, where the flat grasslands touched the sky. There was not a mini-mart in sight.

"We're not lost," Petra assured her. "I know exactly where we are." Then she whispered, "I just don't know how to get to where we were."

Petra was feeling more guilty than scared. The ride into the sawgrass prairie had been her idea, and she had planned well, packing food, water, and a first-aid kit. All the supplies were loaded on the rented horse that carried both girls along the trail. It was not her fault that the horse had wandered off while she and Alicia explored one of the side trails on foot.

"We should stay where we are," Petra said casually, without a trace of care. "The horse will probably return soon. It knows the trail that will take us back."

Alicia shaded her eyes and searched the western region for the missing horse. The bright sun was blinding and hot. That is why they had decided to explore the marsh, where the ground was soggy but the temperature was cooler. Alicia had never ventured into a marsh before. Her boldness had surprised her, but then she had second thoughts. She felt the presence of unknown creatures and wished she had a blunt club to use in defense against those alligators and poisonous snakes that were surely eyeing her soft flesh. All at once her boldness had evaporated. Her skin felt suddenly clammy, and she had run back to the main trail—into a worse nightmare: The horse was gone.

"The horse!" yelled Petra, pointing excitedly. "It's coming back!

"Ah!" sighed Alicia. "We live for another day."

1. Underline the phrase that tells the location of the horizon. Write a sentence using the word *horizon*.

2. Underline the words that have the same meaning as casually. Rewrite the sentence using an antonym for *casually*.

3. Circle the word that tells in what region Alicia searched for the horse. Tell what *region* of the country you live in.

4. Underline the word that describes the marsh. Use *marsh* in a sentence.

5. Underline the sentence that tells why Alicia's boldness had surprised her. Write a sentence using a synonym for *boldness*.

6. Circle the words that tell for what purpose Alicia wanted a blunt club. Write a sentence using an antonym of *blunt*.

7. Underline the words that tell what Alicia wanted a defense against. Write the meaning of *defense*.

8. Underline the words that tell what felt clammy. Rewrite the sentence, using an antonym of *clammy*.

"Rattlesnake Hunt" by Marjorie Kinnan Rawlings
Reading Warm-up B

Read the following passage. Pay special attention to the underlined words. Then, read it again, and complete the activities. Use a separate sheet of paper for your written answers.

Snakes are usually considered the <u>aggressors</u> in stories about snakes biting humans, but that is not always the case. Often it is the humans, known as snake wranglers, who pursue the snakes. Their purpose is not to kill the snakes, but to capture and protect them.

Snake hunting is a dangerous occupation. For example, the death adder in Australia is one of the most poisonous snakes on earth. It awaits its prey while hidden, <u>camouflaged</u> in sand, soil, or leafy <u>vegetation</u>. Its attack is swift, silent, and deadly. The adder's threat to humans depends on <u>varying</u> factors, such as the amount of venom it ejects when it bites. Usually, however, an untreated bite can kill a human within six hours. You have to wonder why snake hunters travel into the <u>wilds</u> of Australia to capture these and other deadly snakes. The answer may surprise you.

Once the snake is captured, the hunter delivers it to a laboratory. There the snake is milked for its venom. Milking is a tricky process. Someone holds the snake by its head and forces it to bite through a sheet of thin rubber stretched over a glass container. The venom is ejected through the snake's hollow fangs into the container. The venom is then prepared for the creation of an antivenin. Antivenin is the only cure for the death adder's bite. Hundreds of milkings are necessary to create a single dose.

The benefit of using antivenin to treat snakebites is well-known. Now <u>scientific</u> research is uncovering other <u>desirable</u> benefits of snake venom. Recent discoveries show that venom may be useful in preventing heart attacks, strokes, cancer, and other diseases. It is clear that protecting, not killing, these <u>reptiles</u> is in the interest of all humankind. The venom from snakes may be deadly, but it may also be life giving.

1. Circle the word that tells what are usually considered aggressors. Write a sentence using an antonym of **aggressors**.

2. Circle the word that is a synonym for <u>camouflaged</u>. Use **camouflaged** in a sentence.

3. Circle the word that describes the <u>vegetation</u>. Write a sentence about **vegetation** growing near your home.

4. Underline the words that describe one <u>varying</u> factor in the threat of snakebites. Describe a **varying** factor that can affect your grades.

5. Circle the words that tell into which <u>wilds</u> snake hunters travel. Describe or name some other **wilds** you know about.

6. Underline the words that tell what <u>scientific</u> research is doing. Use **scientific** in a sentence.

7. Underline the words that describe the <u>desirable</u> benefits of snake venom. Tell why the benefits are **desirable**.

8. Circle the word that names one class of <u>reptiles</u>. Name some other **reptiles**.

Name _____ Date _____

"**Rattlesnake Hunt**" by Marjorie Kinnan Rawlings
Writing About the Big Question

What should we learn?

Big Question Vocabulary

analyze	curiosity	discover	evaluate	examine
experiment	explore	facts	information	inquire
interview	investigate	knowledge	question	understand

A. *Choose one word from the list above to complete each sentence. There may be more than one right answer.*

1. Journalists often _____ dozens of experts before writing an article.

2. Sometimes it's impossible to _____ why something frightens us.

3. The scientist did an _____ to learn how many rattlesnakes he could catch.

B. *Follow the directions in responding to each of the items below.*

1. Write about a time when you learned about something that frightens you. Write your response in complete sentences. Use at least one of the Big Question vocabulary words. You may use the words in different forms (for example you can change *analyze* to *analyzing*).

   _____

   _____

2. Write about a common fear you find difficult to understand. Write your response in complete sentences. Use at least one of the Big Question vocabulary words. You may use the words in different forms (for example you can change *analyze* to *analyzing*).

   _____

   _____

C. *Complete the sentence below. Use the completed sentence as the beginning of a short paragraph in which you discuss the big question.*

The more we understand something, _____

   _____

   _____

"Rattlesnake Hunt" by Marjorie Kinnan Rawlings
Reading: Use Resources to Check Facts

A **fact** is information you can prove. An **opinion** is a judgment.

Fact: Ross Allen is a young herpetologist from Florida.

Opinion: "The scientific and dispassionate detachment of the material and the man made a desirable approach to rattlesnake territory."

Be aware that some writers present opinions or beliefs as facts. To get to the truth, **use resources to check facts.** You can confirm whether a statement is accurate by using one of these resources:

Resource	Characteristics
almanac	a collection of facts and statistics on the climate, planets, stars, people, places, events and so on, updated yearly
atlas	a collection of maps
geographical dictionary	an alphabetical listing of places with statistical and factual information about them and perhaps some maps
dictionary	an alphabetical listing of words with their pronunciations and definitions
encyclopedia	an alphabetically organized collection of articles on a broad range of subjects
reliable Web sites	Internet pages and articles on an extremely wide variety of topics, sponsored by individuals, companies, governments, and organizations

DIRECTIONS: *Read these passages from and about "Rattlesnake Hunt." Then, identify each one as a* fact *or an* opinion. *If the statement is a fact, indicate the best resource for checking it.*

1. Big Prairie, Florida, is south of Arcadia and west of the northern tip of Lake Okeechobee.

   Fact/opinion: _____ **Resource:** _____

2. Snakes take on the temperature of their surroundings. They can't stand too much heat for that reason, and when the weather is cool, as now, they're sluggish.

   Fact/opinion: _____ **Resource:** _____

3. Snakes are not cold and clammy.

   Fact/opinion: _____ **Resource:** _____

4. The next day was magnificent. The air was crystal, the sky was aquamarine.

   Fact/opinion: _____ **Resource:** _____

5. A rattler will lie quietly without revealing itself if a man passes by and it thinks it is not seen.

   Fact/opinion: _____ **Resource:** _____

"Rattlesnake Hunt" by Marjorie Kinnan Rawlings
Literary Analysis: Word Choice and Diction

A writer's **word choice** and **diction** are important elements of his or her writing. The specific words a writer uses can make writing difficult or easy to read, formal or informal. Diction includes not only the vocabulary the writer uses but also the way in which the sentences are put together. Here are some questions writers consider when deciding which kinds of words to use:

- What does the audience already know about the topic? If an audience is unfamiliar with a topic, the writer will have to define technical vocabulary or use simpler language.
- What feeling will this work convey? Word choice can make a work serious or funny, academic or personal. The length or style of the sentences can make a work simple or complex.

In this passage from "Rattlesnake Hunt," note that the author uses formal language and difficult vocabulary, but she also uses the informal word *varmints:*

> The scientific and dispassionate detachment of the material and the man made a desirable approach to rattlesnake territory. As I had discovered with the insects and varmints, it is difficult to be afraid of anything about which enough is known.

DIRECTIONS: *Read each passage. Then, on the lines that follow, write down examples of technical vocabulary, formal language, and informal language. If there are no examples of a particular kind of language, write* none.

1. They lived in winter, he said, in gopher holes, coming out in the midday warmth to forage, and would move ahead of the flames and be easily taken.

   Technical vocabulary: _____

   Informal language: _____

   Formal language: _____

2. After the rattlers, water snakes seemed innocuous enough. We worked along the edge of the stream and here Ross did not use his L-shaped steel.

   Technical vocabulary: _____

   Informal language: _____

   Formal language: _____

3. Yet having learned that it was we who were the aggressors; that immobility meant complete safety; that the snakes, for all their lightning flash in striking, were inaccurate in their aim, . . . suddenly I understood that I was drinking in freely the magnificent sweep of the horizon, with no fear of what might be at the moment under my feet.

   Technical vocabulary: _____

   Informal language: _____

   Formal language: _____

"Rattlesnake Hunt" by Marjorie Kinnan Rawlings
Vocabulary Builder

Word List

adequate   arid   desolate   forage   mortality   translucent

A. DIRECTIONS: *Write* true *if a statement is true and* false *if it is false. Then, explain your answer.*

1. If a region is *arid*, crops will grow there easily.

   True/false: _____ **Explanation:** _____

   _____

2. If a character in a book faces his *mortality*, he believes he will live forever.

   True/false: _____ **Explanation:** _____

   _____

3. If a scene in a movie is set in a *desolate* location, the mood will likely be lonely.

   True/false: _____ **Explanation:** _____

   _____

4. If you will be around dangerous animals, it is important to take *adequate* precautions.

   True/false: _____ **Explanation:** _____

   _____

5. *Forage* can be an important part of cattle's diet.

   True/false: _____ **Explanation:** _____

   _____

6. Windows are never *translucent*.

   True/false: _____ **Explanation:** _____

   _____

B. WORD STUDY: *The Latin root -sol- means "alone." Use your knowledge of the Latin root -sol- to write a full sentence to answer each question. Include the italicized word in your answer.*

1. How many people can play a game of *solitaire*?

   _____

2. If you seek *solitude*, do you want others around?

   _____

3. Would many people play a *solo* at one time?

   _____

Unit 3 Resources: Types of Nonfiction
191

Name _____ Date _____

"Rattlesnake Hunt" by Marjorie Kinnan Rawlings
Enrichment: Dangerous Snakes

Rattlesnakes are one kind of poisonous snake. Their rattles give warning before they strike, so they are easier to avoid than some other kinds of dangerous snakes. Other poisonous snakes include the water moccasin, the copperhead, the coral snake, the mamba, the viper, and the cobra.

DIRECTIONS: *Choose one of the poisonous snakes mentioned above, and do some research on it in a reference book or on the Internet. You may choose to research one family of snake (for example, cobras) or a particular variety (such as the king cobra). Find information to answer these questions.*

Kind of snake: _____

1. Where does the snake live? _____
_____

2. What does the snake look like? How big does it get? _____
_____
_____
_____
_____

3. What does the snake eat? _____
_____
_____

4. How poisonous is the snake? _____
_____
_____

5. Does the snake give warning before it strikes? If so, how? _____
_____
_____

"The Real Story of a Cowboy's Life" by Geoffrey C. Ward
"Rattlesnake Hunt" by Marjorie Kinnan Rawlings
Integrated Language Skills: Grammar

Compound Subjects and Predicates

A **compound subject** contains two or more subjects that share the same verb. A **compound predicate** contains two or more verbs that share the same subject. Both compound subjects and compound predicates are joined by conjunctions such as *and, or, but,* and *nor.*

Compound subject:	<u>Discipline</u> *and* <u>planning</u> were essential to the success of a cattle drive.
Compound predicate:	"The snake <u>did</u> not <u>coil</u>, *but* <u>lifted</u> its head *and* <u>whirred</u> its rattles lightly."

A. PRACTICE: *In these sentences, underline the compound subjects once and the compound predicates twice.*

1. On trail rides, cowboys keep the herd together and guide them along the trail.
2. Trail bosses and cowboys work together to keep the cattle safe.
3. Sometimes bosses pay homesteaders or face their anger.
4. Most trail bosses forbid gambling and punish cowboys for drinking.
5. Rattlesnakes warn intruders but strike quickly.
6. Snakes and other reptiles are cold-blooded.
7. Sun and warm temperatures bring snakes out of hiding.
8. Snake catchers must move carefully or suffer the consequences.

B. Writing Application: *Imagine that you are describing an attempt at catching a rattlesnake. Follow these instructions.*

1. Write a sentence with a compound predicate; use *walked* and *searched.*

_____

_____

2. Write a sentence with a compound subject; use *insects* and *snakes.*

_____

_____

3. Write a sentence with a compound predicate; use *hissed* and *rattled.*

_____

_____

4. Write a sentence with a compound predicate; use *found* and *caught.*

_____

_____

Name _____ Date _____

"The Real Story of a Cowboy's Life" by Geoffrey C. Ward
"Rattlesnake Hunt" by Marjorie Kinnan Rawlings
Integrated Language Skills: Support for Writing an Adaptation

Prepare to write an **adaptation** of one of the incidents described in "Rattlesnake Hunt" or "The Real Story of a Cowboy's Life," by completing the following graphic organizer. First note the incident you plan to adapt and the audience you plan to present your adaptation to. For examples, tell the incident to a group of kinder garteners or a class of students learning English. Then, in the first column of the chart, copy down the incident. In the second column, write your adaptation, keeping your audience in mind. Finally, look carefully at your adaptation. See if you can simplify it even further. In the last column, note your revisions.

Incident: _____
Audience: _____

Passage	Adaptation	Revision of Adaptation

Now, use your notes to write a final draft of your adaptation.

"The Real Story of a Cowboy's Life" by Geoffrey C. Ward
"Rattlesnake Hunt" by Marjorie Kinnan Rawlings

Integrated Language Skills: Support for Extend Your Learning

Research and Technology

To prepare to write a **help-wanted ad** for a job as snake scientist Ross Allen's or Charles Goodnight's assistant, fill in this chart.

Job title: _____

Job Responsibilities	Education Required	Experience Required	Skills Required	Traits Required

Listening and Speaking

As you work with the members of your group to **plan for a multimedia presentation** about rattlesnakes, write your notes in this chart. In the left-hand column, note details that you would like to include. In the right-hand column, note the type of media you would use to present each detail. (Media might include your voice alone, your voice plus photographs or drawings, sound recordings, video recordings, and so on.)

Topic: _____

Details	Type of Media

"Rattlesnake Hunt" by Marjorie Kinnan Rawlings
Open-Book Test

Short Answer *Write your responses to the questions in this section on the lines provided.*

1. In the first sentence of "Rattlesnake Hunt," author Marjorie Kinnan Rawlings describes Ross Allen as "a young Florida herpetologist." What term in this description is an academic term? What does it mean?

   _____

   _____

2. An author chooses words that can create a formal, an informal, a technical, or a personal feeling, among others. In the beginning of "Rattlesnake Hunt," the author states that Ross Allen had a "scientific and dispassionate detachment." What feeling does this word choice convey? Explain.

   _____

   _____

3. Writers use resources such as almanacs, atlases, encyclopedias, and dictionaries to find and check their facts. Of these choices, which resource would you most likely use to check the location of Big Prairie, mentioned near the beginning of "Rattlesnake Hunt"? Explain.

   _____

   _____

4. Marjorie Kinnan Rawlings describes Big Prairie as desolate in the beginning of "Rattlesnake Hunt." Does she still consider it desolate at the end of the essay? Base your answer on the meaning of *desolate*.

   _____

   _____

5. What feeling does this passage from the middle of "Rattlesnake Hunt" convey? What words convey the feeling?

   I took the snake in my hands. It was not cold, it was not clammy, and it lay trustingly in my hands, a thing that lived and breathed and had mortality like the rest of us. I felt an upsurgence of spirit.

   _____

   _____

6. What does Rawlings learn from holding the water snake in "Rattlesnake Hunt"? Support your answer with details from the essay.

   _____

   _____

   _____

7. What does Marjorie Kinnan Rawlings realize in "Rattlesnake Hunt" when she recognizes the water snake's mortality? Base your response on the meaning of *mortality*.

_____

_____

_____

_____

8. What resource would you most likely use to confirm this information from the middle of "Rattlesnake Hunt"?

    The rattler strikes only for paralyzing and killing its food, and for defense.

_____

_____

_____

_____

9. The reader learns, in "Rattlesnake Hunt," that to catch snakes it is important to be able to move silently and to know snakes' habits. Which is more important? Why?

_____

_____

_____

_____

10. In "Rattlesnake Hunt," Marjorie Rawlings changes from the beginning to the end of the essay. In the chart, describe the way she acts and feels in the beginning of the essay. Then, describe how she acts and feels at the end of the essay. Answer the question that follows the chart.

Majorie Rawlings at the beginning	Marjorie Rawlings at the end

What has Marjorie Kinnan Rawlings learned? _____

_____

_____

Essay

Write an extended response to the question of your choice or to the question or questions your teacher assigns you.

11. In "Rattlesnake Hunt," Marjorie Kinnan Rawlings changes the way she feels about rattlesnakes. In an essay, describe how her feelings change. First, tell what her feelings were at the beginning of her article. Then, tell what her feelings were at the end. Finally, explain why her feelings change. Support your claims with examples from the essay.

12. Throughout "Rattlesnake Hunt," Ross Allen, the herpetologist, provides Marjorie Kinnan Rawlings with factual information about snakes. In an essay, cite two facts that Ross relates and describe the effect they have on Rawlings. What is Ross's purpose in relating these facts? How do they change the way in which Rawlings views snakes?

13. In "Rattlesnake Hunt," Rawlings writes that if she had seen a rattlesnake a week earlier, she "should have lain down and died on top of the rattlesnake, with no need of being struck and poisoned." In an essay, explain the meaning of Rawlings's statement. Then, analyze the diction that is Rawlings's choice of words and the way she composes the sentence. What feeling does she convey?

14. **Thinking About the Big Question: What should we learn?** In "Rattlesnake Hunt," Marjorie Kinnan Rawlings learns an important lesson about herself. In an essay, explain what she learns and why it is important. Use details from Rawlings's essay to support your explanation. Then, consider whether it is a lesson that readers can apply to their own lives. Why or why not?

Oral Response

15. Go back to question 6, 9, or 10 or to the question your teacher assigns you. Take a few minutes to expand your answer and prepare an oral response. Find additional details in "Rattlesnake Hunt" that support your points. If necessary, make notes to guide your oral response.

Name _____ Date _____

"Rattlesnake Hunt" by Marjorie Kinnan Rawlings

Selection Test A

Critical Reading *Identify the letter of the choice that best answers the question.*

____ 1. What feeling does the word choice in this passage from "Rattlesnake Hunt" convey?

> Ross Allen, a young Florida herpetologist, invited me to join him on a hunt in the upper Everglades.

A. casual

B. informal

C. technical

D. humorous

____ 2. What feeling does the word choice in this passage from "Rattlesnake Hunt" convey?

> The scientific and dispassionate detachment of the material and the man made a desirable approach to rattlesnake territory.

A. formal

B. informal

C. technical

D. humorous

____ 3. In "Rattlesnake Hunt," what is one way in which Ross helps the author with her fear?

A. He tells her that he will carry the snakes in the back of his car.

B. He provides her with a great deal of information about snakes.

C. He warns her when she is in danger of being attacked by a snake.

D. He builds a cheerful campfire and helps her forget about the snakes.

____ 4. In which resource would you most likely check the fact that Big Prairie, mentioned in "Rattlesnake Hunt," is "west of the northern tip of Lake Okeechobee"?

A. an atlas

B. a dictionary

C. a biographical dictionary

D. an almanac

____ 5. What does Ross use to catch rattlesnakes in "Rattlesnake Hunt"?

A. a hook

B. an L-shaped prong

C. a net

D. a forked stick

_____ 6. In which resource would you most likely check the fact, stated in "Rattlesnake Hunt," that snakes take on the temperature of their surroundings?

    A. an atlas

    B. an almanac

    C. an encyclopedia

    D. a geographical dictionary

_____ 7. According to "Rattlesnake Hunt," why are the snakes sluggish in January?

    A. It is cool.

    B. It is hot.

    C. They are hungry.

    D. They are hibernating.

_____ 8. When the author of "Rattlesnake Hunt" touches a water snake, what does she realize?

    A. Snakes are not as frightening as she had thought.

    B. Snakes are far more frightening than she had thought.

    C. All reptiles are cold and clammy.

    D. All reptiles are extremely strange.

_____ 9. What does the author of "Rattlesnake Hunt" do when she finds a snake under the violet she picks?

    A. She screams and runs.

    B. She freezes in terror.

    C. She begins to tremble.

    D. She steps back slowly.

_____ 10. How has the author of "Rattlesnake Hunt" changed by the end of the essay?

    A. She fears snakes more than ever.

    B. She is no longer so afraid of snakes.

    C. She no longer cares about snakes.

    D. She admires snakes but fears them.

_____ 11. From "Rattlesnake Hunt," which of these qualities would you infer is most important for catching snakes?

    A. a lack of fear

    B. an ability to move silently

    C. knowledge of snakes' habits

    D. physical strength

Name _____ Date _____

Vocabulary and Grammar

____ 12. What does Rawlings mean when she describes Big Prairie as *desolate*?
A. It is beautiful.
B. It is lonely.
C. It is frightening.
D. It is endless.

____ 13. What might you expect of an *arid* region?
A. Plants will grow abundantly.
B. It will rain almost every day.
C. It will be cold in winter.
D. Few plants will grow.

____ 14. Which of these sentences contains a compound predicate?
A. The author and Ross camped on the prairie.
B. Ross caught and kept many snakes.
C. Snakes strike when they are hungry or threatened.
D. The author admires the beauty of the prairie sunset.

____ 15. Which of these sentences contains a compound subject?
A. Cattlemen and Indians were preparing the land for forage.
B. Snakes crawl slowly and heavily in the cold weather.
C. The author was nervous and frightened at first.
D. The prairie was covered with long grasses and trees.

Essay

16. In "Rattlesnake Hunt," Marjorie Kinnan Rawlings changes the way she feels about rattlesnakes. In an essay, describe how her feelings change, and explain why they change. Support your claims with two references to the selection.

17. Ross Allen, the herpetologist featured in "Rattlesnake Hunt," provides Marjorie Kinnan Rawlings with a great deal of factual information about snakes. In an essay, discuss two or three facts about rattlesnakes that Ross reveals. Point to one fact that Ross verifies by showing that what he says is true.

18. **Thinking About the Big Question: What should we learn?** In "Rattlesnake Hunt," Marjorie Kinnan Rawlings learns an important lesson about herself. In an essay, explain what she learns and why it is important. Use details from Rawlings's essay to support your explanation.

"Rattlesnake Hunt" by Marjorie Kinnan Rawlings
Selection Test B

Critical Reading *Identify the letter of the choice that best completes the statement or answers the question.*

_____ 1. In "Rattlesnake Hunt," what does Majorie Kinnan Rawlings mean by this sentence? The scientific and dispassionate detachment of the material and the man [Ross Allen] made a desirable approach to rattlesnake territory.
   A. Ross's attitude and scientific data make for a good approach to rattlesnake hunting.
   B. Ross's scientific data are essential to his decision about where to hunt for snakes.
   C. Ross is a cold, unfeeling person with a brilliant scientific mind.
   D. Ross does not care about the success of the rattlesnake hunt.

_____ 2. In "Rattlesnake Hunt," the herpetologist helps Rawlings feel less afraid of rattlesnakes by
   A. warning her when it is time for them to proceed more cautiously.
   B. telling her that he will carry the snakes in the back of his car.
   C. informing her of a great many scientific facts about rattlesnakes.
   D. bringing along another hunter and building a cheerful campfire.

_____ 3. How is Marjorie Kinnan Rawlings affected by learning about snakes?
   A. She realizes that it is hard to fear something you know much about.
   B. She realizes that she has even more fears than she had thought.
   C. She learns many scientific reasons to avoid rattlesnakes.
   D. She becomes a lifelong fan and defender of rattlesnakes.

_____ 4. Which resource would you most likely check to confirm that Big Prairie is half marsh, half pasture, with islands of palm trees and cypress and oaks?
   A. an almanac
   B. a geographic dictionary
   C. a biographical dictionary
   D. a dictionary

_____ 5. In "Rattlesnake Hunt," the snake hunters are able to catch rattlesnakes easily because
   A. the snakes are hungry.
   B. the snakes are inactive.
   C. the snakes are overheated.
   D. the snakes are afraid of them.

_____ 6. Which statement best expresses what Rawlings learns by holding the water snake?
   A. "Ross said, 'We couldn't have a better night for catching water snakes.'"
   B. "After the rattlers, water snakes seemed innocuous enough."
   C. "It was not cold, it was not clammy."
   D. "It was . . . a thing that lived and breathed and had mortality like the rest of us."

___ 7. What feeling does this passage from "Rattlesnake Hunt" convey?

I took the snake in my hands. It was not cold, it was not clammy, and it lay trustingly in my hands, a thing that lived and breathed and had mortality like the rest of us. I felt an upsurgence of spirit.

A. amusement
B. detachment
C. triumph
D. fear

___ 8. Which of these passages from "Rattlesnake Hunt" contains an example of technical language?

A. Ross Allen, a young Florida herpetologist, invited me to join him on a hunt in the upper Everglades—for rattlesnakes.
B. That night Ross and Will and I camped out in the vast spaces of the Everglades prairies.
C. The air was crystal, the sky was aquamarine, and the far horizon of palms and oaks lay against the sky.
D. A rattler will lie quietly without revealing itself if a man passes by.

___ 9. Which resource would you most likely check to confirm that rattlers strike only for paralyzing and killing their food and for defense?

A. a reliable Web site
B. a geographical dictionary
C. an almanac
D. a dictionary

___ 10. Which of these passages from "Rattlesnake Hunt" is an example of formal language?

A. The scientific and dispassionate detachment of the material and the man made a desirable approach to rattlesnake territory.
B. Ross dropped the rattler in a crocus sack and Will carried it.
C. Whenever I leave my car or truck with snakes already in it, other rattlers always appear.
D. "I'm awfully sorry," I said, "but you're pushing me a little too fast."

___ 11. Which statement best summarizes Rawlings's main point in "Rattlesnake Hunt"?

A. Rattlesnakes are interesting to study in their natural habitat.
B. Learning to overcome deep-seated fears is a thrilling experience.
C. Ross relies on Rawlings's skills as a writer to convey the excitement of the hunt.
D. She experienced more fear in the first hours of the hunt than she had ever known.

___ 12. How does the author change during the events described in "Rattlesnake Hunt"?

A. She learns how to build a campfire.
B. She loses much of her fear of rattlesnakes.
C. She becomes able to pick up a rattlesnake with her hands.
D. She learns how to tell whether rattlesnakes are in their holes.

Vocabulary and Grammar

____ **13.** In calling Big Prairie *arid*, Marjorie Kinnan Rawlings means that the land is

A. flooded.   C. empty.

B. burned.   D. dry.

____ **14.** In recognizing the water snake's *mortality*, Marjorie Kinnan realizes that

A. it will die eventually.   C. it is afraid.

B. it will try to kill her.   D. it will live forever.

____ **15.** A place that is *desolate* is likely to be

A. densely populated.   C. stark and uninhabited.

B. extremely beautiful.   D. clean and well kept.

____ **16.** In the following sentence, which words form the compound predicate?

Ross and Will trapped the snakes and lifted them with the L-shaped prong.

A. Ross, Will   C. snakes, them

B. trapped, lifted   D. snakes, prong

____ **17.** In the following sentence, which words form the compound subject?

Palms and cypress dotted the prairie and bordered the marsh.

A. palms, cypress   C. prairie, marsh

B. dotted, bordered   D. palms, prairie

____ **18.** What is the compound predicate in the following sentence?

An angry rattler will rise and strike in an instant.

A. will rise   C. will rise, strike

B. rise, strike   D. strike in an instant

Essay

19. Throughout "Rattlesnake Hunt," Ross Allen, the herpetologist, provides Rawlings with factual information about snakes. In an essay, cite two facts that Ross imparts, and describe the effect that they have on Rawlings. What is Ross's purpose in relating these facts? How do they change the way in which Rawlings views snakes?

20. Rawlings writes,

> If this [sighting a rattlesnake up close] had happened the week before, if it had happened the day before, I think I should have lain down and died on top of the rattlesnake, with no need of being struck and poisoned.

In an essay, explain the meaning of Rawlings's statement. Then, analyze the diction—Rawlings's choice of words and the way in which she composes the sentence. What feeling does the diction convey?

21. **Thinking About the Big Question: What should we learn?** In "Rattlesnake Hunt," Marjorie Kinnan Rawlings learns an important lesson about herself. In an essay, explain what she learns and why it is important. Use details from Rawlings's essay to support your explanation. Then consider whether it is a lesson that readers can apply to their own lives. Why or why not?

Vocabulary Warm-up Word Lists

Study these words. Then, complete the activities that follow.

Word List A

bellow [BEL oh] *v.* to roar or cry out loudly
   Our mother would <u>bellow</u> loudly when she called us to dinner.

craning [KRAYN ing] *v.* stretching the neck to see something
   Deb was <u>craning</u> her neck in order to see the band perform.

dread [DRED] *n.* great fear or uneasiness, especially about something in the future
   With some <u>dread</u>, Danielle waited in the dentist's chair.

haul [HAWL] *v.* to drag something by force
   It took all the might of the tow truck to <u>haul</u> the vehicle out of the ditch.

quality [KWAH luh tee] *n.* a trait or property of something
   The old, dusty mirror had all but lost its reflective <u>quality</u>.

raved [RAYVD] *v.* talked in a wild, confused, or enthusiastic way
   For hours, Steven <u>raved</u> about the hardships of the past year.

seldom [SEL duhm] *adv.* rarely; not often
   The best athletes <u>seldom</u> miss practices.

stern [STURN] *adj.* something harsh; firm or uncompromising
   There is <u>stern</u> punishment for breaking the law.

Word List B

alligator [AL i gay tuhr] *n.* a large reptile of the crocodile family
   At the zoo's reptile house, the children saw an <u>alligator</u>.

cattails [KAT taylz] *n.* tall marsh plants with brown, furry flowers at the end
   The long <u>cattails</u> looked pretty in the dried-flower arrangement.

crouched [KROWCHT] *v.* stooped down with the knees bent
   Hiding in the closet, Emma <u>crouched</u> among the shoes.

drenched [DRENCHT] *adj.* wet completely; soaked
   The sudden downpour left us <u>drenched</u> and cold.

ghastly [GAST lee] *adj.* frightening or terrifying; like a ghost; extremely unpleasant
   A <u>ghastly</u> figure loomed in the window of the haunted house.

howled [HOWLD] *v.* made one or more long, drawn-out cries
   The wolves <u>howled</u> at the moon, keeping the campers awake.

situated [SICH oo ay tid] *v.* located; placed in a certain spot
   We were <u>situated</u> at a table near the window.

request [ri KWEST] *n.* something that is asked for
   Dave's only <u>request</u> was for a glass of water to quench his thirst.

"Alligator" by Bailey White
"The Cremation of Sam McGee" by Robert Service
Vocabulary Warm-up Exercises

Exercise A *Fill in each blank in the paragraph below with an appropriate word from Word List A. Use each word only once.*

Cal and Al had only to hear Mr. Summer [1] _____ mightily to know they were in trouble. As they were [2] _____ their necks to see around the corner of the house, they spotted Mr. Summer approaching. The sight of the [3] _____, old man filled them with [4] _____. The two friends tried to run but were too late. Mr. Summer had already scooped them up and began to [5] _____ them back to the house. "First, you dig up my garden. Now, you bring dead mice into the parlor. I'll tell you what I'm going to do with you!" the old man [6] _____. His voice had a deep, commanding [7] _____ that seemed to confirm his authority. Although guilty, Cal and Al looked up with wide, innocent eyes. Mr. Summer's heart began to melt. Luckily, for the two kittens, the old man [8] _____ stayed mad at them for long. "Oh, go on," he muttered as he smiled and let the kittens go.

Exercise B *Answer the questions with complete explanations.*

____ 1. Would a grown alligator be able to hide under a pebble?

____ 2. If you stumbled upon <u>cattails</u> in a marsh, did you likely find tall marsh plants with brown furry flowers there?

____ 3. A cat is <u>crouched</u> behind a bush, eyeing a bird. What might the cat do next?

____ 4. If you wore a long raincoat, would your clothing get <u>drenched</u> in rainstorms?

____ 5. Can a scream be described as <u>ghastly</u>?

____ 6. If a boy <u>howled</u> and held his knee, would you suppose something was wrong?

____ 7. In what seat must a person be <u>situated</u> to drive a car?

____ 8. Are you more likely to say *please* or *thank you* when making a <u>request</u>?

Name _____ Date _____

"**Alligator**" by Bailey White
"**The Cremation of Sam McGee**" by Robert Service
Reading Warm-up A

Read the following passage. Pay special attention to the underlined words. Use a separate sheet of paper for your written answers.

Dear Nick,

How is my favorite big brother? I am having a great time at camp. It's a big difference from being back home in the city. There are a lot more trees here and the air has a <u>quality</u> of freshness I cannot describe. I can only taste it.

My counselor, Mr. Smith, is an excellent hike leader. His movements are sure, and he <u>seldom</u> needs to pause to decide our next direction. He knows the trails by heart.

This morning, Tom and I awoke early and saw Mr. Smith enter the forest. Curious to see where he was going, we decided to <u>haul</u> ourselves out of bed and follow him. We crept to the edge of the trees, and <u>craning</u> our necks around the trunk of a giant pine, we spotted Mr. Smith. He shot us a harsh glance to hint his <u>stern</u> disapproval.

"Don't you boys hear that?" he whispered through his teeth. "Listen. No. Look," he said, as he darted his hand toward the top of the distant ridge.

Sitting high atop the forest, wrapped in mist, was a grizzly bear. It rose to its hind legs and let out a long, powerful <u>bellow</u>. The noise came from deep within the animal and echoed through the trees. Mr. Smith turned to us and spoke. "We don't belong here, boys. This is *his* forest, and he watches us with <u>dread</u>. Believe me, he fears that one day our paths will cross his. Let's go."

Back at camp, the others had awakened. They sat excitedly around the breakfast table and <u>raved</u> to one another about the sound that had roared through the camp that morning. Tom and I just smiled as we washed the dishes. It was a small price to pay.

Your brother,

Danny

1. Circle the word that describes the <u>quality</u> of the air. Name a *quality* that is important in a good friend.

2. Underline the sentence that tells why Mr. Smith <u>seldom</u> needs to pause to decide the group's next direction. Use *seldom* in a sentence.

3. Circle the word that tells what the boys decided to <u>haul</u> themselves out of. What are some other things that people can *haul*?

4. Underline the words that tell what Danny and Tom were <u>craning</u> their necks around. Write a synonym for *craning*.

5. Circle the word that is a synonym for <u>stern</u>.

6. Underline the sentence that helps describe what a <u>bellow</u> is. What other animal might *bellow*?

7. Circle the word that gives a clue to the meaning of <u>dread</u>. Define *dread*.

8. Underline the words that tell what the other campers <u>raved</u> about. Use *raved* in a sentence.

"Alligator" by Bailey White
"The Cremation of Sam McGee" by Robert Service
Reading Warm-up B

Read the following passage. Pay special attention to the underlined words. Use a separate sheet of paper for your written answers.

Last week, Jenny's science class visited the zoo. Although there were plenty of animals to see, only one in particular was of interest to Jenny. She wished to see an <u>alligator</u>, a large reptile that lives in freshwater swamps, lakes, and marshes.

As soon as her class arrived at the zoo that morning, Jenny made a <u>request</u> to first visit the alligator swamp. Her teacher, Mrs. Lewis, explained that the class would not see the reptile exhibit until after they had watched the dolphins perform. At the dolphin pool, Jenny foolishly <u>situated</u> herself too near the tank. She was left <u>drenched</u> by the cascades of water that the unlikely mammals sent spewing into the audience. With her clothing thoroughly soaked, Jenny decided she had seen enough of the marine exhibit. She was ready to go see the alligators.

When the class finally approached the reptile house, the alligator exhibit appeared to be empty. Jenny <u>crouched</u> down to see if she could spot any of the alligators hiding in the <u>cattails</u> and other tall marsh plants that surrounded the artificial swamp. She had bent herself so low that her nose was almost drawn even with an old, slimy log that had propped itself against the opposite side of the exhibit fence. Deflated by the alligators' collective refusal to appear, Jenny huffed a sigh of disappointment and began to stand up.

Suddenly, the slimy log snapped back into the air and flashed its enormous mouth full of razor sharp teeth. Jenny leapt back from the fence and <u>howled</u> with fright.

"It's an alligator!" she yelped. "Run!"

She scrambled to her feet, swung around, and ran smack into the zookeeper, who had heard her <u>ghastly</u> scream from across the way.

"Are you all right?" asked the zookeeper. "You look terrified."

"No, Sir!" replied Jenny. "There's a huge alligator on the other side of that fence."

The zookeeper threw his head back and chuckled. "Well, what did you expect?"

1. Underline the words that describe an <u>alligator</u>.

2. What was Jenny's <u>request</u>? Write a sentence that makes a *request*.

3. Underline the words that tell where Jenny <u>situated</u> herself. Define *situated*.

4. Underline the phrase that tells what caused Jenny to be <u>drenched</u>. Describe the last time you were *drenched*.

5. Underline the words that tell why Jenny <u>crouched</u>. What does *crouched* mean?

6. Circle the words that give clues to the meaning of <u>cattails</u>. Define *cattails*.

7. Circle the word that tells with what emotion Jenny <u>howled</u>. Write a sentence using the word *howled*.

8. Circle the word that tells what was <u>ghastly</u>. Write a synonym for *ghastly*.

"**Alligator**" by Bailey White
"**The Cremation of Sam McGee**" by Robert Service
Writing About the Big Question

What should we learn?

Big Question Vocabulary

analyze	curiosity	discover	evaluate	examine
experiment	explore	facts	information	inquire
interview	investigate	knowledge	question	understand

A. *Choose one word from the list above to complete each sentence. There may be more than one right answer.*

1. I think _____ made the alligator visit shore.

2. The characters in "The Cremation of Sam McGee" hoped to _____ gold.

3. I would like to _____ the Yukon.

B. *Follow the directions in responding to each of the items below.*

1. Write about what makes you laugh. Write your response in complete sentences. Use at least one of the Big Question vocabulary words. You may use the words in different forms (for example you can change *analyze* to *analyzing*).

_____

_____

2. Explain one way you think laughter is important. Write your response in complete sentences. Use at least one of the Big Question vocabulary words. You may use the words in different forms.

_____

_____

C. *Complete the sentence below. Use the completed sentence as the beginning of a short paragraph in which you discuss the big question.*

The funniest things happen when _____

_____

_____.

Name _____ Date _____

"**Alligator**" by Bailey White

"**The Cremation of Sam McGee**" by Robert Service

Literary Analysis: Comparing Humorous Essays

Humorous essays are works of nonfiction meant to amuse readers. To entertain, authors may use one or more of these comic techniques:

- presenting an illogical, inappropriate, improper, or unusual situation
- contrasting reality with characters' mistaken views
- exaggerating the truth or exaggerating the feelings, ideas, and actions of characters

While most humorists want to entertain the reader, many also want to convey a serious message.

Writers of humorous essays often develop the humor through the characters they present. For example, humorous characters are central to "Alligator" and "The Cremation of Sam McGee."

DIRECTIONS: *Explain your answers to the following questions, using examples from the selections.*

Question	"Alligator"	"The Cremation of Sam McGee"
1. Does the essay describe illogical, inappropriate, improper, or unusual situations?		
2. Does the writer contrast reality with characters' mistaken views?		
3. Does the writer exaggerate the truth or the feelings, ideas, and actions of characters?		
4. Which character did you find the most humorous? How is that character's appearance described? How are his or her actions described? What does the character say, or what do other characters say about him or her, to add to the humor?		

Unit 3 Resources: Types of Nonfiction

210

Name _____ Date _____

"Alligator" by Bailey White
"The Cremation of Sam McGee" by Robert Service
Vocabulary Builder

Word List

    bellow   cattails   exultant   loathed   whimper

A. DIRECTIONS: *Read each sentence, paying attention to the italicized word from the Word List. Then, explain whether the sentence makes sense. If it does not make sense, rewrite the sentence using the Word List word correctly, or write a new sentence using the word.*

1. On our trip to the desert, we found *cattails* growing everywhere.

   Explanation: _____

   New sentence: _____

2. The crowds in the arena *bellow* when the referee makes an unfair call.

   Explanation: _____

   New sentence: _____

3. When she discovered she had come in last place, the student was *exultant*.

   Explanation: _____

   New sentence: _____

4. We hated to hear our dog *whimper* when we left him home alone.

   Explanation: _____

   New sentence: _____

5. Maria *loathed* eating things she found delicious.

   Explanation: _____

   New sentence: _____

B. DIRECTIONS: *Write the letter of the word that is most similar in meaning to the word from the Word List.*

____ **1.** exultant
    A. depressed   **B.** overjoyed   **C.** safe   **D.** dangerous

____ **2.** cattails
    A. plants   **B.** clothes   **C.** cat   **D.** pattern

____ **3.** bellow
    A. write   **B.** shout   **C.** whisper   **D.** read

____ **4.** whimper
    A. sing   **B.** shout   **C.** whine   **D.** drive

____ **5.** loathed
    A. hated   **B.** loved   **C.** cherished   **D.** ignored

"Alligator" by Bailey White
"The Cremation of Sam McGee" by Robert Service

Integrated Language Skills:
Support for Writing to Compare Literary Works

To prepare to write an essay **comparing humorous essays,** complete this graphic organizer.

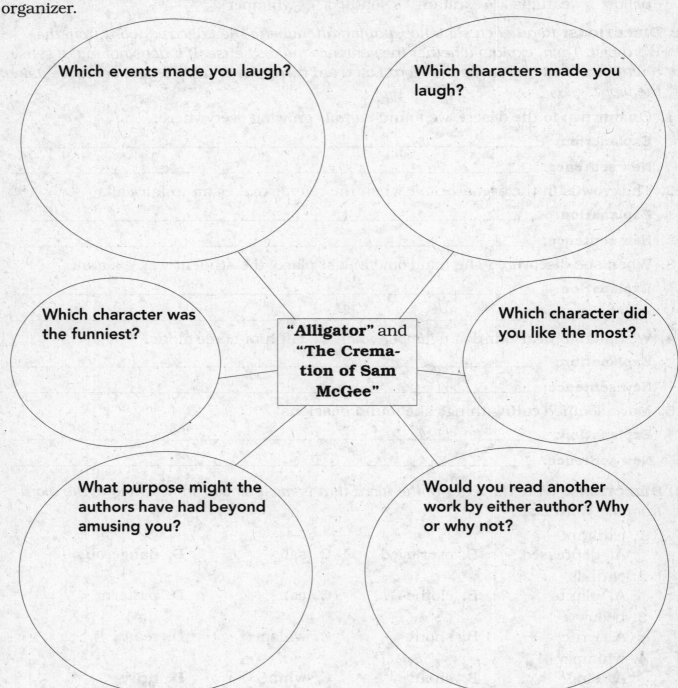

Which events made you laugh?

Which characters made you laugh?

Which character was the funniest?

"Alligator" and "The Cremation of Sam McGee"

Which character did you like the most?

What purpose might the authors have had beyond amusing you?

Would you read another work by either author? Why or why not?

Now, use your notes to write an essay explaining why you found "Alligator" funnier than "The Cremation of Sam McGee" or why you found "The Cremation of Sam McGee" funnier than "Alligator."

"Alligator" by Bailey White and
"The Cremation of Sam McGee" by Robert Service
Open-Book Test

Short Answer *Write your responses to the questions in this section on the lines provided.*

1. In the beginning of "Alligator," the alligator flops back into the water when Aunt Belle jumps up and down and shouts "Whoo!" What does this tell you about the alligator?

   _____

   _____

   _____

2. In the middle of "Alligator," author Bailey White describes the alligator's bellow as "a sound you hear in your bones." How else does a bellow sound? Base your answer on the meaning of *bellow*.

   _____

   _____

   _____

3. Toward the end of "Alligator," why is Aunt Belle spending a lot of time at the pond?

   _____

   _____

   _____

4. In the first stanza of "The Cremation of Sam McGee," the speaker says he "cremated Sam McGee." What feeling does this information give to the opening of the poem?

   _____

   _____

5. Why does the speaker of "Sam McGee" continue to carry his dead friend, even though in his heart he "cursed that load" in line 34 of the poem?

   _____

   _____

   _____

6. What was it that Sam McGee *loathed* about the Yukon Territory? Base your answer on the meaning of *loathed*.

   _____

   _____

   _____

7. Record the unusual situation in each work on the chart. Then, answer the question that follows the chart.

	Unusual Situation
"Alligator"	
"The Cremation of Sam McGee"	

Which situation do you find more humorous? Why? _____
_____

8. When an author uses exaggeration as a comic technique, he or she stretches the truth. Give an example of exaggeration from each work.

"Alligator": _____
_____

"The Cremation of Sam McGee": _____
_____

9. Review the author's use of the word *Whoo!* near the beginning of "Alligator," and the author's use of the word *chum* in line 43 of "Sam McGee." Which word strikes you as more humorous? Why?

_____
_____

10. "Alligator" and "Sam McGee" end on very different notes. How do you think each author wants you to feel at the end of the story or poem?

_____
_____

Essay

Write an extended response to the question of your choice or to the question or questions your teacher assigns you.

11. Both Aunt Belle in "Alligator" and Sam McGee in "The Cremation of Sam McGee" are unusual characters. In an essay, explain what makes each character unusual. What action does the character take that is humorous? What does the character say, or have said about them, that is humorous? In your view, which character is more humorous? Why?

12. Humor is often used to convey a serious theme or central idea. Choose either "Alligator" or "The Cremation of Sam McGee" and write an essay in which you identify a serious theme of that work. Explain how the author uses humor to communicate the theme. In your view, does the author succeed? Why or why not?

13. Both "Alligator" and "The Cremation of Sam McGee" are humorous works. In an essay, describe what makes these works funny. Cite a passage from each selection that strongly contributes to the work's humor. Identify the techniques used in that passage to create the humor. Does the passage present an illogical, inappropriate, improper, or unusual situation? Does it contrast reality with a character's mistaken views? Does it exaggerate the truth or some aspect of a character? Be sure that you provide specific examples and details from each text to support your ideas.

14. **Thinking About the Big Question: What should we learn?** Authors of humorous works want to entertain us, but they also want us to learn something. Choose either "Alligator" or "Sam McGee" and tell what you think the author wants the reader to learn. Why do you think this lesson is worth learning?

Oral Response

15. Go back to question 7, 8, or 10 or to the question your teacher assigns you. Take a few minutes to expand your answer and prepare an oral response. Find additional details in the relevant text or texts that support your points. If necessary, make notes to guide your oral response.

"Alligator" by Bailey White
"The Cremationof Sam McGee" by Robert Service
Selection Test A

Critical Reading *Identify the letter of the choice that best answers the question.*

____ 1. In "Alligator," why does the narrator's aunt crawl through the marsh grass at the edge of a pond?
   A. She is looking for something she lost.
   B. She is going to meet an alligator face to face.
   C. She is afraid an alligator will see her if she stands up.
   D. She is entertaining the children in her care.

____ 2. According to Bailey White, what is the size of the alligator that the children saw?
   A. unusually small
   B. medium size
   C. medium to large
   D. extremely large

____ 3. What impression of her aunt does Bailey White convey in "Alligator"?
   A. She is angry.
   B. She is unfeeling.
   C. She is happy.
   D. She is unusual.

____ 4. What phrase best describes the relationship between the alligator and Aunt Belle?
   A. amused indifference
   B. affectionate respect
   C. fearful caution
   D. cheerful tolerance

____ 5. The opening of "The Cremation of Sam McGee" states that "the Arctic trails have their secret tales." What does this statement suggest about the atmosphere, or mood, of the poem?
   A. It will be jolly.
   B. It will be sad.
   C. It will be strange.
   D. It will be humorous.

____ 6. Why might Alaska's extreme cold have been particularly difficult for Sam McGee to endure?

    A. He was a frail man.

    B. He was a constant complainer.

    C. He was from a warm place.

    D. He wasn't wearing warm clothing.

____ 7. What does McGee mean when he tells the speaker that he will "cash in this trip"?

    A. McGee will collect his wages.

    B. McGee will have his paycheck sent back home.

    C. McGee will become a dealer at a casino.

    D. McGee will soon die.

____ 8. Why does the speaker agree to McGee's request?

    A. McGee is the speaker's best friend.

    B. The speaker likes to please people.

    C. McGee is a difficult man to argue with.

    D. The speaker can't refuse a last request.

____ 9. Which aspect do "Alligator" and "The Cremation of Sam McGee" share?

    A. rhyme scheme

    B. exaggeration

    C. setting

    D. genre

____ 10. In what way are the narrator in "Alligator" and the speaker in "The Cremation of Sam McGee" alike?

    A. They are both related to the main character.

    B. They are both amused by the main character.

    C. They are both involved in the plot.

    D. They are both adult men.

Vocabulary

____ 11. Where are *cattails* most likely to be found?

    A. in a cage   **B.** in a desert   **C.** in a swamp   **D.** in a zoo

____ 12. How might you feel after acing a tough test?

    A. ominous   **B.** apathetic   **C.** perilous   **D.** exultant

____ **13.** Which of the following words refers to a sound?

    A. solicitous

    B. vibrant

    C. bellow

    D. vast

____ **14.** If you *loathed* someone, how would you feel about that person?

    A. You would respect the person.

    B. You would like the person.

    C. You would neither like nor dislike the person.

    D. You would hate the person.

____ **15.** What kind of cry is a *whimper*?

    A. a loud cry

    B. a small cry

    C. an irritating cry

    D. an inaudible cry

Essay

16. The essay "Alligator" and the poem "The Cremation of Sam McGee" both include humor. In an essay, compare the humor in these selections. Use specific details in your comparison.

17. In both "Alligator" and "The Cremation of Sam McGee," the setting is very important to the action of the plot. Write an essay in which you explain why the setting is critical to "Alligator" and "The Cremation of Sam McGee."

18. **Thinking About the Big Question: What Should We Learn?** Authors of humorous works want to entertain us, but they also want us to learn something. Choose either "Alligator" or "The Cremation of Sam McGee" and tell what you think the author wants the reader to learn. Do you think this lesson is worth learning?

Unit 3 Resources: Types of Nonfiction
218

"Alligator" by Bailey White
"The Cremation of Sam McGee" by Robert Service
Selection Test B

Critical Reading *Identify the letter of the choice that best completes the statement or answers the question.*

_____ 1. What is amusing about the following passage from "Alligator"?

Then my aunt would jump up, wave her arms in the air, and shout, "Whoo!" With a tremendous leap and flop the alligator would throw himself into the water.

A. Aunt Belle is not scared of the alligator, but the alligator may be scared of her.
B. Aunt Belle is jumping around and waving her arms because she is scared of the alligator.
C. Aunt Belle is too old to be jumping around, waving her arms, and scaring alligators.
D. Aunt Belle is scaring the alligator just as much as the alligator is scaring her.

_____ 2. In "Alligator," the alligator is described as
A. bellowing loudly.
B. the biggest alligator they had ever seen.
C. swimming fiercely toward Aunt Belle.
D. feared by everyone.

_____ 3. What is significant about the fact that the alligator bellows after Belle turns off the truck's engine?
A. The alligator bellows when he is hungry.
B. Belle knows when the alligator is about to bellow.
C. The alligator does not like the noise the truck makes.
D. Belle has trained the alligator to bellow when she cuts the engine.

_____ 4. Near the end of "Alligator," why is Aunt Belle spending a lot of time at the pond?
A. She enjoys being outdoors because her house is empty and quiet.
B. The alligator cannot be found, and she is spending her time looking for him.
C. Her children are grown, she is lonely, and the alligator keeps her company.
D. She enjoys watching the alligator swim out to the middle of the pond and disappear.

_____ 5. At the end of "Alligator," why does Aunt Belle walk "around and around the pond looking, listening, and sniffing"?
A. The alligator killed an animal whose carcass is decaying.
B. The alligator has not come to sit with her and has probably died.
C. Belle has dementia and believes that the alligator is hiding from her.
D. Belle is entertaining the children who are watching from high up on the bank.

____ 6. What does Sam McGee mean when he says that he would "sooner live in hell"?
   A. He thinks that living in the Arctic is like living in hell.
   B. He would rather be in hell than feel cold all the time.
   C. He thinks that living in Tennessee is like living in hell.
   D. He believes that he will soon be living in hell.

____ 7. What does Sam McGee tell the speaker before the men go to sleep on Christmas night?
   A. He is returning to Tennessee.
   B. He has discovered gold.
   C. He will die soon.
   D. He is very hungry.

____ 8. Why is the setting of "The Cremation of Sam McGee" important to the poem's conflict?
   A. It brings the two characters together.
   B. It is beyond the experience of most readers.
   C. It creates the conflict by causing Sam's death.
   D. It creates the conflict by causing Sam to go insane.

____ 9. What makes "The Cremation of Sam McGee" a narrative poem?
   A. It uses regular rhythm and rhyme.
   B. The speaker is a character in the poem.
   C. It contains a surprise ending.
   D. It is a poem that tells a story.

____ 10. Which is an example of simile from "The Cremation of Sam McGee"?
   A. "cotton blooms and blows"
   B. "it stabbed like a driven nail."
   C. "the stars o'erhead were dancing heel and toe."
   D. "I hurried, horror-driven,"

____ 11. Which statement is *not* true of both "Alligator" and "The Cremation of Sam McGee"?
   A. The narrator uses exaggeration to create humor.
   B. The narrator describes an illogical or unusual situation.
   C. The narrator concludes in a more serious tone.
   D. The narrator writes about both family members and animals.

____ 12. In which scene is the writer of "Alligator" or "The Cremation of Sam McGee" presenting an unusual situation in order to create humor?
   A. Aunt Belle gets used to seeing the alligator.
   B. Aunt Belle teaches an alligator to bellow.
   C. Sam McGee has a last request.
   D. The narrator promises to honor McGee's request.

____ 13. Which of the following scenes from "Alligator" or "The Cremation of Sam McGee" is
an example of exaggeration?
A. Aunt Belle crawls through the marsh to meet an alligator face to face.
B. Aunt Belle drives down to the pond and guns the engine.
C. Sam McGee mushes a dog team down the Dawson trail on Christmas day.
D. Sam McGee whimpers over the cold.

____ 14. In what way are Aunt Belle and Sam McGee similar?
A. Both characters come from a cold climate.
B. Both characters are adventurous.
C. Both characters have a mistaken view of reality.
D. Both characters are training an animal to do something unusual.

Vocabulary

____ 15. Sam McGee loathed the Yukon's cold climate. That means he _____ it.
A. loved
B. tolerated
C. accepted
D. despised

____ 16. A *pungent* odor is one that is
A. pleasant.
B. strong.
C. dangerous.
D. poisonous.

Essay

17. After reading "Alligator" and "The Cremation of Sam McGee," you might conclude that
Aunt Belle and Sam McGee are unusual and memorable characters. In an essay, compare Aunt Belle with Sam McGee. Explain what makes each character memorable. For
example, what does the character say or do that is unusual? How does the narrator
seem to react to the character? Finally, state which character you believe is more successfully portrayed and explain why.

18. **Thinking About the Big Question: What Should We Learn?** Authors of humorous
works want to entertain us, but they also want us to learn something. Choose either
"Alligator" or "Sam McGee" and tell what you think the author wants the reader to
learn. Why do you think this lesson is worth learning?

Name _____   Date _____

Exposition: Comparison-and-Contrast Essay

Prewriting: Gathering Details

Use the following Venn diagram to organize the details of your comparison-and-contrast essay by filling in details about one subject on the left side of the diagram and details about the other on the right side of the diagram. Use the middle for features the subjects have in common.

Subject 1: _____   **Subject 2:** _____

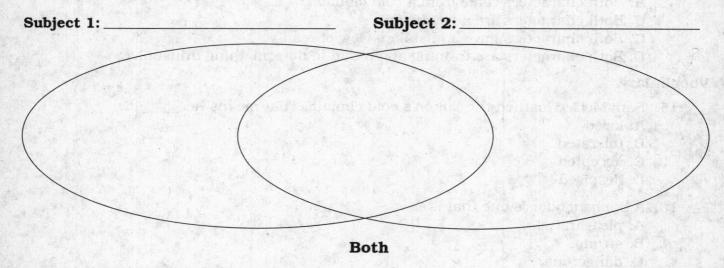

Both

Drafting: Using the SEE Method

Develop strong elaboration for your comparison-and-contrast essay by using the following graphic organizer.

State the main idea in every paragraph to make sure you stay on topic. Write the main idea here:

	List specific examples that prove the main idea:	**Provide further details to describe your example:**
Paragraph 1:		
Paragraph 2:		
Paragraph 3:		
Paragraph 4:		
Paragraph 5:		

Writing Workshop—Unit 3, Part 2

Comparison-and-Contrast Essay: Integrating Grammar Skills

Revising Errors in Adjective and Adverb Use

Adjectives modify nouns and pronouns. **Adverbs** modify verbs, adjectives, or other adverbs. Be careful not to use an adjective when you should use an adverb.

    Incorrect: Cindy ran *real quickly.*   **Correct:** Cindy ran *really quickly.*

    Bad is an adjective; *badly* is an adverb.

    Incorrect: She felt *badly* about losing the race.   **Correct:** She felt *bad* about losing the race.

    Good is an adjective; *well* can be either an adjective or an adverb.

    Incorrect: The winner ran especially *good.*   **Correct:** The winner ran especially *well.*

    The adjective *fewer* answers the question *How many?* The adjective *less* answers *How much?*

    Incorrect: There are less cats in the yard.   **Correct:** There are fewer cats in the yard.

Identifying Correct Adjectives and Adverbs

A. DIRECTIONS: *Complete each sentence by circling the correct choice in parentheses.*

  1. There were (fewer, less) students back then.

  2. The academy is now doing very (good, well).

  3. Classes are (real, really) popular.

  4. Mr. Wong feels (bad, badly) about turning students away.

Fixing Incorrect Adjective and Adverbs

B. DIRECTIONS: *On the lines provided, rewrite these sentences so that they use adjectives and adverbs correctly. If a sentence is correct as presented, write* correct.

  1. Jack is performing real good in karate.

_____

  2. Amy has taken far less classes than Jack.

_____

  3. Amy is learning slow but sure.

_____

  4. She feels bad about her lack of experience.

_____

Name _____ Date _____

Unit 3 Vocabulary Workshop—1
Words with Multiple Meanings

Words that have more than one meaning are called **multiple-meaning words**. There are many of them in the English language. When you come to a multiple-meaning word in your reading, use context clues to figure out which meaning the author intends. This chart gives an example of a multiple-meaning word and the context clues that help to unlock its meaning.

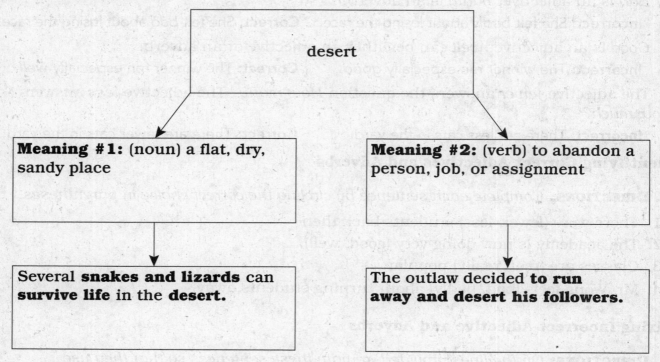

A. DIRECTIONS: *Each sentence contains a pair of multiple-meaning words. Use context clues to define each one.*

1. Please *place* Grandmother's glass dish in a very safe *place*.

   _____

2. After his solo, the violinist put down his *bow* and took a *bow* as the audience cheered.

   _____

3. Jim's *related* to some interesting people, and he has *related* some funny stories about them.

   _____

4. Now that I'm feeling and looking more *fit*, my clothes *fit* better.

   _____

5. I'm sure that Mr. Stone didn't *mean* for his remarks to sound so *mean*.

   _____

Name _____ Date _____

Unit 3 Vocabulary Workshop—2
Words with Multiple Meanings

B. DIRECTIONS: *Fill out the following chart. First, write two definitions for each multiple-meaning word. Include the word's part of speech (noun, verb, adjective, adverb, etc.). Use a dictionary check your definitions. Then write a sentence using each meaning of the word. Include context clues that provide clear hints about the word's meaning.*

Word	Meanings	Sentences
1. junk	Meaning 1 and part of speech:	Sentence 1:
	Meaning 2 and part of speech:	Sentence 2:
2. mail	Meaning 1 and part of speech:	Sentence 1:
	Meaning 2 and part of speech:	Sentence 2:
3. refuse	Meaning 1 and part of speech:	Sentence 1:
	Meaning 2 and part of speech:	Sentence 2:
4. mush	Meaning 1 and part of speech:	Sentence 1:
	Meaning 2 and part of speech:	Sentence 2:

Name _____ Date _____

Evaluating a Persuasive Presentation

After choosing your sales pitch, listen to it with your partner. Fill out the following chart and evaluate what you hear.

Title of sales pitch: _____

What is the speaker's statement of position?
What convincing arguments are given?
What questions need to be asked?
What statements do you agree with?
What statements do you disagree with?
What overall impact did the presentation have on you?

Unit 3: Types of Nonfiction
Benchmark Test 6

MULTIPLE CHOICE

Reading Skill: Fact and Opinion

1. What is a critical difference between statements of fact and opinions?
   A. Facts are more valuable than opinions.
   B. Facts can be proved or disproved, but opinions cannot.
   C. Facts are dull, and opinions are interesting.
   D. Facts are the result of research, but opinions are not.

2. Which of the following phrases signals an opinion?
   A. in spite of   B. in summary   C. in my view   D. in essence

3. Which resource would be the best place to check the fact in the following sentence?

   The word *ambience* can also be spelled *ambiance*

   A. dictionary   B. almanac   C. atlas   D. encyclopedia

4. Which resource would be the best place to check the information in the following sentence?

   In 776 BC, Koroibos of Elis became the first winner of an Olympics.

   A. almanac   B. atlas   C. dictionary   D. encyclopedia

5. Which resource would be the best place to find the distance between two cities?
   A. almanac   B. atlas   C. dictionary   D. encyclopedia

Reading Skill: Understand Structure and Purpose

Read the selection. Then, answer the questions that follow.

New Sources of Energy

The developed nations of the world have become more and more dependent on oil and gas as sources of energy. However, rising prices and serious shortages of these fuels compel us to explore new sources of energy.

Nuclear Energy

To produce electricity from nuclear energy, radioactive sources of heat are used instead of fossil fuels. The heat from the radioactive fuel is then used to produce steam, which turns the blades of a turbine. The turning motion of the turbine is used to run a generator that produces electricity. Although nuclear energy is effective, some people fear it is too dangerous.

Geothermal Power

Geothermal energy comes from the heat in the earth's crust. To tap this source of energy, wells are drilled into the underground deposits of hot water to recover steam. The steam is brought to the surface, where it is filtered to remove small particles of rock. Then, the steam is used to turn turbines that generate electricity. Northern California has been producing electricity from geothermal sources for over 40 years.

Solar Energy

If we could capture even a small amount of the energy from the sun, our energy problems would disappear. Solar energy is harnessed through the use of solar panels, which gather and convert the energy from the sun. Besides solar panels, a storage unit is needed to store the energy for long periods of time. Although at present there is no way to store enough of this energy for widespread use, improvements in technology might one day make this possible.

6. In which of the following would this selection most likely be found?
   A. science textbook for middle school students
   B. editorial section of a popular science magazine
   C. local news section of a newspaper
   D. professional journal for scientists

7. What is the main purpose of the selection?
   A. to explain how geothermal energy is harnessed from the earth
   B. to persuade readers to use solar energy over nuclear energy
   C. to provide information on alternative energy sources
   D. to discuss why we are facing shortages of oil and gas

8. Which of the following subheadings would most logically come next in the selection?
   A. The Energy Crisis
   B. Electricity Production
   C. Drilling for Oil
   D. Wind Power

Literary Analysis: Essays

9. In what way is a humorous essay different from other types of essays?
   A. It might present an illogical or improper situation.
   B. Its goal is to affect readers' thoughts and emotions.
   C. It tries to persuade readers to do or believe something.
   D. It attempts to explain how to make or do something.

10. What is the main purpose of a humorous essay?
   A. to persuade   B. to entertain   C. to describe   D. to explain

11. Which of the following are some techniques writers of humorous essays often use?
   A. appeals to emotions and logic
   B. descriptions of heart-rending, real-life situations
   C. exaggerated feelings and actions of characters
   D. references to authority figures and respected resources

Read the selection. Then, answer the questions that follow.

(1) Let me introduce Javier Solas, who is running for president of student council. (2) As Than Liu, last year's president, said, "I can't imagine voting for anyone but Javier. (3) He's clearly the best-qualified candidate. (4) Nearly every other member of last year's student council has endorsed him, as well." (5) Most of you know that Javier arrived in this country a few years ago knowing not a word of English. (6) Now he

speaks English fluently. (7) Shouldn't that determination be rewarded? (8) Not only that, but Javier is an Eagle Scout and the editor-in-chief of the school newspaper. (9) His ability to lead is unparalleled. (10) Vote for Javier!

12. What kind of essay is the selection?
    A. persuasive   B. reflective   C. expository   D. descriptive

13. Which sentence appeals to authority?
    A. sentence two   B. sentence six   C. sentence eight   D. sentence ten

14. What sentence appeals to emotion?
    A. sentence two   B. sentence six   C. sentence seven   D. sentence ten

Literary Analysis: Diction

15. How might a writer's word choice and diction in a letter to a friend most likely be described?
    A. difficult and informal   C. difficult and formal
    B. easy and formal   D. easy and informal

16. Which of the following is the best definition of *diction*?
    A. a writer's use of clues to hint at what might happen later in the story
    B. a writer's word choice and the way the writer puts words together
    C. the feeling created in a reader by a literary work or passage
    D. the writer's attitude toward his or her audience and subject

17. Which of the following would most strongly shape an author's choice of diction?
    A. readers' knowledge of the subject
    B. readers' gender and age
    C. readers' enjoyment of reading
    D. readers' purpose for reading the selection

Vocabulary: Roots

18. Based on your knowledge of the root *-leg-*, what does a *legislator* do?
    A. keeps the peace   C. makes laws
    B. judges cases   D. manages affairs

19. Using your knowledge of the root *-peti-*, what is the meaning of *impetus* in the following sentence?

The approaching deadline gave impetus to the investigation.

    A. a driving force   C. panic
    B. a new direction   D. a solution

20. Using your knowledge of the root *-vers-*, what does the word *diversion* mean in the following sentence?

The dam caused a diversion of the stream.

A. increase in movement

B. act of turning aside

C. remaining on course

D. act of stopping

21. Using your knowledge of the root *-sol-*, what does the word *desolate* mean in the following sentence?

With no trees or signs of life for miles, the desert was indeed a desolate place.

A. uninspiring   B. boring   C. deserted   D. hot

22. Based on your knowledge of the root *-leg-*, who would most likely do something *illegal*?

A. comedian   B. firefighter   C. farmer   D. crook

23. Based on your knowledge of the root *-sol-*, what kind of speech is a *soliloquy*?

A. one said to more than one character

B. one said when alone

C. one said at the very beginning of a play

D. one said with strong feeling

Grammar: Subjects and Predicates

24. How many parts does every sentence have?

A. one   B. two   C. three   D. four

25. What part of speech is the simple subject?

A. an adjective or adverb

B. a conjunction or interjection

C. a noun or pronoun

D. a verb or verb phrase

26. What part of speech is the simple predicate?

A. a verb or verb phrase

B. an adjective or adverb

C. a noun or pronoun

D. a conjunction or interjection

27. What is a compound subject?

A. a noun or pronoun that has two or more verbs

B. a verb or verb phrase that has one subject

C. two or more verbs that share the same noun

D. two or more nouns that share the same verb or verbs

28. What is a compound predicate?

A. a noun or pronoun that has two or more verbs

B. a verb or verb phrase that has one subject

C. two or more verbs that share the same subject

D. two or more nouns that share the same verb

29. Which word in the following sentence joins *tourist* to create a compound subject?

Both tourists and all-year residents often see iguanas and armadillos crossing the highway.

A. notice   B. iguanas   C. armadillos   D. residents

Grammar: Adjective and Adverb Usage

30. What is the best way to revise the following sentence using the word *just* as an adverb that means "no more than"?

    Do you just want to borrow one shirt for the play?

    A. Do you want to borrow just one shirt for the play?
    B. Do you want to just borrow one shirt for the play?
    C. Do you want to borrow one shirt just for the play?
    D. Do you want just to borrow one shirt for the play?

31. What is the best way to revise the following sentence so that *only* means the sole person?

    As president, I can choose only the committee members.

    A. As president, I can only choose the committee members.
    B. As president, only I can choose the committee members.
    C. As president, I can choose only the committee members.
    D. Only as president can I choose the committee members.

Spelling

32. Which of the following resources is the best place to check the spelling of a word?
    A. almanac   C. dictionary
    B. atlas   D. encyclopedia

33. How is an incorrectly spelled word usually noted on a computer spell checker?
    A. An alarm sounds.   C. The correct spelling appears.
    B. The computer shuts down.   D. The word is underlined.

34. What must the user do before a spell checker can find the correct spelling of a word?
    A. Highlight the word.   C. Delete the word.
    B. Underline the word.   D. Italicize the word.

ESSAY

Writing

35. What issue at school or in your community really gets you excited? What would you like people to do about it? Write a letter to the editor of your local newspaper in which you try to persuade readers to take action.

36. Write an adaptation of one of your favorite short works of nonfiction or fiction. Adapt the work for an audience much younger than the one for which the original selection was intended.

37. Express your opinions in a comparison-and-contrast essay. Compare two movies or television shows you have seen recently that are the same genre. Describe similarities and differences and conclude by recommending one over the other.

Name _____ Date _____

Vocabulary in Context

Identify the answer choice that best completes the statement.

1. In the distance, we could see snow at the very top of the_____ .
   A. winter
   B. plains
   C. clearing
   D. mountain

2. The sky looks dark and_____ today.
   A. fog
   B. watery
   C. dreary
   D. steady

3. After swimming for some time, I decided just to_____ .
   A. flick
   B. float
   C. plunge
   D. harbor

4. I wanted to be successful, so I_____ worked as hard as possible.
   A. hardly
   B. simply
   C. awfully
   D. scarcely

5. Anything that I do, my little sister will_____ .
   A. mimic
   B. glare
   C. tease
   D. amuse

6. The yellow flowers are in bloom on the_____ bush.
   A. violet
   B. forsythia
   C. blossoms
   D. cypress

7. The day of my test is coming soon, and I have been_____ for it.
   A. panting
   B. toiling
   C. preparing
   D. trembling

8. As soon as we eat dinner, let's _____ away the dishes.
   A. aside
   B. clear
   C. below
   D. onward

9. I heard such a beautiful _____ on the radio.
   A. melody
   B. fragrance
   C. enchanted
   D. formation

10. I didn't like being teased, so I decided to give him a taste of his own _____ .
    A. medicine
    B. ointment
    C. physician
    D. injury

11. Father claims he was a serious person during the time of his _____ .
    A. century
    B. former
    C. spring
    D. youth

12. If you will not be able to keep them, don't make worthless _____ .
    A. impressions
    B. leftovers
    C. fortunes
    D. promises

13. The oysters should have stayed in the deep _____ .
    A. sea
    B. coral
    C. puddles
    D. forge

14. Frederick Douglass wanted to be free so _____ .
    A. envious
    B. extremely
    C. ordinarily
    D. desperately

15. They had to travel far to attend the king's wedding, but his_____ still came.
    A. buyers
    B. adults
    C. kinsmen
    D. majority

16. For my English class, I have to write a two-page_____ .
    A. topic
    B. collage
    C. composition
    D. conversation

17. The color of the sofa faded as it was_____ to sunlight.
    A. proposed
    B. exposed
    C. published
    D. registered

18. John Singer Sargent painted many_____ .
    A. lenses
    B. portraits
    C. photographs
    D. advertisements

19. The chemists wrote a report that explains their_____ .
    A. destiny
    B. fiction
    C. analysis
    D. certainty

20. After he was cleared of all charges, he was able to_____ his good name.
    A. arise
    B. regain
    C. pursue
    D. classify

Diagnostic Tests and Vocabulary in Context
Use and Interpretation

The Diagnostic Tests and Vocabulary in Context were developed to assist teachers in making the most appropriate assignment of *Prentice Hall Literature* program selections to students. The purpose of these assessments is to indicate the degree of difficulty that students are likely to have in reading/comprehending the selections presented in the *following* unit of instruction. Tests are provided at six separate times in each in each grade level—a *Diagnostic Test* (to be used prior to beginning the year's instruction) and a *Vocabulary in Context,* the final segment of the Benchmark Test appearing at the end of each of the first five units of instruction. Note that the tests are intended for use not as summative assessments for the prior unit, but as guidance for assigning literature selections in the upcoming unit of instruction.

The structure of all Diagnostic Tests and Vocabulary in Context in this series is the same. All test items are four-option, multiple-choice items. The format is established to assess a student's ability to construct sufficient meaning from the context sentence to choose the only provided word that fits both the semantics (meaning) and syntax (structure) of the context sentence. All words in the context sentences are chosen to be "below-level" words that students reading at this grade level should know. All answer choices fit *either* the meaning or structure of the context sentence, but only the correct choice fits *both* semantics and syntax. All answer choices—both correct answers and incorrect options—are key words chosen from specifically taught words that will occur in the subsequent unit of program instruction. This careful restriction of the assessed words permits a sound diagnosis of students' current reading achievement and prediction of the most appropriate level of readings to assign in the upcoming unit of instruction.

The assessment of vocabulary in context skill has consistently been shown in reading research studies to correlate very highly with "reading comprehension." This is not surprising as the format essentially assesses comprehension, albeit in sentence-length "chunks." Decades of research demonstrate that vocabulary assessment provides a strong, reliable prediction of comprehension achievement— the purpose of these tests. Further, because this format demands very little testing time, these diagnoses can be made efficiently, permitting teachers to move forward with critical instructional tasks rather than devoting excessive time to assessment.

It is important to stress that while the Diagnostic and Vocabulary in Context were carefully developed and will yield sound assignment decisions, they were designed to *reinforce*, not supplant, teacher judgment as to the most appropriate instructional placement for individual students. Teacher judgment should always prevail in making placement—or indeed other important instructional—decisions concerning students.

Diagnostic Tests and Vocabulary in Context
Branching Suggestions

These tests are designed to provide maximum flexibility for teachers. Your *Unit Resources* books contain the 40-question **Diagnostic Test** and 20-question **Vocabulary in Context** tests. At *PHLitOnline*, you can access the Diagnostic Test and complete 40-question Vocabulary in Context tests. Procedures for administering the tests are described below. Choose the procedure based on the time you wish to devote to the activity and your comfort with the assignment decisions relative to the individual students. Remember that your judgment of a student's reading level should always take precedence over the results of a single written test.

Feel free to use different procedures at different times of the year. For example, for early units, you may wish to be more confident in the assignments you make—thus, using the "two-stage" process below. Later, you may choose the quicker diagnosis, confirming the results with your observations of the students' performance built up throughout the year.

The **Diagnostic Test** is composed of a single 40-item assessment. Based on the results of this assessment, make the following assignment of students to the reading selections in Unit 1:

Diagnostic Test Score	Selection to Use
If the student's score is 0–25	more accessible
If the student's score is 26–40	more challenging

Outlined below are the three basic options for administering **Vocabulary in Context** and basing selection assignments on the results of these assessments.

1. For a one-stage, quicker diagnosis using the *20-item* test in the *Unit Resources*:

Vocabulary in Context Test Score	Selection to Use
If the student's score is 0–13	more accessible
If the student's score is 14–20	more challenging

2. If you wish to confirm your assignment decisions with a *two-stage* diagnosis:

Stage 1: Administer the 20-item test in the *Unit Resources*	
Vocabulary in Context Test Score	Selection to Use
If the student's score is 0–9	more accessible
If the student's score is 10–15	(Go to Stage 2.)
If the student's score is 16–20	more challenging

Stage 2: Administer items 21–40 from *PHLitOnline*	
Vocabulary in Context Test Score	Selection to Use
If the student's score is 0–12	more accessible
If the student's score is 13–20	more challenging

3. If you base your assignment decisions on the full 40-item **Vocabulary in Context** from *PHLitOnline*:

Vocabulary in Context Test Score	Selection to Use
If the student's score is 0–25	more accessible
If the student's score is 26–40	more challenging

Name _____ Date _____

Grade 7—Benchmark Test 5
Interpretation Guide

For remediation of specific skills, you may assign students the relevant Reading Kit Practice and Assess pages indicated in the far-right column of this chart. You will find rubrics for evaluating writing samples in the last section of your Professional Development Guidebook.

Skill Objective	Test Items	Number Correct	Reading Kit
Reading Skill			
Main Idea	1, 2, 3, 4, 5, 6		pp. 100, 101
Analyze Author's Argument	7, 8, 9		pp. 102, 103
Literary Analysis			
Expository Essay	10, 12, 13, 14		pp. 104, 105
Reflective Essay	11, 15, 16, 17		pp. 106, 107
Biography and Autobiography	18, 19, 20		pp. 108, 109
Vocabulary			
Suffixes and Roots -*ness*, -*able*, -*just*-, -*rupt*-	21, 22, 23, 34, 25, 26		pp. 110, 111
Grammar			
Conjunctions and coordinating conjunctions	27, 28, 29, 30, 31		pp. 112, 113, 116, 117
Prepositions and Propositional Phrasess	32, 33, 34		pp. 114, 115
Writing			
Comparison-and-Contrast Essay	35	Use rubric	pp. 118, 119
Outline	36	Use rubric	pp. 120, 121
How-to Essay	37	Use rubric	pp. 122, 123

Grade 7—Benchmark Test 6
Interpretation Guide

For remediation of specific skills, you may assign students the relevant Reading Kit Practice and Assess pages indicated in the far-right column of this chart. You will find rubrics for evaluating writing samples in the last section of your Professional Development Guidebook.

Skill Objective	Test Items	Number Correct	Reading Kit
Reading Skill			
Fact and Opinion	1, 2, 3, 4, 5		pp. 124, 125
Understand Structure and Purpose	6, 7, 8		pp. 126, 127
Literary Analysis			
Persuasive Essay	12, 13, 14		pp. 128, 129
Diction	15, 16, 17		pp. 130, 131
Humorous Essay	9, 10, 11, 12		pp. 132, 133
Vocabulary			
Roots -peti-, -leg-, -vers-, -sol-	18, 19, 20, 21, 22, 23		pp. 134, 135
Grammar			
Subjects and Predicates	24, 25, 26		pp. 136, 137
Compound Subjects and Predicates	27, 28, 29		pp. 138, 139
Revising errors in Adjective and Adverb use	30, 31		pp. 140, 141
Spelling			
Tools for checking spelling	32, 33, 34		pp. 142, 143
Writing			
Persuasive letter	35	Use rubric	pp. 144, 145
Adaptation	36	Use rubric	pp. 146, 147
Comparison-and-Contrast Essay	37	Use rubric	pp. 148, 149

Unit 3 Resources: Types of Nonfiction
238

ANSWERS

Big Question Vocabulary—1, p. 1

Answers will vary. Possible responses are shown.

1. How heavy are clouds? How can we measure the speed of light? What is acid rain?

To satisfy my curiosity, I could do research to answer the questions.

2. Derek Jeter, Al Sharpton, Hillary Clinton

In my interview, I'd ask Derek Jeter, "How did you train for major-league baseball?

3. California is on the Pacific Ocean. It is the home of Disneyland. Its largest city is Los Angeles.

The second fact would be most interesting. Children love to go to Disneyland.

4. Read the poem carefully. Look for key words and phrases. Look for rhymes.

By breaking the poem into its parts and looking at each one carefully, you can understand how the elements work together.

Big Question Vocabulary—2, p. 2

A. 1. c
2. a
3. c
4. b
5. a

B. 1. inquire
2. evaluate
3. discover
4. explore
5. experiment

Big Question Vocabulary—3, p. 3

A. 1. information
2. investigate
3. examine
4. understand
5. question

B. Sentences will vary. Possible responses are shown.

1. False; Most information is based on facts and details that can be proved true.
2. True
3. False; If you don't understand the question, you'll probably get the wrong answer.e
4. False; A person who investigates a crime might be a police officer or a detective.
5. False; It is wise to question the claims in an advertisement.

"What Makes a Rembrandt a Rembrandt?"
by Richard Mühlberger

Vocabulary Warm-up Exercises, p. 8

A. 1. portrait
2. military
3. glorious
4. emblems
5. details
6. Ordinarily
7. standard
8. opportunity

B. Sample Answers

1. F; when you are contrasting colors, you are using colors that are different from each other.
2. T; polishing a table with wax would make it shine.
3. F; rivals are competitors, not supporters.
4. F; a traditional costume is one whose style has remained the same for some time.
5. F; a former teacher is one you had in the past.
6. T; to impress someone, you would do a good job.
7. T; individuals, or persons, make up a team when they work together.
8. T; a sash is often given to a winner as an honor.

Reading Warm-up A, p. 9

Words that students are to circle appear in parentheses.

Sample Answers

1. to go on a guided tour at the art museum; *chance*
2. she just wandered from room to room on her own, looking at the paintings and other art; Ordinarily, I play soccer on Saturdays.
3. regular admission; children's admission, seniors' admission
4. a young woman; For my portrait, I would pose with my dog.
5. Men in uniforms, marched, soldiers, officers and soldiers, battle, soldiers, emblems, wars; *Military* means "having to do with the armed forces or warfare."
6. (marched proudly, heads held high); *Glorious* means "deserving great honor and praise."
7. they had fought in earlier wars; They might have been wearing medals, ribbons, pins.
8. (her pearls, her rings, and other jewelry) (strong, healthy horses); The details in the painting revealed the poverty of the subjects.

Reading Warm-up B, p. 10

Words that students are to circle appear in parentheses.

Sample Answers

1. <u>Her right hand gracefully rests on her left wrist as she sits</u>; We sang traditional songs during the holiday season.

2. (friendliness and distance); *Contrasting* means "different."

3. (over her left shoulder); I would wear a sash around my waist.

4. He uses light; A sheen would not show up in the dark because light is needed for something to shine.

5. She is called the former Mona Lisa because her name changed after she married; The former Miss Jones is now called Ms. Smith.

6. <u>how Leonardo managed to make Mona Lisa look alive</u>; *Individuals* means "persons."

7. Leonardo's rivals were also artists; The rivals shook hands before the competition began.

8. <u>talk about Leonardo</u>; If I wanted to impress my friends, I would say that I was interested in the things they were interested in.

Richard Mühlberger

Listening and Viewing, p. 11

Sample answers and guidelines for evaluation:

Segment 1. Students may answer that Richard Mühlberger decided to write books about art history because he did not get the chance to study them in school when he was a young student and he wants to make this information available to a young audience. Students may agree that the most famous paintings are most important to focus on, or they may wish to hear about less famous works of art.

Segment 2. Richard Mühlberger thinks that essays appeal to both the heart and the mind; essays about art represent an appreciation and a spirit of the times and attempt to explain why a piece of art still speaks to us after hundreds of years. Students may answer that they would write an essay to describe or explain something in a concise way; they may say that they would write an essay in order to share information as well as enthusiasm or emotion.

Segment 3. As an illustration in the book, the painting is much smaller, so Richard Mühlberger must accurately describe the details of the painting that a reader might not be able to see. Richard Mühlberger also needs to be very descriptive with his language in order to explain something visual with words. Students may answer that he writes in a conversational tone to appeal to his audience of young people who do not have advanced knowledge about art.

Segment 4. Richard Mühlberger hopes his readers will apply their knowledge about artists and artwork in their writing and interests and explore the subject themselves. Students may answer that art history books are important to society because they record history and provide examples of universal themes like love, happiness, and sadness.

Learning About Nonfiction, p. 12

A. 1. B; A
   2. A; B
   3. D; B

B. 1. humorous; it is meant to entertain
   2. persuasive; it is meant to persuade the reader
   3. expository; it presents ideas and facts

"What Makes a Rembrandt a Rembrandt?"
by Richard Mühlberger

Model Selection: Nonfiction, p. 13

1. It is an essay; it is a short nonfiction work about a subject

2. comparison-and-contrast; he compares the appearance of Cocq with that of van Ruytenburgh

3. the artist Rembrandt and the militia captain Frans Banning Cocq

4. He uses an expository format to present facts about the painting and explain the process that Rembrandt used to compose it.

5. C and E

Open-Book Test, p. 14

Short Answer

1. The writing is a nonfiction journal because it is the personal thoughts and reflections of a real person. A persuasive essay would try to convince the reader to adopt a particular point of view.
   Difficulty: *Easy* **Objective:** *Literary Analysis*

2. Expository writing will present facts, discuss ideas, or explain a process.
   Difficulty: *Average* **Objective:** *Literary Analysis*

3. Reflective writing talks about an event or experience. The writer uses the event to share his or her insights.
   Difficulty: *Challenging* **Objective:** *Literary Analysis*

4. The article would most likely be organized by comparison and contrast. Because it discusses how two things are similar and different.
   Difficulty: *Average* **Objective:** *Literary Analysis*

5. Rembrandt didn't like the traditional portraits. Instead, he wanted to show a realistic scene that would be more interesting for viewers.
   Difficulty: *Average* **Objective:** *Interpretation*

6. The painting uses many sharp contrasts of dark and light. Students might note that the artist used light to highlight the military honors and *chiaroscuro* to create dramatic effects.
   Difficulty: *Challenging* **Objective:** *Interpretation*

7. The student meant that it was a greater painting than any other of its kind and that it would be famous long after other paintings faded from memory.
   Difficulty: *Easy* **Objective:** *Interpretation*

8. Real person: Rembrandt, Banning Cocq; Real place: Netherlands; Real idea: Most famous Dutch painting of all time. The author hopes the reader will experience viewing the painting *The Night Watch* as he did.

   Difficulty: *Average*   **Objective:** *Literary Analysis*

9. Descriptive: The author describes *Night Watch* in great detail.

   Expository: The author explains what the militia does. He also explains how Rembrandt was chosen to paint *Night Watch*.

   Difficulty: *Average*   **Objective:** *Literary Analysis*

10. Mühlberger probably wanted to describe and analyze the features of *Night Watch*. He obviously finds it fascinating, and his detailed description shows he wanted to share his insights.

    Difficulty: *Challenging*   **Objective:** *Literary Analysis*

Essay

11. Students may select either the man in gold and yellow, Captain Banning Cocq, or the girl with the dead chicken, because they are all attention-grabbing. Students should support choices with details and reasons.

    Difficulty: *Easy*   **Objective:** *Essay*

12. Students should note that militia companies were groups of ordinary citizens who were trained to fight if their cities were attacked. They held meetings, but other than that they led ordinary lives.

    Difficulty: *Average*   **Objective:** *Essay*

13. Students should note that most paintings of militia companies were formal portraits. By contrast, Rembrandt chose to show the men posed informally. They are dressed in historical costumes and are preparing for a parade. The painting is similar to others in that it shows real men in a militia unit and was intended to be hung in a meeting hall. Students might note that the differences resulted in a painting that was unique and memorable.

    Difficulty: *Challenging*   **Objective:** *Essay*

14. Students may note that it is important to learn that Rembrandt used light and darkness differently from other painters of his day. His use of chiaroscuro, a style of light and shade, created dramatic effects that make his paintings more memorable than those of other painters.

    Difficulty: *Average*   **Objective:** *Essay*

Oral Response

15. Oral responses should be clear, well organized, and well supported by appropriate examples from the selection.

    Difficulty: *Average*   **Objective:** *Oral Interpretation*

Selection Test A, p. 17

Learning About Nonfiction

1. ANS: C	DIF: Easy	OBJ: Literary Analysis
2. ANS: A	DIF: Easy	OBJ: Literary Analysis

3. ANS: D	DIF: Easy	OBJ: Literary Analysis
4. ANS: B	DIF: Easy	OBJ: Literary Analysis
5. ANS: C	DIF: Easy	OBJ: Literary Analysis

Critical Reading

6. ANS: B	DIF: Easy	OBJ: Literary Analysis
7. ANS: C	DIF: Easy	OBJ: Comprehension
8. ANS: A	DIF: Easy	OBJ: Comprehension
9. ANS: D	DIF: Easy	OBJ: Comprehension
10. ANS: A	DIF: Easy	OBJ: Comprehension
11. ANS: B	DIF: Easy	OBJ: Comprehension
12. ANS: C	DIF: Easy	OBJ: Comprehension
13. ANS: D	DIF: Easy	OBJ: Comprehension
14. ANS: B	DIF: Easy	OBJ: Interpretation
15. ANS: D	DIF: Easy	OBJ: Literary Analysis

Essay

16. He meant that it was a great painting that would still be honored long after other paintings of its type were forgotten. While other militia company portraits may have been less exciting, this painting was truly a masterpiece.

    Difficulty: *Easy*

    Objective: *Essay*

17. Answers should be supported by details and reasons. Students will probably select either the man in gold and yellow, Captain Banning Cocq, or the girl with the dead chicken, because they are all attention-grabbing.

    Difficulty: *Easy*

    Objective: *Essay*

18. Students may note that it is important to learn that Rembrandt used light and darkness differently from other painters of his day. His use of light and shade created dramatic effects that make his paintings more interesting than those of other painters.

    Difficulty: *Average*

    Objective: *Essay*

Selection Test B, p. 20

Learning About Nonfiction

1. ANS: C	DIF: Average	OBJ: Literary Analysis
2. ANS: A	DIF: Average	OBJ: Literary Analysis
3. ANS: C	DIF: Average	OBJ: Literary Analysis
4. ANS: D	DIF: Average	OBJ: Literary Analysis
5. ANS: B	DIF: Challenging	OBJ: Literary Analysis
6. ANS: B	DIF: Average	OBJ: Literary Analysis

Critical Reading

7. ANS: C	DIF: Average	OBJ: Literary Analysis
8. ANS: B	DIF: Challenging	OBJ: Interpretation

9. ANS: D	DIF: Average	OBJ: Comprehension
10. ANS: C	DIF: Average	OBJ: Comprehension
11. ANS: A	DIF: Average	OBJ: Comprehension
12. ANS: B	DIF: Challenging	OBJ: Interpretation
13. ANS: C	DIF: Challenging	OBJ: Comprehension
14. ANS: B	DIF: Challenging	OBJ: Comprehension
15. ANS: B	DIF: Challenging	OBJ: Comprehension
16. ANS: D	DIF: Average	OBJ: Comprehension
17. ANS: C	DIF: Average	OBJ: Comprehension
18. ANS: D	DIF: Challenging	OBJ: Literary Analysis
19. ANS: B	DIF: Challenging	OBJ: Literary Analysis

Essay

20. Students should note that militia companies were groups of ordinary citizens who were trained to fight as soldiers if their cities were attacked. They were "citizen" soldiers because they were not full-time military personnel. Aside from meetings, they led nonmilitary lives and held other jobs.

    Difficulty: *Average*

    Objective: *Essay*

21. Students should note that the paintings of most militia companies were formal portraits, in which the men were all lined up in an even row, giving each man equal treatment. By contrast, Rembrandt chose to show the men posed informally. They are preparing for a parade. Some are in front, and others are in the background or on the steps. They are not dressed in regular uniforms but in historical costumes. They are similar in that they picture real men, all members of a militia unit. Also, they are similar in purpose: The paintings were hung in the meeting halls of the militia companies.

    Difficulty: *Average*

    Objective: *Essay*

22. Students may note that it is important to learn that Rembrandt used light and darkness differently from other painters of his day. His use of chiaroscuro, a style of light and shade, created dramatic effects that make his paintings more memorable than those of other painters.

    Difficulty: *Average*

    Objective: *Essay*

"Life Without Gravity" by Robert Zimmerman

Vocabulary Warm-up Exercises, p. 24

A.
1. effort
2. installed
3. securely
4. relax
5. organized
6. orbit
7. gravity
8. missions

B. Sample Answers
1. Sylvia thought the roller-coaster ride was downright exciting.
2. Stanley found it difficult to breathe deeply through his stuffy nose.
3. Myra's skin tissue was badly damaged by her serious sunburn.
4. After losing fourteen games in a row, the team had an unexpected win.
5. Josh needs an operation to repair the damaged disks in his spine.
6. Mark's feeble muscles made it impossible for him to lift 200 pounds.
7. It took great courage for Heather to overcome her fear of flying.
8. The two friends split the money evenly, each one taking 50 percent.

Reading Warm-up A, p. 25

Words that students are to circle appear in parentheses.

Sample Answers
1. put a man on the moon; One other great mission in history was for women to earn the right to vote.
2. The men were firmly strapped in.
3. (around the Earth), (the lunar orbit); Two moons are in orbit around Mars.
4. (team); *Organized* means "arranged in an orderly way."
5. (We're breathing again.) One thing I do to relax is listen to music.
6. the moon's weak gravity; Two activities that take a lot of effort are running and studying for science tests.
7. weak; Gravity is the force that keeps us on Earth.
8. a U.S. flag and a plaque; Electric lights, computers, and desks are installed in my classroom.

Reading Warm-up B, p. 26

Words that students are to circle appear in parentheses.

Sample Answers
1. (nose); Another thing that might be described as stuffy is the air in a room.
2. just came up; An unexpected event that happened recently at home was that our dog got lost.
3. (feeble); I find it downright annoying to have to deal with flies.
4. excuses; *Feeble* means "weak."
5. (your own laziness); Someone might have to overcome a fear of flying.
6. muscle; Tissue is a group of cells in a plant or an animal that are somewhat alike and work together to perform a certain function.
7. (in your spine); Surgery repaired the damaged disks in Tom's spine.
8. *Percent* means "a hundredth part."

Writing About the Big Question, p. 27

A. 1. curiosity; knowledge
2. discover; explore; investigate
3. question

B. Sample Answers

1. I learned how to swim at the YMCA; I learned to speak Spanish from my grandmother.
2. My grandmother gave me a wonderful gift when she shared her **knowledge** of Spanish with me. Learning to speak Spanish helped me **understand** her better. Now I would like to **experiment** with some other languages.

C. Sample Answer

Our assumptions about unfamiliar experiences are often wrong. For example, I always thought astronauts were lucky and that traveling into space was fun. I never realized that an astronaut might suffer from physical difficulties like feeling sick to his stomach. We should learn to understand our assumptions and grow beyond them.

Reading: Adjust Your Reading Rate to Recognize Main Ideas and Key Points, p. 28

A. 1. The paragraph mentions the muscles, the inner ear, blood, the legs, and the heart.
2. The paragraph mentions cornflakes and milk.

B. Sample answers are provided for items 2 and 4:

1. Our bodies have adapted to gravity.
2. Our muscles are strong so that we can overcome the pull of gravity; our hearts are strong so that they can pump blood to the brain.
3. In a weightless environment, you cannot eat the way you do in an environment where there is gravity.
4. Cornflakes cannot be poured into a bowl: They will float around. Milk cannot be poured at all: The liquid will float in large blobs.

Literary Analysis: Expository Essay, p. 29

Sample Answers

The blood: Weightlessness causes the blood to flow from the legs to the head. This change causes the legs to become very thin and the head to swell.

The spine: Weightlessness causes the bones in the spine to straighten out and the disks to "spread apart and relax." This change causes people to "grow" by as much as three inches.

The bones: Weightlessness causes bones to lose 10 percent or more of their tissue.

The muscles: Weightlessness causes muscles to weaken.

The stomach: Weightlessness causes people to feel nausea. This change causes them to lose their appetite and perhaps vomit a good deal.

Vocabulary Builder, p. 30

A. Sample answers follow the identification of the statements as true or false:

1. T; The spine is the backbone, one of the strongest parts of the body.
2. F; A feeble voice is weak and so would probably not be heard across a room.
3. T; Pepper is spicy, so foods made without it would have less taste than foods made with it.
4. T; All of the astronauts in the story eventually regained their strength on Earth.
5. F; Astronauts are currently living in space for up to a year.
6. F; Globules are balls of liquid and have nothing to do with exercising.

B. 1. *Weightlessness* is fun when you fly around in the air or watch items float around the spaceship.
2. *Feebleness* can result from the lack of gravity.
3. Astronauts need a *willingness* to try new things because living in space is like living in another world.

Enrichment: Astronaut Training, p. 31

A. Sample Answers

1. A person might want to be an astronaut if he or she is interested in science and space and likes adventure. Nothing provides more adventure than exploring space.
2. The most difficult part would be the survival training. It would be physically and emotionally demanding.

B. Students should base the information in their letters on "Life Without Gravity" and the preceding passage. They might mention the excitement, the experience of floating around in a weightless environment, the experience of eating in a weightless environment, and so on.

Open-Book Test, p. 32

Short Answer

1. Tito means that life without gravity is very strange. It is hard to get used to it.
   Difficulty: *Challenging*   **Objective:** *Interpretation*
2. Astronauts lose 10 percent of bone tissue after several months in microgravity. The main idea is that weaker gravity makes the human body change in unexpected ways.
   Difficulty: *Challenge*   **Objective:** *Reading*
3. The handshake would feel limp and weak, perhaps because of loss of muscle strength due to long months in microgravity.
   Difficulty: *Average*   **Objective:** *Vocabulary*
4. Astronauts become nauseous, lose their appetites, and throw up.
   Difficulty: *Easy*   **Objective:** *Reading*

5. Food with less taste than usual may have something to do with the effects of microgravity, or it may be because the food actually lacks spices and seasonings that would add to the taste.

   Difficulty: *Easy* **Objective:** *Vocabulary*

6. Students may choose the following details:

   [col 2, row 2] blood is rerouted; spines spread out and relax; the inner ear becomes unbalanced

   [col 2, row 3] you can't pour milk or use a spoon; you have to drink through a straw

   Sample key point: Weightlessness brings new problems in space.

   Difficulty: *Average* **Objective:** *Reading*

7. Linenger means that he was not used to gravity, and the sudden force of it made him feel very heavy.

   Difficulty: *Easy* **Objective:** *Interpretation*

8. It is an expository essay. It is a short work of nonfiction that explains the effects and problems of weightlessness.

   Difficulty: *Average* **Objective:** *Literary Analysis*

9. The author uses cause and effect to tell about the effects of microgravity. He uses problem and solution to explain how astronauts handle the effects.

   Difficulty: *Challenging* **Objective:** *Literary Analysis*

10. He claims that being weightless has unpleasant effects on the body, and he describes its effects on blood, bones, and general well-being, even after returning to Earth.

    Difficulty: *Average* **Objective:** *Interpretation*

Essay

11. Students should include three effects of weightlessness on the body as they are described in the essay. They might include effects on balance, effects on the stomach, and difficulty eating.

    Difficulty: *Easy* **Objective:** *Essay*

12. Students should name two advantages and two disadvantages of weightlessness as they are presented in "Life Without Gravity." Their reasons for wishing or not wishing to travel in space should be logical and should reflect the details they cite.

    Difficulty: *Average* **Objective:** *Essay*

13. Students may note that astronauts face problems with nausea, dizziness, swelling, and bone loss. They should detail the solutions astronauts have found. Some students may say that the difficulties with bone loss will prevent extended space travel.

    Difficulty: *Challenging* **Objective:** *Essay*

14. Students may cite the idea that microgravity can be difficult for astronauts as the most important. They should explain that it is important because it illustrates how challenging an astronaut's job can be.

    Difficulty: *Average* **Objective:** *Essay*

Oral Response

15. Oral responses should be clear, well organized, and well supported by appropriate examples from the selection.

    Difficulty: *Average* **Objective:** *Oral Interpretation*

Selection Test A, p. 35

Critical Reading

1. ANS: B	DIF: Easy	OBJ: Interpretation
2. ANS: D	DIF: Easy	OBJ: Interpretation
3. ANS: B	DIF: Easy	OBJ: Comprehension
4. ANS: B	DIF: Easy	OBJ: Reading
5. ANS: A	DIF: Easy	OBJ: Reading
6. ANS: C	DIF: Easy	OBJ: Comprehension
7. ANS: C	DIF: Easy	OBJ: Comprehension
8. ANS: A	DIF: Easy	OBJ: Comprehension
9. ANS: B	DIF: Easy	OBJ: Interpretation
10. ANS: C	DIF: Easy	OBJ: Reading
11. ANS: D	DIF: Easy	OBJ: Literary Analysis

Vocabulary and Grammar

12. ANS: B	DIF: Easy	OBJ: Vocabulary
13. ANS: A	DIF: Easy	OBJ: Vocabulary
14. ANS: C	DIF: Easy	OBJ: Grammar
15. ANS: C	DIF: Easy	OBJ: Grammar

Essay

16. Students should incorporate into their essays three effects of weightlessness on the body as they are described in "Life Without Gravity."

    Difficulty: *Easy*

    Objective: *Essay*

17. Students should define an expository essay as a short piece of nonfiction that explains, defines, or interprets ideas, events, or processes. They should recognize that "Life Without Gravity" explains the processes involved in the human body's experience of weightlessness, and they should cite one example from the essay to illustrate that point.

    Difficulty: *Easy*

    Objective: *Essay*

18. Students might argue that the most important idea is that microgravity can be difficult for astronauts. They should explain that it is important because it illustrates how challenging an astronaut's job can be.

    Difficulty: *Average*

    Objective: *Essay*

Selection Test B, p. 38

Critical Reading

1. ANS: A	DIF: Average	OBJ: Interpretation
2. ANS: A	DIF: Average	OBJ: Interpretation
3. ANS: B	DIF: Average	OBJ: Interpretation
4. ANS: D	DIF: Average	OBJ: Interpretation
5. ANS: C	DIF: Average	OBJ: Reading
6. ANS: D	DIF: Challenging	OBJ: Interpretation
7. ANS: C	DIF: Average	OBJ: Comprehension
8. ANS: D	DIF: Challenging	OBJ: Interpretation
9. ANS: C	DIF: Average	OBJ: Comprehension
10. ANS: B	DIF: Average	OBJ: Interpretation
11. ANS: B	DIF: Challenging	OBJ: Reading
12. ANS: B	DIF: Average	OBJ: Literary Analysis
13. ANS: C	DIF: Average	OBJ: Reading
14. ANS: C	DIF: Challenging	OBJ: Reading

Vocabulary and Grammar

15. ANS: B	DIF: Average	OBJ: Vocabulary
16. ANS: A	DIF: Average	OBJ: Vocabulary
17. ANS: C	DIF: Average	OBJ: Grammar
18. ANS: D	DIF: Average	OBJ: Grammar

Essay

19. Students should name two advantages and two disadvantages of weightlessness as they are presented in "Life Without Gravity." Their reasons for wishing or not wishing to travel in space should be thoughtful and logical.

    Difficulty: *Average*

    Objective: *Essay*

20. Students should define an expository essay as a short piece of nonfiction that explains, defines, or interprets ideas, events, or processes. They should recognize that "Life Without Gravity" explains the processes involved in the human body's experience of weightlessness, and they should cite three examples from the essay to illustrate that point.

    Difficulty: *Average*

    Objective: *Essay*

21. Students may cite the idea that microgravity can be difficult for astronauts as the most important. They should explain that it is important because it illustrates how challenging an astronaut's job can be.

    Difficulty: *Average*

    Objective: *Essay*

"Conversational Ballgames"
by Nancy Masterson Sakamoto

Vocabulary Warm-up Exercises, p. 42

A. 1. confused
   2. consider
   3. challenge
   4. tennis
   5. extremely
   6. interesting
   7. lack
   8. conversation

B. Sample Answers

1. No; a twelve-year-old is not old enough to drive a car.
2. No; I would not be able to relax around a dog that might become violent at any time.
3. I would expect to see and hear a performance of music, dance, or drama.
4. I would wear a dress, dressy shoes, and nice jewelry; I would wear a suit and tie.
5. When introduced to someone for the first time, I say, "Hello. It's a pleasure to meet you."
6. In a discussion, more than one person speaks; in a speech, only one person speaks.
7. Yes, I would try to find that book because it is obviously important.
8. Yes, I do think a powerful flea powder would kill fleas on a dog because the word *powerful* suggests strength.

Reading Warm-up A, p. 43

Words that students are to circle appear in parentheses.

Sample Answers

1. <u>historians</u>;

   "Good morning, Elaine," said Tom.

   "Good morning, Tom," said Elaine.

   "What would you like for breakfast?" asked Tom.

   "I would like some oatmeal," said Elaine.
2. (the origins); "Anyone for tennis?" asked Nigel.
3. <u>how the game began</u>; *Confused* means "mixed up."
4. (sounds); *Interesting* means "worthy of attention."
5. <u>Tinnis</u>, <u>rahat</u>; Please consider your cousin's feelings.
6. (evidence of any form of tennis before the year 1000); I would like to see more books in our classroom.
7. <u>the idea of more ancient origins</u>; I challenge the idea that haste makes waste.
8. (the game); *Extremely* means "very."

Reading Warm-up B, p. 44

Words that students are to circle appear in parentheses.

Sample Answers

1. (tradition); Going to the ballet was a new cultural experience for Sean.
2. <u>kimono</u>; I would wear a suit and tie on a formal occasion.
3. (a similar bow); My response to his rudeness was to ignore him.
4. <u>decorations</u>; *Suitable* means "appropriate."
5. (limited); conversation

6. comments; *Occasional* means "occurring now and then."

7. (the beauty of the teahouse); Let me refer to the comments made by the previous speaker.

8. (power); *Powerful* means "strong and mighty."

Writing About the Big Question, p. 45

A. 1. Interview
   2. Knowledge
   3. understand

B. Sample Answers

1. I learned that Latina girls have big parties to celebrate their fifteenth birthdays. I learned that Chinese people eat with chopsticks.

2. As an **experiment**, my father took us out to eat in a Chinese restaurant. I was **curious** to try the new kind of food. I **discovered** that I like many Chinese dishes. I also got to try using chopsticks. For me, it was very challenging.

C. Sample Answer

Cultural knowledge can change the way you see the world and the people you meet.

People from different cultures can see the same facts differently. We should learn to recognize these differences. Reading can help because it teaches us how people from other cultures think.

Reading: Adjust Your Reading Rate to Recognize Main Ideas and Key Points, p. 46

A. 1. tennis
   2. bowling

B. Sample answers are provided for items 2 and 4:

1. Western-style conversations involve an exchange of ideas.

2. If one person introduces a topic, the next person is expected to respond; agreement is not required.

3. Japanese-style conversations are structured.

4. Speakers wait their turn; when someone speaks depends on his or her relationship to the other speakers in the conversation.

Literary Analysis: Expository Essay, p. 47

Sample Answers

Western-Style Conversations / Japanese-Style Conversations

1. People speak whenever they want to. / People wait their turn to speak, and their turn depends on their social position in the group.

2. Speakers may interrupt or join in. / People listen quietly as each person speaks.

3. Everyone replies to everyone else. / Each speaker begins with the same point.

4. People might argue or attack others' opinions. / People do not argue or respond to what others say.

5. People carry on long conversations during meals. / People do not carry on long conversations during meals.

Vocabulary Builder, p. 48

A. Sample Answers

1. The lines will not intersect.

2. He or she might be asked to talk more loudly.

3. It is difficult to learn a foreign language without consulting a dictionary.

4. I would provide details.

5. It could be difficult if they wanted to hold the meeting at different times.

6. If you do something unconsciously, you aren't aware of what you're doing.

B. 1. A capable person doesn't need help.

2. If an experience is enjoyable, you are not eager to have it end.

3. Unbreakable plates are a good choice for a picnic.

Enrichment: Writing Dialogue, p. 49

Sample Answers for Western-Style Conversation

Speaker 1: I don't understand people who wait till the last minute to do their homework. I do it the minute I get home. Otherwise, I can't enjoy the rest of the day—I would have homework hanging over my head every minute.

Speaker 2: Aren't you exhausted when you get home? You don't have a snack and watch some TV? I do my homework in the evening. I feel more refreshed then.

Speaker 1: No, I'm more tired in the evening. The way I do it, I can relax and do whatever after I'm done with my homework.

Speaker 2: I don't think that would work for me.

Sample Answers for Japanese-Style Conversation

Speaker 1: It's best for me to do my homework as soon as I get home. I don't like to have it hanging over my head during the evening. If I get it done right away, I can relax for the rest of the day.

Speaker 2: I usually do mine in the evening. I find I'm too tired when I get home to start doing homework right away. I like to have a snack, watch some TV, and relax first. That way, I'm refreshed when I start.

"Life Without Gravity" by Robert Zimmerman
"Conversational Ballgames"
by Nancy Masterson Sakamoto

Integrated Language Skills: Grammar, p. 50

A. Conjunctions are followed by the words, phrases, or clauses they connect.

1. but; Some astronauts adjust well to living without gravity, others have problems

2. and; the bones, the muscles

3. for; Astronauts are not surprised by zero gravity, they are trained to expect it

4. yet; Sakamoto had mastered Japanese, she was having trouble communicating

5. or; agree, question, challenge

6. so; Sakamoto learned the art of Japanese conversation, she was able to participate fully

B. Sample Answers

1. Astronauts can easily do somersaults and flips.

2. In response to every question, we nodded or disagreed.

3. I was excited when we took off, but I was also scared.

4. You cannot eat out of a bowl or drink from a glass.

5. Being an astronaut is scary yet exciting.

Open-Book Test, p. 53

Short Answer

1. In both, the ball (topic) is batted back and forth. Each player (speaker) takes a turn and adds a twist or a spin.

   Difficulty: *Average*   **Objective:** *Interpretation*

2. In Japanese conversations, you must wait your turn and you know your place in line.

   Difficulty: *Easy*   **Objective:** *Reading*

3. The author means that all the topics move in the same direction and keep a distance between them. They do not intersect.

   Difficulty: *Average*   **Objective:** *Vocabulary*

4. The author paid no attention to whose turn it was to speak, and she tried to hold a back-and-forth conversation. She was speaking in a western style, not "playing" the Japanese conversational "game."

   Difficulty: *Challenging*   **Objective:** *Interpretation*

5. Both cultures agree that it is rude to speak with your mouth full. The Japanese do not speak during dinner; westerners alternate between eating and speaking.

   Difficulty: *Average*   **Objective:** *Interpretation*

6. Japanese-style Conversation: People take turns speaking; speakers do not refer to previous conversation; people do not interrupt

   Western-style Conversation: People elaborate on others' ideas; people get excited; speakers jump into the conversation

   Sample Titles: A Comparison of Conversation in Two Cultures; Conversational Customs

   Difficulty: *Average*   **Objective:** *Reading*

7. It is an expository essay, because it is a short work of nonfiction that explains Japanese and western styles of conversation.

   Difficulty: *Average*   **Objective:** *Literary Analysis*

8. The two processes are Japanese-style conversations and western-style conversations. The essay uses comparison and contrast to explain the differences between them.

   Difficulty: *Easy*   **Objective:** *Literary Analysis*

9. Students may choose a title such as "Styles of Conversation." They should explain that their title choice reflects the essay's main idea.

   Difficulty: *Challenging*   **Objective:** *Reading*

10. Sample answer: Japanese conversation is like bowling, in which people line up and take turns. There is encouragement but no interruption from others. Japanese conversation, like bowling, is orderly, polite, and players (speakers) do not interact.

    Difficulty: *Easy*   **Objective:** *Interpretation*

Essay

11. Students should describe the conversational style they chose, alluding to tennis or volleyball to describe western-style conversation, or bowling to describe Japanese-style conversation. Advantages: western-style conversation lends itself to a free exchange of ideas; Japanese-style conversation allows a speaker to speak without interruption. Disadvantages: a shy person might have trouble taking part in western-style conversation; a person might not receive feedback to ideas in Japanese-style conversation.

    Difficulty: *Easy*   **Objective:** *Essay*

12. Students should note the key characteristics of a Japanese-style conversation. They might say that there would be fewer differences of opinion or arguments, conversations would proceed more slowly, speakers would be more polite, or topics might not be explored in depth.

    Difficulty: *Average*   **Objective:** *Essay*

13. Students might note that the author's difficulty in "just listening" reflects westerners' impatience with the Japanese style of conversation, whereas Japanese students' hesitancy to engage in western-style conversations reflects their discomfort with the unstructured nature of the style. Students might cite the ballgame analogies to support their explanations.

    Difficulty: *Challenging*   **Objective:** *Essay*

14. Students should point out that the author wants the reader to learn that the Japanese and westerners approach conversation very differently, reflecting a basic cultural difference. They might point out that the differences include a basic impatience and a desire to exchange ideas on the part of westerners and a basic politeness and respect for the speaker on the part of the Japanese. The information is important because understanding those differences can help the two groups to understand each other and to communicate more effectively.

    Difficulty: *Average*   **Objective:** *Essay*

Oral Response

15. Oral responses should be clear, well organized, and well supported by appropriate examples from the selection.

    Difficulty: *Average*   **Objective:** *Oral Interpretation*

Selection Test A, p. 56

Critical Reading

1. ANS: C	DIF: Easy	OBJ: Comprehension
2. ANS: C	DIF: Easy	OBJ: Comprehension
3. ANS: A	DIF: Easy	OBJ: Reading
4. ANS: B	DIF: Easy	OBJ: Reading
5. ANS: A	DIF: Easy	OBJ: Interpretation
6. ANS: A	DIF: Easy	OBJ: Interpretation
7. ANS: C	DIF: Easy	OBJ: Interpretation
8. ANS: A	DIF: Easy	OBJ: Comprehension
9. ANS: B	DIF: Easy	OBJ: Comprehension
10. ANS: D	DIF: Easy	OBJ: Literary Analysis

Vocabulary and Grammar

11. ANS: A	DIF: Easy	OBJ: Vocabulary
12. ANS: B	DIF: Easy	OBJ: Vocabulary
13. ANS: B	DIF: Easy	OBJ: Grammar
14. ANS: C	DIF: Easy	OBJ: Grammar

Essay

15. Students should describe the conversational style they choose, alluding to tennis or volleyball if they are describing western-style conversation, or to bowling if they are describing Japanese-style conversation. They should then describe one advantage (for example, that western-style conversation lends itself to a free exchange of ideas or that Japanese-style conversation allows a speaker to speak without interruption) and one disadvantage (for example, that a shy person might have trouble expressing himself or herself in a western-style conversation or that a person may not receive a response to his or her ideas in a Japanese-style conversation).
    Difficulty: *Easy*
    Objective: *Essay*

16. Students should note that Sakamoto explains the differences between western-style and Japanese-style conversations. They may note that the way in which she explores the differences is by comparing and contrasting the two styles, and they may refer to the analogies of tennis, volleyball, and bowling that the author uses to illustrate her points.
    Difficulty: *Easy*
    Objective: *Essay*

17. Students should point out that the author wants the reader to learn that the Japanese and westerners approach conversation very differently. This reflects differences in the two cultures. Westerners are more impatient and eager to exchange ideas. The Japanese are more polite and show more respect to the speaker. The information is important because understanding those

differences can help the two groups to understand each other and to communicate more effectively.
Difficulty: *Average*
Objective: *Essay*

Selection Test B, p. 59

Critical Reading

1. ANS: C	DIF: Average	OBJ: Comprehension
2. ANS: B	DIF: Average	OBJ: Comprehension
3. ANS: C	DIF: Average	OBJ: Comprehension
4. ANS: B	DIF: Average	OBJ: Interpretation
5. ANS: D	DIF: Challenging	OBJ: Reading
6. ANS: A	DIF: Average	OBJ: Comprehension
7. ANS: C	DIF: Average	OBJ: Interpretation
8. ANS: A	DIF: Average	OBJ: Interpretation
9. ANS: B	DIF: Average	OBJ: Comprehension
10. ANS: D	DIF: Average	OBJ: Literary Analysis
11. ANS: D	DIF: Challenging	OBJ: Reading

Vocabulary and Grammar

12. ANS: C	DIF: Challenging	OBJ: Vocabulary
13. ANS: B	DIF: Average	OBJ: Vocabulary
14. ANS: A	DIF: Challenging	OBJ: Grammar
15. ANS: D	DIF: Challenging	OBJ: Grammar
16. ANS: B	DIF: Average	OBJ: Grammar

Essay

17. Students should note the key characteristics of a Japanese-style conversation: that speakers speak in turn, that one's turn is determined by one's relationship to the other speakers present, that speakers never interrupt one another, that they are supportive of one another's statements, and so on. Students might say that there would be fewer arguments or differences of opinion, that conversations would proceed more slowly, that speakers were apt to be more polite, or that topics might not be explored in depth.
    Difficulty: *Average*
    Objective: *Essay*

18. Students might note that the author's difficulty in "just listening" reflects westerners' impatience with the Japanese style of conversation, in which one waits one's turn and one's turn is determined by one's relationship to the others present, whereas Japanese students' hesitancy to engage in western-style conversations reflects their discomfort with the unstructured nature of that style. Students might cite the ballgame analogies to support their explanations.
    Difficulty: *Challenging*
    Objective: *Essay*

19. Students should point out that the author wants the reader to learn that the Japanese and westerners approach conversation very differently, reflecting a basic cultural difference. They might point out that the differences include a basic impatience and a desire to exchange ideas on the part of westerners and a basic politeness and respect for the speaker on the part of the Japanese. The information is important because understanding those differences can help the two groups to understand each other and to communicate more effectively.

Difficulty: *Average*

Objective: *Essay*

"I Am a Native of North America"
by Chief Dan George

Vocabulary Warm-up Exercises, p. 63

A. 1. presence
2. creative
3. values
4. creation
5. worthy
6. abuses
7. shameful
8. privacy

B. Sample Answers
1. erasing; This vacation is erasing the memory of all the hard work I did.
2. friendship; Your friendship is important to me.
3. suspicion; After their misunderstanding, there was suspicion between the two boys.
4. authentic; The antique coin was appraised and found to be authentic.
5. encourage; Our club will work to encourage donations to the food drive.
6. comforting; A comforting hug always feels good!
7. pains; The pains of hard times were known to many immigrants.
8. aid; The government will arrange for aid to the homeless.

Reading Warm-up A, p. 64

Words that students are to circle appear in parentheses.

Sample Answers
1. (heroes); *Worthy* means "having value or meriting something."
2. Alan thought long and hard about who, in all the universe, was his biggest hero. In all creation, my biggest heroes are my parents, President Lincoln, and Arthur Ashe.
3. I would have to share a bedroom with my brother, I would have less privacy; The presence of a clown at the party made it a lot of fun.
4. (my parents); *Privacy* is the condition of being private or alone.

5. my attitude toward him; *proud*
6. He showed me the beautiful kitchen table he was building for us; Some things I think are creative are well-written books, beautiful sculptures, and people who solve problems in an interesting way.
7. how to get along with and respect others; Values are social principles that people live by and think are important.
8. it does not feel good; *Abuses* means "mistreats or uses wrongly."

Reading Warm-up B, p. 65

Words that students are to circle appear in parentheses.

Sample Answers
1. European explorers; *Blotting* means "erasing" or "getting rid of."
2. (They also included the settlers' attempt to change or do away with the Indians' culture); It is hard to watch the sufferings of others without trying to help them.
3. (much of their culture has been kept alive by the Native Americans who still live in this region); Some things I find reassuring are having a home, a family, friends, and enough to eat.
4. the idea that the land and its bounty are gifts to be used wisely; *Promote* means "to help to bring about."
5. They enjoyed the companionship of others during the winter. People might enjoy the companionship of others when they are at school, at dinner, or playing a game.
6. Giving food to visitors and those in need was a system of welfare because it took care of people in need. Welfare is the programs concerned with giving aid to those in need.
7. When Europeans landed on the shores of Vancouver, some Native Americans warned of the dangers brought by the new settlers; *Distrust* is a lack of confidence in someone or something.
8. (openness); *false; fake*

Writing About the Big Question, p. 66

A. 1. discover; examine; explore; investigate; understand
2. knowledge
3. interview; questions

B. Sample Answers
1. People in this country used to keep slaves. Japanese Americans had to stay in labor camps during World War II. People in Washington D.C. cannot vote in elections.
2. In history class, we learned that Japanese-Americans were put in labor camps during World War II. This policy was based on fear, not **facts**. I find this hard to **understand** or accept. I think of America as a fair country – a notion I had to **question** after learning about this policy. In time, I've decided that even great countries can make mistakes.

C. Sample Answer

In order for people to live together in a society, they must understand one another. Understanding others is not difficult for people with natural curiosity. Ask an honest question of a new acquaintance. You might learn something!

Reading: Make Connections Between Key Points and Supporting Details to Understand the Main Idea, p. 67

Sample Answers

Main idea: The most important part of life for human beings is love.

1. It is important to respect and love nature.
2. The earth is a gift from the Great Spirit. It is a "second mother." We show our thanks for the gifts of nature by using them with respect.
3. Love nourishes the human spirit.
4. Without love, people have no courage, they have weak self-esteem, they have no confidence to face the world, and they destroy themselves.

Literary Analysis: Reflective Essay, p. 68

Sample Answers

A. Author's Thoughts / My Thoughts

1. Chief George believes that growing up in a smoke house teaches people to live with one another, to serve one another, to respect one another's rights. / I wonder how these concepts can be taught in a modern environment.
2. Chief George learns from his father that we are part of nature, nature is part of us, and we must therefore respect nature. / Sometimes people have thought that nature must be feared or conquered. Chief George's thoughts about nature are gentler.
3. Chief George claims that Indian culture is dying out, that soon only white culture will be left. / I think that Indians have made an effort to preserve their culture. I don't think it will die out. In addition, I think many cultures are represented in American society today. Maybe things have changed since Chief George wrote his essay.

B. In their paragraphs, students should clearly state the topic on which they are writing and their main idea.

Vocabulary Builder, p. 69

A. Sample Answers

1. The speaker wanted to promote the use of hybrid cars.
2. In a communal garden in the city, neighbors got together and grew tomatoes and corn.
3. The crisis of world hunger justifies a conference on the topic.
4. In science class, we learned to recognize the distinct features of various species.

5. During hurricane season, the *hoarding* of water is widespread.
6. Some immigrants believe *integration* is good for their children.

B. 1. An *unjust* decision is not fair.
2. You are not free from blame if your mistake has no *justification*.
3. A justifiable *complaint should be taken seriously.*

Enrichment: Promoting a Message, p. 70

Students should come up with a succinct statement that relates to the essay. Their responses to the items should demonstrate an understanding of the components of a unified commercial message.

Open-Book Test, p. 71

Short Answer

1. a) His family lived in a communal home where members accepted and depended on each other. b) His people loved and respected the earth and all creatures.
   Difficulty: *Average* **Objective:** *Reading*
2. Communal living teaches people to live with one another, serve one another, and respect the rights of one another.
   Difficulty: *Average* **Objective:** *Literary Analysis*
3. It supports the main idea that we must show respect for all living things.
   Difficulty: *Challenging* **Objective:** *Reading*
4. The neighbors live separately and do not know or care about each other.
   Difficulty: *Easy* **Objective:** *Interpretation*
5. The author concludes that he cannot understand a culture that justifies war over education and welfare.
   Difficulty: *Challenging* **Objective:** *Literary Analysis*
6. Sample answer: Chief Dan George writes that he believes that people have not learned to love nature. This suggests that he thinks people can change. They can learn to love nature and to treat the planet with more respect.
   Difficulty: *Challenging* **Objective:** *Interpretation*
7. The author sees privacy as something that is harmful. He believes it leads to distrust.
   Difficulty: *Easy* **Objective:** *Literary Analysis*
8. White culture: live privately; do not love nature; wage war; hoard private possessions

   Indian culture: live communally; love nature; love all people; share their possessions
   Love can help both cultures.
   Difficulty: *Average* **Objective:** *Interpretation*
9. The main idea is that we must learn to love each other and all of creation.
   Difficulty: *Easy* **Objective:** *Reading*
10. The distinct culture is separate and different from another culture, or way of life.
    Difficulty: *Average* **Objective:** *Vocabulary*

Essay

11. Students may note that his childhood experiences living communally taught Chief George to live with and respect and love other people. He learned, when fishing with his father, to love and respect the earth and all of nature.

    Difficulty: *Easy* **Objective:** *Essay*

12. Students should note that Chief George criticizes white culture's past wars, weapons manufacturing, and destruction of the environment. He believes that the solution lies in learning to love.

    Difficulty: *Average* **Objective:** *Essay*

13. Students should recognize that Chief George describes as an ideal, a community in which people love and respect each other and their environment. Students may note that he believes communal living is best because it fosters love and respect. He feels that people in today's communities live in isolation and do not know, love, or care for one another.

    Difficulty: *Challenging* **Objective:** *Essay*

14. Students should note that Chief George's concept of love involves people learning to live with one another, serve one another, and respect one another and all of nature. Students may point out that Chief George suggests that love can end hatred, war, and feelings of isolation, making it one of the most important things to learn.

    Difficulty: *Average* **Objective:** *Essay*

Oral Response

15. Oral responses should be clear, well organized, and well supported by appropriate examples from the selections.

    Difficulty: *Average* **Objective:** *Oral Interpretation*

Selection Test A, p. 74

Critical Reading

1. ANS: C	DIF: Easy	OBJ: Comprehension
2. ANS: B	DIF: Easy	OBJ: Comprehension
3. ANS: A	DIF: Easy	OBJ: Interpretation
4. ANS: B	DIF: Easy	OBJ: Interpretation
5. ANS: C	DIF: Easy	OBJ: Literary Analysis
6. ANS: C	DIF: Easy	OBJ: Literary Analysis
7. ANS: B	DIF: Easy	OBJ: Interpretation
8. ANS: A	DIF: Easy	OBJ: Interpretation
9. ANS: D	DIF: Easy	OBJ: Reading
10. ANS: A	DIF: Easy	OBJ: Comprehension
11. ANS: C	DIF: Easy	OBJ: Reading
12. ANS: C	DIF: Easy	OBJ: Reading

Vocabulary and Grammar

13. ANS: D	DIF: Easy	OBJ: Vocabulary
14. ANS: C	DIF: Easy	OBJ: Vocabulary
15. ANS: C	DIF: Easy	OBJ: Grammar

Essay

16. Students should recognize that George makes these two points: His family lived in a communal home whose residents learned to accept and depend on one another, and his people learned to love and respect the earth and all its creatures. Students should cite two details that support each main point.

    Difficulty: *Easy*

    Objective: *Essay*

17. Students may note that because he was exposed to communal living as a child, Chief George learned to live with and love other people and that he learned from his father to love and respect the earth and all of nature. They may point out that as an adult, he concludes that privacy promotes distrust, hoarding is shameful, and love of the earth and of all people is necessary to survival.

    Difficulty: *Easy*

    Objective: *Essay*

18. Students should note that Chief George's concept of love involves people learning to live with one another, serve one another, and respect one another and all of nature. Students may point out that Chief George suggests that love can end hatred and war. This power of love makes it one of the most important things to learn.

    Difficulty: *Average*

    Objective: *Essay*

Selection Test B, p. 77

Critical Reading

1. ANS: C	DIF: Average	OBJ: Comprehension
2. ANS: C	DIF: Average	OBJ: Literary Analysis
3. ANS: D	DIF: Challenging	OBJ: Reading
4. ANS: D	DIF: Average	OBJ: Comprehension
5. ANS: B	DIF: Average	OBJ: Interpretation
6. ANS: C	DIF: Challenging	OBJ: Literary Analysis
7. ANS: B	DIF: Average	OBJ: Interpretation
8. ANS: A	DIF: Average	OBJ: Interpretation
9. ANS: A	DIF: Average	OBJ: Interpretation
10. ANS: A	DIF: Average	OBJ: Reading
11. ANS: A	DIF: Average	OBJ: Comprehension
12. ANS: C	DIF: Challenging	OBJ: Reading
13. ANS: C	DIF: Average	OBJ: Reading
14. ANS: A	DIF: Average	OBJ: Literary Analysis

Vocabulary and Grammar

15. ANS: B	DIF: Challenging	OBJ: Vocabulary
16. ANS: A	DIF: Challenging	OBJ: Vocabulary
17. ANS: B	DIF: Average	OBJ: Grammar
18. ANS: B	DIF: Challenging	OBJ: Grammar

Essay

19. Students should note that Chief George's concept of love involves people learning to live with one another, serving one another, and respecting one another and all nature. Students may point to Chief George's idea that if they feel the love of white society, Native Americans can begin to "forgive and forget" the horrors they suffered at the hands of that society. Students may also note that Chief George suggests that love can end hatred, war, and feelings of isolation.

    Difficulty: *Average*

    Objective: *Essay*

20. Students should note that Chief George criticizes white culture's justifying its past wars, manufacturing weapons, and harming the environment. He believes that the solution lies in learning to love "fully."

    Difficulty: *Average*

    Objective: *Essay*

21. Students should recognize that Chief George describes as ideal a community in which people love and respect one another and their environment. Students may note that he suggests that communal living is best because it fosters love and respect. He believes that people in today's communities neither know nor care for one another because they live in isolation.

    Difficulty: *Challenging*

    Objective: *Essay*

22. Students should note that Chief George's concept of love involves people learning to live with one another, serve one another, and respect one another and all of nature. Students may point out that Chief George suggests that love can end hatred, war, and feelings of isolation, making it one of the most important things to learn.

    Difficulty: *Average*

    Objective: *Essay*

"Volar: To Fly"
by Judith Ortiz Cofer

Vocabulary Warm-up Exercises A, p. 81

A. 1. fantasy
   2. patiently
   3. ermine
   4. dismal
   5. refuse
   6. interrupted
   7. obsession
   8. clinging

B. Sample Answers
   1. T; An avid fan would want to watch every game.
   2. F; If she was scattering her books, they would not be in a neat pile.

3. F; If they didn't like discussing things, they wouldn't talk for very long.
4. T; Plastic chairs would look incongruous with an old oak table.
5. T; Yes, recurring fees are charged over and over again.
6. T; A responsible consumer would do research before she bought something.
7. T; That would be a logical desire for a grandmother.
8. F; If the author had been inspired by the response to his story, he would have kept on writing.

Reading Warm-up A, p. 82

Sample Answers
1. our studies; No, I don't like being *interrupted* when I am talking.
2. Yes, it is usually hard to wait patiently; impatiently
3. The vine was *clinging* to the tree. sticking, holding onto
4. *Fantasy* books and games are good because they let you use your imagination.
5. the weather, someone's mood; bright, cheerful, sunny
6. No, people keep our neighborhood clean and don't throw *refuse* on the street. garbage, trash
7. My friend has an *obsession* with video games (or) my father has an *obsession* with football. An *obsession* is stronger and more intense than just liking or being interested in something.
8. An *ermine* cloak would be made of white fur tipped with black.

Reading Warm-up B, p. 83

Sample Answers
1. to determine the function of dreams; my coach *inspired* me to work harder at soccer.
2. random images; Highway toll collector, artist, writer
3. eager, enthusiastic; I am an *avid* fan of NBA basketball.
4. I am a *consumer* of television shows, fantasy books, fast food.
5. to try to understand themselves; talking about, arguing, chatting about
6. No, I have never had the same dream happen over again (or) Yes, I often have the same dreams several times; frequent, returning over and over
7. wish, want, craving, longing for something. A *desire* might be hidden if it was for something that a person was ashamed of wanting.
8. bizarre; out of place, odd, strange, not going together

Writing About the Big Question, p. 84

A. 1. explore; investigate
   2. experiment
   3. understand; analyze

B. Sample Answers

1. I learned that my mother was allergic to corn. I learned that my father once rode his bicycle to Chicago. I learned that my grandmother was a Reds fan.

2. At dinner the other night, I **discovered** that my father had an interesting adventure as a young man. He rode his bike from Cincinnati to Chicago to visit my mother. It was winter at the time! Guess what? My mother was out of town visiting relatives. I think my father should have called and asked a few **questions** before setting out.

C. Sample Answer

Family connections are often not easy to understand. For example, everyone in my family roots for different football teams. We fight a lot about which team is best. We should learn to emphasize our common love of the game, instead of arguing so much.

Reading: Make Connections Between Key Points and Supporting Details to Understand the Main Idea, p. 85

Main idea: Dreaming or daydreaming of being able to fly allows you to imagine a greater, richer, more fulfilling life for yourself, beyond the limitations of current circumstances.

1. Having superpowers such as flying and X-ray vision allows me to see into the lives of other people and manipulate their lives to my satisfaction.

2. I could see our landlord greedily counting his money. Knowing my family does not like him, I used my super-breath to scatter his piles of money so he would have to keep re-counting.

3. I could program or adjust my Supergirl dreams to focus on things that interested or obsessed me.

4. I could look into the private lives of my teachers and boys that I had crushes on.

Literary Analysis: Reflective Essay p. 86

Sample answers for Author's Thoughts; My Thoughts will vary:

1. She fantasized that she could be a superhero and fly.

2. As Supergirl, she created imaginary lives for the people she knew.

3. She realizes that her mother also wishes she could fly.

Vocabulary Builder, p. 87

A. 1. *Adolescence* is an emotional time for many kids.

2. Mark is an *avid* basketball fan.

3. The early reports about the plane crash were *dismal.*

4. Grandpa hated when anyone *interrupted* his computer time.

5. He had an *obsession* with macaroni and cheese.

6. *Refuse* blew around the empty stadium.

B. 1. A quiet conversation would disrupt science class.

2. Traffic would be heavy if a water main ruptured.

3. A baby couldn't sleep through a disruption.

Enrichment: Botany, p. 88

Superman—Superpowers: Flying, X-ray vision, super strength, super speed, super breath, bullet-proof body; Real name or secret identity: Clark Kent, newspaper reporter; TV versions: (selected) *Superman* (1952–1958); *Lois and Clark, the New Adventures of Superman* (1993–1997); Movie versions: *Superman* (1978), *Superman II* (1980), *Superman III* (1983), *Superman IV, The Quest for Peace* (1987), *Superman Returns* (2006). Spiderman—Superpowers: spiderlike powers: can cling to most surfaces, super strength and reflexes; uses shooters on his wrists to shoot thin strands of a special web fluid; Real name or secret identity: Peter Parker, teen science whiz; TV versions: various animated series (1967–2008); Movie versions: *Spider-Man (2002), Spider-Man 2* (2004); *Spider-Man 3* (2007). Batman—Superpowers: no superpowers—relies on intelligence, strength, and gadgets; Real name or secret identity: Bruce Wayne, playboy; TV versions: *Batman* (1966–1968); Movie versions: *Batman* (1966); *Batman* (1986); *Batman* (1989); *Batman Returns* (1992); *Batman Forever* (1995); *Batman & Robin* (1997).

The Hulk—Superpowers: unlimited physical strength; Real name or secret identity: Robert Bruce Banner, nuclear physicist; TV versions: *The Incredible Hulk* (1977–1982); Movie versions: *Hulk* (2003). Wonder Woman—Superpowers: super strength and agility, flying at super speeds, super breath; Real name or secret identity: Princess Diana, an Amazon from Greek mythology; TV versions: *Wonder Woman* (1975–1979); Movie versions: none. Green Lantern—Superpowers: almost unlimited powers, provided by power ring; Real name or secret identity: Alan Scott, Hal Jordan, John Stewart, Guy Gardner, and Kyle Rayner; TV versions: appearances in various animated series; Movie versions: none. Captain America—Superpowers: no superpowers but has great strength and endurance; Real name or secret identity: Steve Rogers, sickly young man given strength serum to help U.S. in World War II; TV versions: *Captain America* and *Captain America II* (1979); Movie versions: *Captain America* (1944 serial); *Captain America* (1990).

"Volar: To Fly" by Judith Ortiz Cofer
"I Am a Native of North America" by Chief Dan George

Integrated Language Skills: Grammar, p. 89

1. of my super-breath; into his fireplace

2. above the mountaintop; in the early morning

3. for everything; in nature

4. In my dream; to the top; of our apartment building

5. inside the homes; of people

6. In the course; of my lifetime; in two distinct cultures

7. <u>with</u> him; <u>up</u> Indian River
8. <u>beyond</u> the few blocks; <u>of</u> our barrio

Open-Book Test, p. 92

Short Answer

1. Sample answer: Cofer still thinks fondly of Supergirl because Supergirl gave her strength and power when she felt small and powerless.
Difficulty: *Easy* **Objective:** *Literary Analysis*

2. Sample answer: This detail shows how important Supergirl was to the author.
Difficulty: *Easy* **Objective:** *Interpretation*

3. Sample answer: The author dreams she can fly and has super-breath and X-ray vision.
Difficulty: *Easy* **Objective:** *Reading*

4. Sample answer: This detail supports the idea that her family was poor, and by making life a bit harder for the landlord, she could ease her own family's hardships.
Difficulty: *Average* **Objective:** *Reading*

5. She means that she imagined or dreamed about how they lived and what they did in the privacy of their own homes.
Difficulty: *Average* **Objective:** *Interpretation*

6. Sample answer: The mother and father's relationship seems tender and honest but also focused on everyday cares such as money and parenting.
Difficulty: *Challenging* **Objective:** *Interpretation*

7. The clock has a prayer for patience and grace on it. The author includes this detail because she believes that if we have patience and grace, we will someday "fly."
Difficulty: *Challenging* **Objective:** *Literary Analysis*

8. No, she did not treat the comic books as if they were garbage. She treasured them and stored them safely in her closet.
Difficulty: *Average* **Objective:** *Vocabulary*

9. Sample answers: Author's Thoughts—Cofer fondly remembers wanting to be a superhero; Cofer remembers her mother's patience and resignation at not being able to travel.
Students should name a book or story title and write a reflection about it.
Difficulty: *Average* **Objective:** *Literary Analysis*

10. They both long to fly.
Difficulty: *Average* **Objective:** *Interpretation*

Essay

11. Students may note that being able to buy the comics must have been empowering to Cofer as a young girl. Keeping them must have provided a sense of security and comfort, like relying on an old, trusted friend. In both the comic book and in Cofer's dream, the main character has superpowers, has freedom and is unchallenged, and is in control of her own destiny.
Difficulty: *Easy* **Objective:** *Essay*

12. Students may say that Cofer feels nostalgic about her old comic books and that they help her express the idea that our imagination can help carry us to the places we need to go.
Difficulty: *Average* **Objective:** *Essay*

13. Students should recognize that the title reflects one of the author's personal desires and that it is intended both literally, from the point of view of the 12-year-old, and figuratively, in terms of flying from her identity. Students should also note that the title points to the essay's main idea: with patience and grace, a person will eventually learn to "fly"—though it may be in a way different from the one imagined as a child.
Difficulty: *Challenging* **Objective:** *Essay*

14. Students may say that Cofer wants us to learn that our most important superpower is our imagination, or that our most important "super" identity is the one we are born with. Accept all reasonable responses.
Difficulty: *Average* **Objective:** *Essay*

Oral Response

15. Oral responses should be clear, well organized, and well supported by appropriate examples from the selections.
Difficulty: *Average* **Objective:** *Oral Interpretation*

Selection Test A, p. 95

1.	ANS: A	Diff: Easy	Obj: Comprehension
2.	ANS: C	Diff: Average	Obj: Comprehension
3.	ANS: D	Diff: Average	Obj: Interpretation
4.	ANS: A	Diff: Easy	Obj: Comprehension
5.	ANS: B	Diff: Average	Obj: Comprehension
6.	ANS: A	Diff: Average	Obj: Literary Analysis
7.	ANS: B	Diff: Challenging	Obj: Literary Analysis
8.	ANS: A	Diff: Average	Obj: Interpretation
9.	ANS: D	Diff: Average	Obj: Interpretation
10.	ANS: C	Diff: Average	Obj: Literary Analysis
11.	ANS: A	Diff: Average	Obj: Reading
12.	ANS: A	Diff: Challenging	Obj: Reading
13.	ANS: B	Diff: Average	Obj: Interpretation
14.	ANS: A	Diff: Average	Obj: Vocabulary
15.	ANS: C	Diff: Challenging	Obj: Vocabulary
16.	ANS: B	Diff: Average	Obj: Vocabulary
17.	ANS: C	Diff: Easy	Obj: Vocabulary
18.	ANS: A	Diff: Easy	Obj: Vocabulary
19.	ANS: A	Diff: Average	Obj: Vocabulary
20.	ANS: A	Diff: Easy	Obj: Vocabulary

Essay

21. Students should understand that the writer and her mother have different reasons for wanting to fly. The

writer wants to see into the lives of people who interest her. Her mother wants to escape her deary life and return to her family in Puerto Rico.

Difficulty: *Easy*

Objective: *Essay*

22. Expect some variation in answers to this question. Students should mention that many people wish to escape from their everyday lives and/or their limitations.

Difficulty: *Average*

Objective: *Essay*

23. The author does seem sympathetic toward her mother's longing. She describes her mother in gentle terms. Even when disappointed, she moves "not abruptly." She seems to aim for patience and grace. Some students may point out that the writer respects her parents by giving them time alone together. Some students may grasp the fact that although the writer is sympathetic toward her mother, she does not share her longings.

Difficulty: *Challenging*

Objective: *Essay*

24. Students may say that Cofer wants us to learn that our most important superpower is our imagination. It gives us the power to hope and dream of a different and better way of life. She might also say that our most important "super" identity is the one we are born with.

Difficulty: *Average*

Objective: *Essay*

Selection Test B, p. 98

1.	**ANS:** B	**Diff:** Average	**Obj:** Interpretation
2.	**ANS:** A	**Diff:** Average	**Obj:** Comprehension
3.	**ANS:** D	**Diff:** Challenging	**Obj:** Literary Skill: Reflective Essay
4.	**ANS:** C	**Diff:** Easy	**Obj:** Reading Skill: Main Idea
5.	**ANS:** A	**Diff:** Easy	**Obj:** Comprehension
6.	**ANS:** D	**Diff:** Challenging	**Obj:** Literary Analysis: Reflective Essay
7.	**ANS:** C	**Diff:** Average	**Obj:** Comprehension
8.	**ANS:** C	**Diff:** Challenging	**Obj:** Interpretation
9.	**ANS:** B	**Diff:** Easy	**Obj:** Reading Skill: Main Idea
10.	**ANS:** D	**Diff:** Average	**Obj:** Reading Skill: Main Idea
11.	**ANS:** D	**Diff:** Challenging	**Obj:** Literary Skill: Reflective Essay
12.	**ANS:** C	**Diff:** Easy	**Obj:** Comprehension
13.	**ANS:** B	**Diff:** Challenging	**Obj:** Interpretation
14.	**ANS:** A	**Diff:** Challenging	**Obj:** Literary Skill: Reflective Essay
15.	**ANS:** B	**Diff:** Average	**Obj:** Interpretation

16.	**ANS:** C	**Diff:** Average	**Obj:** Vocabulary
17.	**ANS:** A	**Diff:** Easy	**Obj:** Vocabulary
18.	**ANS:** A	**Diff:** Challenging	**Obj:** Vocabulary
19.	**ANS:** B	**Diff:** Average	**Obj:** Grammar
20.	**ANS:** C	**Diff:** Challenging	**Obj:** Grammar

Essay

21. Answers will vary. Students should identify a known character from the realm of fiction—books, movies, comic books, or TV—and clearly identity the characteristics of that character that they most admire and explain why they consider them important or admirable.

Difficulty: *Esay*

Objective: *Essay*

22. Students should clearly identify at least two other uses of superpowers and explain why they think those uses are better—more useful, more productive, etc.—than the ones chosen by the narrator.

Difficulty: *Average*

Objective: *Essay*

23. Students might note that both the narrator and her mother use the fantasy of flying as a way of imagining a better life for themselves. For the narrator, as a young adolescent, flying and the other superpowers make her feel more control of her life and better able to imagine how she would feel if she were more independent. For the mother, the ability to fly represents an ability to soar beyond the limitations of her life in the barrio, which prevents her even from returning to Puerto Rico, her homeland, to visit her relatives.

Difficulty: *Challenging*

Objective: *Essay*

"A Special Gift: The Legacy of Snowflake Bentley" by Barbara Eaglesham
"No Gumption" by Russell Baker

Vocabulary Warm-up Exercises, p. 102

A.
1. dreaded
2. delayed
3. advise
4. worthwhile
5. absorbed
6. buyer
7. eventually
8. solution

B. Sample Answers
1. T; If someone has faced obstacles and overcome them, he or she has succeeded despite, or in spite of, them.
2. F; If we regularly take a walk, we do it on a daily basis or a set schedule.

3. T; *Superior* means "higher," so superior workmanship would be high-quality work.

4. F; If the woman indicated which scarf she wanted, then she pointed it out. Thus, we would know which one she wanted.

5. T; A perfect record of wins means that the football team completed the season with a high degree of success, which is an accomplishment.

6. F; A man bored by the sights of the city was clearly not very interested or enchanted by it. Thus, he was not fascinated by what he saw.

7. T; An explorer on a long journey with a goal is on a quest.

8. T; *Image* means picture, and a yearbook is a record in words and pictures. So a school yearbook usually contains an image of each student and teacher.

Reading Warm-up A, p. 103

Words that students are to circle appear in parentheses.

Sample Answers

1. new fads and inventions: My mind has been absorbed by the ideas of playing piano in a jazz band and learning to knit a sweater that I could eventually wear.

2. The item would be paid for later: A buyer is someone who purchases something.

3. (payment): We delayed going to the game until everyone was ready to leave.

4. by saying it was stable: *Advise* means "to notify" or "give advice or an opinion."

5. (the thought of losing their money): *feared*

6. after Franklin Delano Roosevelt was elected president in 1932: *finally*

7. direct large amounts of government money and effort into public works; projects that built roads and buildings; big programs . . . for the media and arts: She raised her hand because she knew the solution to the hardest math problem.

8. these projects provided jobs for thousands of unemployed people: I stayed after school to help a younger child with her reading homework when she was having trouble.

Reading Warm-up B, p. 104

Words that students are to circle appear in parentheses.

Sample Answers

1. (picture): I might see photographic images everyday on a computer, in a newspaper, magazine, or book.

2. interested: I am fascinated by electric cars and by cellphones that can play music and show movies, too.

3. (*daguerreotype*): A synonym for *accomplishment* is achievement.

4. This means that in spite of the fact that lots of people liked the daguerreotype method, it stopped being used after a while. The reason it was replaced was that newer methods of photography were easier to use and worked more quickly. They also allowed pictures to be printed on paper instead of on metal.

5. methods: *Superior* means "better, or higher than."

6. magazines, newspapers, and books: The opposite of *regularly* is rarely or irregularly.

7. (how important these images were becoming all over the world): The dog wagged its tail, which *indicated* that it was happy.

8. the invention of digital cameras for home use in 1995: A *quest* is a journey or an effort to find something or to achieve a goal.

Writing About the Big Question, p. 105

A. 1. analyze; experiment

2. discover

3. interview

B. Sample Answers

1. I learned that I'm good at fixing mechanical things. I learned that I make very good pie crust.

2. The other day my family's clothes dryer broke. **Curiosity** led me to take off the knob. Inside I **discovered** a broken plastic piece. I **experimented** with glueing it together, and now the dryer works again. My family thinks I'm a mechanical genius!

C. Sample Answer

When you discover something you love to do, you should be thankful. Many people never develop a passion in life. I think that makes their life more difficult, and much less interesting. Having a passion for your work or a hobby is a wonderful gift. We should learn to experience as much as possible until we find something we love.

Literary Analysis: Comparing Biography and Autobiography, p. 106

A. 1. autobiography / use of "I"

2. autobiography / tells information a researcher is unlikely to know

3. biography / tone, use of third person

B. 1. personal, engaging, meaty, fun, etc. "you learn interesting things about people," etc.

2. informative, well-researched, objective, etc.

Vocabulary Builder, p. 107

A. 1. The young artist had an *aptitude* for business.

2. A hot oven is *crucial* to success when baking popovers.

3. Sweat *evaporated* on his back.

4. The stunt man had plenty of *gumption*.

5. *Hexagons* have six sides.

6. The cheap *microscope* was not very powerful.

7. The photographers' *negatives* filled an entire filing cabinet.

8. She thought *paupers* was an unpleasant word.

B. 1. A. 2. D; 3. C; 4. B; 5. A; 6. A

Open-Book Test, p. 109

Short Answer

1. "A labor of love" means that although he didn't make much money, Bentley had a passion for snowflakes and wanted to share their beauty with others.
   Difficulty: *Essay*   **Objective:** *Interpretation*

2. Musician: played the piano, violin, and clarinet; Scientist: kept a daily log of local weather conditions and measured the size of raindrops
   Difficulty: *Easy*   **Objective:** *Literary Analysis*

3. No, because if a snow crystal has changed into a vapor, it is no longer visible.
   Difficulty: *Average*   **Objective:** *Vocabulary*

4. The mother means that Russell is not motivated to set goals or work or improve himself.
   Difficulty: *Average*   **Objective:** *Interpretation*

5. Sample answer: Baker includes details that show how much "gumption" his sister has. These details contrast and emphasize in a humorous way Russell's own lack of "gumption."
   Difficulty: *Challenging*   **Objective:** *Interpretation*

6. Sample answer: The comment shows that the mother is still determined to make something of her son. It also shows that she is flexible enough to consider his talents and inclinations.
   Difficulty: *Average*   **Objective:** *Interpretation*

7. "The Legacy of 'Snowflake' Bentley" is based on research. "No Gumption" is based on personal memory.
   Difficulty: *Easy*   **Objective:** *Literary Analysis*

8. Bentley is persistent and motivated, spending hours attempting to draw snowflake crystals before they melt. Baker lacks "gumption." He prefers to lie in front of the radio and look at books. Both boys have a parent who believes they waste most of their time.
   Difficulty: *Challenging*   **Objective:** *Literary Analysis*

9. Sample answer: Both mothers encourage their sons to succeed.
   Difficulty: *Average*   **Objective:** *Literary Analysis*

10. "Snowflake" Bentley: biography; Both: tell about someone's life; "No Gumption": autobiography. Biography tells the life story of someone else, and autobiography tells the writer's own life story.
    Difficulty: *Average*   **Objective:** *Literary Interpretation*

Essay

11. Students will most likely respond that Baker's mother would, in fact, enjoy having Bentley as a son, because he demonstrates interest in and commitment to a particular kind of work. Some students may conclude, however, that Baker's mother would find the "work" of drawing snowflakes useless, as did Bentley's own father.
    Difficulty: *Easy*   **Objective:** *Essay*

12. Students may say that "The Legacy of 'Snowflake' Bentley" as an autobiography, readers would give a better

sense of Bentley's personality, but that the story would not be able to place Bentley in history as an important scientist and photographer. As a biography, "No Gumption" would lose much of its humor, replacing Baker's insights and narratives with the facts relating to his childhood, but perhaps giving a more objective picture of his mother and her concerns.
    Difficulty: *Average*   **Objective:** *Essay*

13. Students may say that Bentley most values the beauty of nature or the challenge of capturing nature's tiniest details, and that Baker most values the free flow of creative ideas. Evaluate students' essays for logic, clarity, and support.
    Difficulty: *Challenging*   **Objective:** *Essay*

14. Students may respond that Bentley believes we should learn all we can about the world around us, because only then will we be able to truly love, celebrate, and care for it. They may also say that Baker believes we should learn what it is that we truly enjoy—and don't enjoy—in life, because we will only flourish by pursuing work that is suited to our nature.
    Difficulty: *Average*   **Objective:** *Essay*

Oral Response

15. Oral responses should be clear, well organized, and well supported by appropriate examples from the selections.
    Difficulty: *Average*   **Objective:** *Oral Interpretation*

Selection Test A, p. 112

Critical Reading

1. ANS: A
2. ANS: D
3. ANS: C
4. ANS: B
5. ANS: A
6. ANS: A
7. ANS: B
8. ANS: A
9. ANS: A
10. ANS: C
11. ANS: B
12. ANS: C
13. ANS: B
14. ANS: C

Vocabulary and Grammar

15. ANS: A
16. ANS: A
17. ANS: C
18. ANS: D

19. ANS: A
20. ANS: A

Essay

21. A. "Snowflake" Bentley's father is described as "a serious, hardworking farmer" who "felt that looking through a microscope was a waste of time." Students should draw the conclusion the Bentley's father probably wanted him to help out on their farm, or concern himself with other money-making matters. "Snowflake" Bentley seems to have been little interested in money himself. His passion was photographing snow crystals.

    B. Russell Baker's mother wants him to "make something of himself." She thinks selling newspapers will teach him valuable skills for a career in business. Russell himself would prefer to stay home and read comics.

22. Students should list at least three examples of how Baker's writing style is different from Eaglesham's. For instance, he exaggerates (saying he is "working in journalism" at age 8, quoting his mother as saying they read the *Saturday Evening Post* with "religious devotion," ringing most of Belleville's 30,000 doorbells, etc.), he includes dialogue, his tone is more light-hearted. Students may express a preference for either writer, as long as they explain their reasoning (perhaps they think Baker is funny or prefer Eaglesham's more measured tone).

23. Each selection contains many engaging details, so students should be able to successfully argue that either "Snowflake" Bentley or Russell Baker is more vividly drawn. An autobiography often contains more interior thoughts and emotions, so it can be easier to draw a picture of someone in an autobiography. That said, some of a selection's success depends on the author's talent and style, and the audience's preferences. Some may prefer biography.

24. Students may respond that Bentley believes we should learn all we can about the world around us. Only then will we be able to truly love and care for it. They may also say that Baker believes we should learn what it is that we truly enjoy—and don't enjoy—in life. He believes that we will do best by doing work that we can do well.

    Difficulty: *Average*
    Objective: *Essay*

Selection Test B, p. 115

Critical Reading

1. ANS: A
2. ANS: D
3. ANS: C
4. ANS: B
5. ANS: A
6. ANS: A
7. ANS: B

8. ANS: B
9. ANS: A
10. ANS: C
11. ANS: B
12. ANS: C
13. ANS: B
14. ANS: C

Vocabulary and Grammar

15. ANS: A
16. ANS: A
17. ANS: C
18. ANS: D
19. ANS: A
20. ANS: A

Essay

21. A. "Snowflake" Bentley's father is described as "a serious, hardworking farmer" who "felt that looking through a microscope was a waste of time." Students should draw the conclusion that Bentley's father probably wanted him to help out on their farm or concern himself with other money-making matters. "Snowflake" Bentley seems to have been little interested in money. His passion was photographing snow crystals.

    B. Russell Baker's mother wants him to "make something of himself." She thinks selling newspapers will teach him valuable skills for a career in business. Russell Baker would prefer to stay home and read comics.

    Parents and children often have different ideas about how they should spend their time because: parents focus on practical concerns, parents and children grow up in different times and have different expectations, values, and knowledge, they are different people.

22. Students should identify Baker's style as humorous and Eaglesham's as serious, journalistic, or straightforward. They should list at least three examples of how the two writers' styles differ. For instance, Baker exaggerates (saying he is "working in journalism" at age 8, quoting his mother as saying they read *The Saturday Evening Post* with "religious devotion," ringing most of Belleville's 30,000 doorbells, etc.), he includes dialogue, his tone is more lighthearted.

    Autobiography contains more emotion, thoughts, and dialogue. Biography is more fact-based and reasoned.

    Students may express a preference for either writer, as long as they explain their reasoning (perhaps they think Baker is funny or prefer Eaglesham's more measured tone).

23. Each selection contains many engaging details, so students should be able to successfully argue that either "Snowflake" Bentley or Russell Baker is more vividly drawn. An autobiography often contains more interior

thoughts and emotions, so it can be easier to paint a picture of someone in an autobiography. That said, some of a selection's success depends on the author's talent and style, as well as the audience's preferences. Some may prefer biography or feel that they can trust the facts reported in a biography more than those in an autobiography.

24. Students may respond that Bentley believes we should learn all we can about the world around us, because only then will we be able to truly love, celebrate, and care for it. They may also say that Baker believes we should learn what it is that we truly enjoy—and don't enjoy—in life, because we will only flourish by pursuing work that is suited to our nature.

Difficulty: *Average*
Objective: *Essay*

Writing Workshop

How-to Essay: Integrating Grammar Skills, p. 119

A. 1. and; 2. but; 3. or; 4. if
B. Sample Sentences

1. Many dieters eat vegetables because they are low in fat.
2. Raw carrots are rich in vitamin A, although cooking them loses some vitamins.
3. You can eat spinach raw, or you can cook it in a little olive oil.
4. You must wash spinach thoroughly before you add it to salad.

Benchmark Test 5, p. 120
MULTIPLE CHOICE

1. ANS: D
2. ANS: C
3. ANS: D
4. ANS: A
5. ANS: A
6. ANS: B
7. ANS: D
8. ANS: B
9. ANS: D
10. ANS: B
11. ANS: D
12. ANS: C
13. ANS: D
14. ANS: D
15. ANS: B
16. ANS: A
17. ANS: C
18. ANS: D
19. ANS: C
20. ANS: B
21. ANS: A
22. ANS: C
23. ANS: D
24. ANS: B
25. ANS: C
26. ANS: A
27. ANS: A
28. ANS: C
29. ANS: A
30. ANS: C
31. ANS: B
32. ANS: D
33. ANS: C
34. ANS: D

ESSAY

35. Students' essays should include at least two advantages and two disadvantages.
36. Students' outlines should follow formal outline form, including Roman numerals and indented heads and subheads.
37. Students' how-to essays should describe needed materials and include in sequential order all the steps necessary to make or do a project of their choice.

"The Eternal Frontier" by Louis L'Amour

Vocabulary Warm-up Exercises, p. 128

A. 1. considered
2. scarcely
3. vehicle
4. achieve
5. automobile
6. system
7. outer
8. enable

B. Sample Answers

1. No, lights that run on solar power cannot be recharged at night because they need sunlight to be recharged.
2. In the first year of development, a baby learns to sit up, crawl, and stand.
3. I could eat well and exercise regularly.
4. My favorite atmospheric condition is low humidity and a moderate termperature.

5. A spaceship traveling through the orbit of asteroids would be in danger of getting hit by one.

6. I would rather drive on paved roads because unpaved roads are bumpy, uncomfortable, and dangerous.

7. *Telephone* is a common word from another language.

8. Obvious signs that someone has a cold are a runny nose, sneezing, sniffles, and stuffiness.

Reading Warm-up A, p. 129

Words that students are to circle appear in parentheses.

Sample Answers

1. (Model T); Skip's father buys a new automobile every four years.

2. motor; A vehicle is a device used to carry something.

3. He made it possible for ordinary workers to buy a car; *accomplish*

4. producing cars; To get something done, I make a list and check off each step as I do it.

5. (limits); Steven Spielberg's movies take us to the outer limits of the imagination.

6. reckless; *Considered* means "regarded as" or "thought to be."

7. (could believe); The child is scarcely able to reach the shelf in the closet.

8. buy cars of their own; A raise in pay might allow someone to buy a house.

Reading Warm-up B, p. 130

Words that students are to circle appear in parentheses.

Sample Answers

1. the telescope; The development of the computer has changed modern life.

2. (planets); Asteroids are small heavenly bodies that usually orbit between Mars and Jupiter.

3. system; Three objects in our *solar* system are the sun, any of the planets, and any of the planets' moons.

4. (gathered); Atmospheric conditions changed drastically during the storm.

5. unknown; I would like to believe that my own destiny is to be a useful member of society.

6. (later space probes that were able to orbit the planets); *Paved the way* means "prepared a path for something else to follow in." When a road is *paved*, it is prepared for vehicles to ride on it.

7. Jupiter; The country of origin is stamped on the soles of my shoes.

8. (the answers will not be known soon); It is obvious that the planets are in orbit around the sun.

Writing About the Big Question, p. 131

A. 1. explore; discover; analyze; investigate; understand

2. curiosity

3. interview

B. Sample Answers

1. **Exploring** space can teach humans to better appreciate Earth. Earth is the one place in the universe that can support human life. **Experimenting** with living in freezing, airless space is a great way to make you appreciate the comforting climate of home.

C. Sample Answer

When we stop asking questions about the unknown, we doom ourselves to never learn anything new. If scientists didn't ask questions, we would never have new medicines. If writers didn't ask questions, we would never have a works of fiction. We should learn to ask more questions. Asking questions leads to progress.

Reading: Fact and Opinion, p. 132

Sample answers follow the identification of each statement as *Fact* or *Opinion*:

1. Opinion / There is no information in this statement that can be proved. In addition, the word *All* suggests that the statement is a personal judgment.

2. Fact / The statement consists of statistics that can be verified by checking a reference work.

3. Opinion / There is no way to prove that in every situation there will be a "nay-sayer." The word *always* indicates that this statement is a personal judgment.

4. Opinion / There is no way to prove that a person is driven to see what lies beyond the frontier.

5. Fact / The information can be verified and proved true.

6. Opinion / One cannot prove that there are no limits to the ability of the human mind. In addition, the use of the phrase "at all" indicates that the statement is a personal judgment.

Literary Analysis: Persuasive Essay, p. 133

Sample Answers

Appeals to Emotion:

1. "Outer space is a frontier without end, the eternal frontier, an everlasting challenge to explorers not [only] of other planets and other solar systems but also of the mind of man."

2. "It is our destiny to move out, to accept the challenge, to dare the unknown. It is our destiny to achieve."

Appeals to Reason:

1. "We have been preparing ourselves mentally for what lies ahead. . . . In the past seventy years we have developed the automobile, radio, television, transcontinental and transoceanic flight, and the electrification of the country, among a multitude of other such developments."

2. "Yet we must not forget that along the way to outer space whole industries are springing into being that did not exist before. The computer age has arisen in part from the space effort, which gave great impetus to the development of computing devices."

Vocabulary Builder, p. 134

A. Sample Answers

1. I would like to learn more about the frontier of the American West.
2. My antidote for an hour spent working in the hot sun is a cool glass of lemonade.
3. The impetus for studying for a test is the desire to earn a good grade.
4. A preliminary examination is sometimes given before a major exam.
5. Earth's *atmospheric* gases help keep the planet warm.
6. I believe humankind's *destiny* is on Earth, not in space.

B. 1. When you petition the principal, you are hoping for a response.
2. Competition can motivate a person to improve her skills.
3. Repetition helps me learn new words.

Enrichment: Space Exploration, p. 135

Sample answers follow. Students may report other information about any of these missions. Note that all except *Venera 7* were launched by NASA; *Venera 7* was launched by the Soviet Union.

Apollo 11: First manned craft to land on the moon, 1969

Venera 7: First probe (unmanned craft) to land on Venus and return information from that planet, 1970

Mariner 9: First craft to orbit another planet (Mars), 1971

Pioneer 10: First craft to fly close to Jupiter and return images of that planet, 1973; first craft to pass Pluto (the last planet in the solar system) and fly beyond the solar system, 1983

Mariner 10: First craft to fly by Mercury and Venus, recording images and large quantities of information, 1974

Ulysses: Settled into an orbit over the sun's polar regions and began returning information about the sun, 1994

Galileo: Reached Jupiter's atmosphere and began returning data, 1995

Open-Book Test, p. 136

Short Answer

1. L'Amour means that everything that happened before has led to the exploration of space.
   Difficulty: *Average*   **Objective:** *Vocabulary*

2. The author wants to show the reader that progress is occurring quickly and will continue on the same path.
   Difficulty: *Easy*   **Objective:** *Interpretation*

3. It is a fact. It can be proved by measuring the miles of surfaced road.
   Difficulty: *Easy*   **Objective:** *Reading*

4. The nay-sayers are those who do not believe we should explore outer space. L'Amour thinks they are wrong and short-sighted.
   Difficulty: *Average*   **Objective:** *Interpretation*

5. L'Amour means that if we had been the sort of beings to concentrate on the here and now, we would never have invented and explored as we have. We have evolved because of our need to explore.
   Difficulty: *Challenging*   **Objective:** *Interpretation*

6. L'Amour means that the space effort gave force to the development of computers. Without that forward force, many computer devices might never have developed.
   Difficulty: *Average*   **Objective:** *Vocabulary*

7. The statement appeals to reason. It uses a logical argument based on facts.
   Difficulty: *Challenging*   **Objective:** *Literary Analysis*

8. It appeals to emotion by using the strongly emotional phrase "we have no future."
   Difficulty: *Easy*   **Objective:** *Literary Analysis*

9. Facts: In the past 70 years, we have developed cars, radios, TVs, airplanes, and electrification; we have landed men on the moon; the computer age, Teflon, and new medicines were affected by the space effort; there are now over 3,000,000 miles of paved roads.

   Opinions: The mind of mankind is not limited; the moon is just a stepping stone; it is our destiny to dare the unknown; we need leaders with perspective.

   Sample answer: The facts are more persuasive because they show what mankind is capable of in technological development and that space exploration is possible and has benefits.
   Difficulty: *Average*   **Objective:** *Reading*

10. L'Amour tries to persuade the reader to show interest in space exploration. He uses strongly emotional arguments to show that space exploration is vital to human development.
    Difficulty: *Average*   **Objective:** *Literary Analysis*

Essay

11. Students should demonstrate their understanding of appeals to emotion, pointing to places in the text where L'Amour uses language that conveys strong feelings, or appeals to reason, pointing to L'Amour's use of statistics or facts to support his arguments.
    Difficulty: *Easy*   **Objective:** *Essay*

12. Students might note that L'Amour thinks we should explore space because humans have always been explorers and outer space is the next logical step in the progression of human civilization. Students should refer to points L'Amour makes to defend their opinions of his message.
    Difficulty: *Average*   **Objective:** *Essay*

13. Students defending the statement might refer to the technological advances L'Amour cites and his statement that "we would still be hunters and gatherers" if we had not embraced progress. Students who disagree with the statement should present a well-reasoned defense of their position. They may claim that it is now too important to solve problems here on Earth to waste resources exploring space.
    Difficulty: *Challenging*   **Objective:** *Essay*

14. Students should note that L'Amour's references to the past stress that humans need to explore and invent to keep on evolving. They might point out that he believes what we have learned before now has prepared us for the future. Students might state that L'Amour feels that the past teaches us to keep reaching forward.

Difficulty: *Average* **Objective:** *Essay*

Oral Response

15. Oral responses should be clear, well organized, and well supported by appropriate examples from the selection.

Difficulty: *Average* **Objective:** *Oral Interpretation*

Selection Test A, p. 139

Critical Reading

1. ANS: A	DIF: Easy	OBJ: Reading
2. ANS: A	DIF: Easy	OBJ: Comprehension
3. ANS: A	DIF: Easy	OBJ: Interpretation
4. ANS: B	DIF: Easy	OBJ: Reading
5. ANS: D	DIF: Easy	OBJ: Comprehension
6. ANS: C	DIF: Easy	OBJ: Reading
7. ANS: C	DIF: Easy	OBJ: Comprehension
8. ANS: D	DIF: Easy	OBJ: Comprehension
9. ANS: C	DIF: Easy	OBJ: Literary Analysis
10. ANS: B	DIF: Easy	OBJ: Literary Analysis

Vocabulary and Grammar

11. ANS: A	DIF: Easy	OBJ: Vocabulary
12. ANS: C	DIF: Easy	OBJ: Vocabulary
13. ANS: D	DIF: Easy	OBJ: Grammar
14. ANS: B	DIF: Easy	OBJ: Grammar

Essay

15. Students should recognize that L'Amour is trying to persuade his readers to support the idea—to believe—that the exploration of outer space is essential to the progress of human civilization. To support their point, they might refer to the many statements L'Amour makes to support his argument—for example, that the frontier "has been a part of our thinking, waking, and sleeping since men first landed on this continent."

Difficulty: *Easy*

Objective: *Essay*

16. Students should demonstrate their understanding of appeals to emotion, pointing to places in the text where L'Amour uses language that conveys strong feelings or appeals to reason, pointing to L'Amour's use of statistics or facts to support his arguments.

Difficulty: *Easy*

Objective: *Essay*

17. Students should note that L'Amour discusses the past to show that humans need to explore and invent to move forward. They might point out that he believes what we have learned before now has prepared us for the future. Students might state that L'Amour feels that the past teaches us to keep moving forward.

Difficulty: *Average*

Objective: *Essay*

Selection Test B, p. 142

Critical Reading

1. ANS: D	DIF: Challenging	OBJ: Interpretation
2. ANS: C	DIF: Average	OBJ: Comprehension
3. ANS: A	DIF: Average	OBJ: Interpretation
4. ANS: A	DIF: Average	OBJ: Reading
5. ANS: C	DIF: Average	OBJ: Comprehension
6. ANS: B	DIF: Challenging	OBJ: Interpretation
7. ANS: B	DIF: Challenging	OBJ: Interpretation
8. ANS: D	DIF: Challenging	OBJ: Reading
9. ANS: C	DIF: Average	OBJ: Reading
10. ANS: D	DIF: Challenging	OBJ: Literary Analysis
11. ANS: D	DIF: Challenging	OBJ: Literary Analysis
12. ANS: D	DIF: Challenging	OBJ: Literary Analysis

Vocabulary and Grammar

13. ANS: A	DIF: Average	OBJ: Vocabulary
14. ANS: C	DIF: Average	OBJ: Vocabulary
15. ANS: B	DIF: Average	OBJ: Grammar
16. ANS: C	DIF: Challenging	OBJ: Grammar
17. ANS: C	DIF: Challenging	OBJ: Grammar

Essay

18. Among other reasons, students might note that L'Amour thinks we should explore outer space because human beings have always been explorers and because outer space is the logical next step in the progression of human civilization. Students should refer to points made by L'Amour (for example, that all the problems on Earth need not be solved before space exploration proceeds) in defending their opinions of his message.

Difficulty: *Average*

Objective: *Essay*

19. In defense of the statement, students may refer to the technological advances that L'Amour cites and to L'Amour's statement that "we would still be hunters and gatherers" if we had not embraced the notion of progress. Students who disagree with L'Amour should present a well-reasoned defense of their position.

Difficulty: *Challenging*

Objective: *Essay*

20. Students should note that L'Amour's references to the past stress that humans need to explore and invent to keep on evolving. They might point out that he believes what we have learned before now has prepared us for the future. Students might state that L'Amour feels that the past teaches us to keep reaching forward.

Difficulty: *Average*

Objective: *Essay*

"All Together Now" by Barbara Jordan

Vocabulary Warm-up Exercises, p. 146

A. 1. relations
2. civil
3. create
4. community
5. concerned
6. century
7. equality
8. society

B. Sample Answers

1. No; tolerance is an attitude toward others that is fair and free from emotional bias regardless of beliefs, so if someone gets annoyed when another person expresses an opinion he or she disagrees with, that person is not showing tolerance.

2. Sadly, not every country welcomes people of all backgrounds. The United States, on the other hand, does not discriminate on the basis of people's education or experience.

3. No; the practice of segregation involves separating people on the basis or race or religion, not on the basis of age or ability level.

4. No; issues of national importance are problems that affect the nation as a whole and topics that people will want to read about. Therefore, they are more likely to be found on the front page than on the sports pages of a newspaper.

5. People with positive attitudes believe they can accomplish things; and when people believe that they can be constructive, they usually are.

6. By definition, prejudices are not fair because they are based on too little information or experience with whatever is being judged.

7. A group of ninth graders would be considered an ethnic group only if all the students shared the same language, culture, and customs.

8. One fundamental belief in sports is fair play; it is essential to play by the rules.

Reading Warm-up A, p. 147

Words that students are to circle appear in parentheses.

Sample Answers

1. (the first half of the twentieth century); The twentieth century saw great advances in science.

2. the National Association for the Advancement of Colored People (NAACP); *Create* means "to cause to come into existence."

3. (only through protest and change); Society is "all of the people living at any one time."

4. the African American community; The community in which I live is racially and culturally diverse.

5. (rights); It is extremely important to protect our civil rights.

6. Washington's plan would only worsen race relations; *Concerned* means "involved or interested in."

7. (race); Relations among the people on my block are good.

8. freedom; Another figure in the struggle for equality for African Americans was Martin Luther King, Jr.

Reading Warm-up B, p. 148

Words that students are to circle appear in parentheses.

Sample Answers

1. public support; One of the important issues we face today is health care.

2. A person might demonstrate a spirit of tolerance by appreciating different cultural customs.

3. changes; One of my fundamental beliefs is that we should treat others as we want to be treated.

4. Civil rights leaders wanted an America free of segregation because segregation is demeaning and not in the best interests of society.

5. Prejudices can divide a country by leading to distrust, hatred, and unfair treatment.

6. (reasons); *Positive* means "making a definite contribution" or "constructive."

7. groups; Many ethnic groups were represented at the music festival.

8. One thing that is different about the backgrounds of people from England and people from Argentina is that they speak different languages.

Writing About the Big Question, p. 149

A. 1. information; facts
2. examine
3. analyze

B. Sample Answers

1. I had a classmate named Jill. She had her whole life planned out at the age of 15. She had already **investigated** colleges and knew where she wanted to go. She knew what kind of job she wanted and even how many children she would like to have. I am making it up as I go along.

2. Jill taught me that it is a good idea to **examine** your goals in life. After I learned about all of her plans, I began to ask **questions** about different colleges.

C. Sample Answer

Asking questions can help us get to know other people better. We should learn not to draw conclusions about people based on what they look like or what kind of job they do. Ask people questions about their lives instead. You may discover something amazing.

Reading: Fact and Opinion, p. 150

Sample Answers

1. Fact / The statement describes historical events that can be verified by checking a reference work.
2. Opinion / There is no information in the statement that can be proved true. In addition, the word *must* suggests that it is a personal judgment.
3. Fact / This statement has been proved true (by research in the field of psychology).
4. Opinion / The statement cannot be proved true. In addition, the phrase "I absolutely believe" makes clear that this is a personal judgment.
5. Opinion / The statement cannot be proved true. In addition, the use of the word *all* suggests that it is a personal judgment.

Literary Analysis: Persuasive Essay, p. 151

Sample Answers

Appeals to Authority:

1. "Think about the 1960s when Dr. Martin Luther King, Jr., was in his heyday and there were marches and protests against segregation and discrimination."
2. "President Lyndon B. Johnson pushed through the Civil Rights Act of 1964, which remains the fundamental piece of civil rights legislation in this century."

Appeals to Emotion:

1. "One thing is clear to me: We, as human beings, must be willing to accept people who are different from ourselves."

Appeals to Reason:

1. "The Voting Rights Act of 1965 ensured that everyone in our country could vote. At last, black people and white people seemed ready to live together in peace."

Vocabulary Builder, p. 152

A. Sample Answers

1. Civil rights legislation has helped to give all people in the country equal rights.
2. The fundamental rule for getting along with others is to treat everyone with respect.
3. When people are not tolerant of others, there is likely to be violence and even war.
4. Yes, I am an optimist.
5. Barbara Jordan's career culminated when she was elected to the United States House of Representatives.
6. This country was founded on the idea that everyone should enjoy equality.

B. 1. A thief is not likely to give a legitimate account of his actions.
2. I wouldn't expect an honest person to do something illegal.

3. It is not legal to cross the street when the sign reads DON'T WALK.

Enrichment: Advances in Civil Rights, p. 153

Thirteenth Amendment: abolishes slavery in all states and territories of the United States (ratified 1865)

Fourteenth Amendment: declares that all men born or naturalized in the United States are citizens and entitled to equal protection under the law (ratified 1868)

Fifteenth Amendment: declares that no citizen of the United States may be denied the right to vote on the basis of "race, color, or previous condition of servitude" (ratified 1868)

Nineteenth Amendment: gives women the right to vote (ratified 1920)

Brown v. Board of Education: overturns the principle that public schools may be segregated by race ("separate but equal"), paving the way for the integration of public schools (1954)

Montgomery bus boycott: African American boycott of segregated city buses in Montgomery, Alabama, begun by Rosa Parks in 1955, led by Martin Luther King, Jr., lasted through 1956, set off a wave of sit-ins and protests, and drew the nation's attention to the movement

Civil Rights Act of 1960: authorizes the intervention of federal authorities when states attempt to keep African Americans from registering to vote

Twenty-fourth Amendment: forbids the payment of any kind of taxes as a requirement for voting in a federal election (ratified 1964)

Civil Rights Act of 1964: outlaws racial discrimination in voting, education, public places, employment, and all federal programs

Voting Rights Act of 1965: authorizes the intervention of federal authorities to ensure that the right to vote is not denied according to the law

Civil Rights Act of 1968: outlaws discrimination in housing

"The Eternal Frontier" by Louis L'Amour
"All Together Now" by Barbara Jordan

Integrated Language Skills: Grammar, p. 154

A. Each simple subject is followed by the simple predicate.

1. Louis L'Amour, writes
2. outer space [or *simply* space], is
3. All, longs
4. we, can win
5. children, do hate
6. People, learn

B. Students should write a cohesive paragraph of at least four sentences and should demonstrate the ability to recognize simple subjects and simple predicates.

Open-Book Test, p. 157

Short Answer

1. Ms. Jordan means we have the laws we need to create a just society.
   Difficulty: *Easy*   **Objective:** *Vocabulary*

2. Ms. Jordan thinks the government should have no role. It is not the government's job to promote tolerance. She believes it is something that is learned from parents and teachers.
   Difficulty: *Challenging*   **Objective:** *Interpretation*

3. She appeals to authority, because she mentions experts and well-known people.
   Difficulty: *Easy*   **Objective:** *Literary Analysis*

4. Ms. Jordan means this legislation was the basis for other laws and was vitally important.
   Difficulty: *Average*   **Objective:** *Vocabulary*

5. It is a fact because it can be proved true.
   Difficulty: *Easy*   **Objective:** *Reading*

6. It appeals to reason. It uses logical argument backed by facts.
   Difficulty: *Challenging*   **Objective:** *Literary Analysis*

7. Ms. Jordan mentions it because it is an example of people of different ethnic backgrounds who do not get along.
   Difficulty: *Easy*   **Objective:** *Interpretation*

8. The statement uses words that convey strong feelings, such as "must be willing" and "as human beings."
   Difficulty: *Average*   **Objective:** *Literary Analysis*

9. People must tolerate people of all races and backgrounds, accepting those who are different from themselves.
   Difficulty: *Average*   **Objective:** *Interpretation*

10. Sample answer: Facts: The Civil Rights Act was passed in 1964; Voting Rights Act was passed in 1965; In 1963 there was a march on Washington. Opinions: Government cannot bring us together; Parents can do a lot to promote tolerance; Children absorb prejudice from teachers and parents.

    Students might say the opinions are more persuasive, because Ms. Jordan interprets the facts and pulls them together and gives them context through her opinions.
    Difficulty: *Average*   **Objective:** *Reading*

Essay

11. Students should recognize that Jordan believes that parents must teach their children to be tolerant of others and that everyone should work on improving human relationships. Students should demonstrate an understanding of Jordan's idea of starting small to effect widescale change. They should defend their opinion with logical reasons.
    Difficulty: *Easy*   **Objective:** *Essay*

12. Students should present a well-reasoned defense of their opinion of Jordan's remark, backed up by persuasive examples. Some students may mention the role of peers or the media in the acquisition of prejudices.
    Difficulty: *Average*   **Objective:** *Essay*

13. Students should recognize that Ms. Jordan is trying to persuade readers that individuals and especially parents must work together to create a harmonious, tolerant society. In supporting their opinions of the essay, students should present well-reasoned arguments.
    Difficulty: *Challenging*   **Objective:** *Essay*

14. Students should note that Jordan feels children must learn tolerance from adults and must learn to have a broader and more inclusive view of humanity. They may feel that children should also learn such qualities as patience, compassion, and charity from adults in order to create a harmonious society.
    Difficulty: *Average*   **Objective:** *Essay*

Oral Response

15. Oral responses should be clear, well organized, and well supported by appropriate examples from the selection.
    Difficulty: *Average*   **Objective:** *Oral Interpretation*

Selection Test A, p. 160

Critical Reading

1. ANS: C	DIF: Easy	OBJ: Comprehension
2. ANS: B	DIF: Easy	OBJ: Literary Analysis
3. ANS: B	DIF: Easy	OBJ: Interpretation
4. ANS: A	DIF: Easy	OBJ: Interpretation
5. ANS: C	DIF: Easy	OBJ: Reading
6. ANS: B	DIF: Easy	OBJ: Interpretation
7. ANS: C	DIF: Easy	OBJ: Literary Analysis
8. ANS: C	DIF: Easy	OBJ: Comprehension
9. ANS: A	DIF: Easy	OBJ: Literary Analysis
10. ANS: D	DIF: Easy	OBJ: Interpretation

Vocabulary and Grammar

11. ANS: A	DIF: Easy	OBJ: Vocabulary
12. ANS: D	DIF: Easy	OBJ: Vocabulary
13. ANS: C	DIF: Easy	OBJ: Grammar
14. ANS: B	DIF: Easy	OBJ: Grammar

Essay

15. Students should recognize that Jordan believes parents must teach their children to be tolerant of others who are different from them and that everyone should "work on human relationships in every area of our lives." In defending their opinion of the effectiveness of starting

small to effect widescale change, students should demonstrate an understanding of the idea and defend their
opinion with logical reasons.

Difficulty: *Easy*

Objective: *Essay*

16. As an example of an appeal to emotion, students might
cite Jordan's reference to Bosnia, her strong words
about the innocence of young children, or her belief in
the power of love. As an example of an appeal to reason,
they might cite Jordan's ideas about teaching tolerance
to young children. In expressing an opinion of the effectiveness of Jordan's use of emotion and reason, students should make well-reasoned arguments.

Difficulty: *Easy*

Objective: *Essay*

17. Students should note that Jordan feels that what
children should learn from adults is to understand
people from different backgrounds. Students may feel
that children should also learn such qualities as
patience, compassion, and charity from adults.

Difficulty: *Average*

Objective: *Essay*

Selection Test B, p. 163

Critical Reading

1. ANS: C	DIF: Challenging	OBJ: Interpretation
2. ANS: A	DIF: Average	OBJ: Comprehension
3. ANS: A	DIF: Average	OBJ: Literary Analysis
4. ANS: C	DIF: Average	OBJ: Comprehension
5. ANS: D	DIF: Average	OBJ: Comprehension
6. ANS: D	DIF: Challenging	OBJ: Literary Analysis
7. ANS: B	DIF: Average	OBJ: Interpretation
8. ANS: B	DIF: Average	OBJ: Interpretation
9. ANS: D	DIF: Challenging	OBJ: Reading
10. ANS: A	DIF: Average	OBJ: Reading
11. ANS: B	DIF: Average	OBJ: Interpretation
12. ANS: C	DIF: Average	OBJ: Literary Analysis
13. ANS: B	DIF: Average	OBJ: Reading

Vocabulary and Grammar

14. ANS: D	DIF: Average	OBJ: Vocabulary
15. ANS: B	DIF: Challenging	OBJ: Vocabulary
16. ANS: A	DIF: Average	OBJ: Grammar
17. ANS: B	DIF: Average	OBJ: Grammar

Essay

18. Students should present a well-reasoned defense of
their opinion of Jordan's remark, backed up by persuasive examples. Some students may mention the role of
peers in the acquisition of prejudices.

Difficulty: *Average*

Objective: *Essay*

19. Students should recognize that Jordan is trying to
persuade readers that individuals, and especially
parents, must work together on a small scale to create a
harmonious, tolerant society. In supporting their
opinion of the effectiveness of Jordan's essay, students
should present well-reasoned arguments.

Difficulty: *Average*

Objective: *Essay*

20. Students should note that Jordan feels children must
learn tolerance from adults and must learn to have a
broader and more inclusive view of humanity. They may
feel that children should also learn such qualities as
patience, compassion, and charity from adults in order
to create a harmonious society.

Difficulty: *Average*

Objective: *Essay*

"The Real Story of a Cowboy's Life"
by Geoffrey C. Ward

Vocabulary Warm-up Exercises, p. 167

A. 1. series
2. experienced
3. Regardless
4. territory
5. settlement
6. claim
7. alarming
8. rarely

B. Sample Answers

1. control; We taught our dog to control his barking.
2. put into effect; The crossing guard tried to put into
effect the law against jaywalking.
3. dislike; The boy felt a strong dislike for his neighbor's
mean dog.
4. animals; The rancher's animals required a lot of food
and care.
5. place; Ann looked forward to reaching her place.
6. tame; There is no such thing as a tame cheetah.
7. edge; The shy boy stood on the edge of the crowd.
8. responsible; The woman felt responsible for the mess
she was in.

Reading Warm-up A, p. 168

Words that students are to circle appear in parentheses.

Sample Answers

1. the behavior of cattle; I am experienced in gymnastics.
2. because rivers, streams, and other watering places were
plentiful; *seldom*
3. (of events); A series is a number of related things that
follow in order.
4. (to land); The pioneers stated that the land was theirs.

5. (place), (town); The settlement grew into a town.
6. the fences kept cattle away from sources of water; I find the number of homeless people in our cities alarming.
7. (western); They argued that the western region should provide free grazing and water for all animals.
8. the fences stayed, and the days of the long drive came to an end; *Regardless* means "in spite of."

Reading Warm-up B, p. 169

Words that students are to circle appear in parentheses.

Sample Answers

1. (the pasture); just beyond the edge of the pasture
2. They trample the fields and muddy the water; We have to learn to overcome our hostility and make peace with our enemies.
3. by putting up barbed-wire fences; I would like to enforce the rules that prohibit littering.
4. (open-range cattle); My favorite domestic animal is my cat, although she thinks she is a tiger.
5. (cows), (goats); Sometimes, though, cows, goats, and other farm animals would escape through breaks in the fence.
6. the way they worked together on horseback, turning and tightening the herd into a single moving mass; *Discipline* means "control over behavior."
7. (Wichita, Kansas); We reached our destination at 3:30 in the afternoon.
8. knowing how his father disliked them; The woman was proved innocent of all charges against her.

Writing About the Big Question, p. 170

A. 1. question
2. evaluate
3. discover

B. Sample Answers

1. I'd like to **explore** the profession of teaching because I like working with kids. I'd like to help nurture their natural **curiosity** with new **information**.
2. One job that doesn't interest me is police work. I have no **curiosity** about how people break the law. I would not enjoy **discovering** all of the illegal things happening around me.

C. Sample Answer

Talking to people who participated in an event can change the way you view things. Much of what we think we know comes from movies, but screenwriters make things more exciting than they were in real life. Only the people who were there can tell you what really happened. We should learn to be more suspicious of the conventional wisdom and ask more questions.

Reading: Use Resources to Check Facts, p. 171

1. Fact / encyclopedia *or* reliable Web site
2. Fact / atlas

3. Opinion
4. Fact / encyclopedia *or* reliable Web site

Literary Analysis: Word Choice and Diction, p. 172

Sample answers are provided; in some cases, the distinction between *technical vocabulary* and *informal language* is negligible:

1. *Technical vocabulary:* "on herd," "into a mill," "duct banks"; *Informal language:* "jump for your horse," "trying to head them," "a dead run," "land you in a shallow grave"; *Formal language:* none
2. *Technical vocabulary:* "Texas fever," "quarantine lines"; *Informal language:* "deadlines; *Formal language:* "devastated . . . livestock," "at the western fringe of settlement," "insisted that trail drives not cross them"

Vocabulary Builder, p. 173

A. 1. ultimate
2. diversions
3. gauge
4. discipline
5. emphatic
6. Longhorns

B. 1. If you reverse direction, you go in the opposite way.
2. If you behave in a subversive manner, you are not being supportive.
3. A versatile employee can handle many different responsibilities.

Enrichment: Cowboy Songs, p. 174

Sample Answers

1. He does not want to be buried alone in a deserted place far from his home and family.
2. He warns the others not to leave home for the prairie. He is miserable because he is dying far from his family, and he does not want the others to suffer as he is suffering.
3. He loves his home and family and despises the prairie. The other cowboys may love the adventure of their work and so may not share the dying cowboy's thoughts.

Open-Book Test, p. 175

Short Answer

1. An encyclopedia, because it would give an explanation of the history of the cowboy. Students might also suggest checking an online encyclopedia.
   Difficulty: *Easy*   **Objective:** *Reading*
2. The terms "point" and "swing," which have a specific meaning in cowboy life, are explained as the head and sides of a long herd.
   Difficulty: *Challenging*   **Objective:** *Literary Analysis*
3. The choice of the words "gauge" and "temperament" are formal.
   Difficulty: *Easy*   **Objective:** *Literary Analysis*

4. A cowboy has to judge how the cattle might behave. If he didn't, they might get out of control before he could stop it.
Difficulty: *Challenging*   **Objective:** *Vocabulary*

5. It suggests that cattle are jittery. The essay describes how the cowboys have to work hard to keep them calm and how a sound, smell, or movement could make them stampede.
Difficulty: *Easy*   **Objective:** *Interpretation*

6. An atlas, because an atlas is a book of maps that includes landforms and water.
Difficulty: *Average*   **Objective:** *Reading*

7. It conveys an informal feeling, because the author has chosen to include the slang term "punkins."
Difficulty: *Average*   **Objective:** *Literary Analysis*

8. It tells the reader that a cowboy's life could be very dangerous. The fact that they rode with their guns across the saddle implies that they faced danger every day.
Difficulty: *Challenging*   **Objective:** *Interpretation*

9. The cowboys might have paid too little attention to their jobs if there had been many amusements to distract them.
Difficulty: *Average*   **Objective:** *Vocabulary*

10. Traits a Cowboy Needs: ability to work in a team; ability to gauge the temperament of cattle
   Traits a Trail Boss Needs: ability to keep order and apply discipline; ability to make decisions
   Trail boss. Essay says the most experienced men rode at the head.
Difficulty: *Average*   **Objective:** *Interpretation*

Essay

11. Students should recognize that the informal language is found in the cowboys' speech. This has the effect of giving readers a sense of how cowboys spoke and what their interests were.
Difficulty: *Easy*   **Objective:** *Essay*

12. Students should recognize that the "article of agreement" suggests that cowboys were rough and inclined to resort to violence. Strict discipline was required to keep cattle drives under control. Students might recognize that Goodnight felt his agreement helped to maintain peace, but there is no evidence to suggest that there were shootings on other bosses' drives or that the agreement was necessarily what kept Goodnight's drives peaceful.
Difficulty: *Average*   **Objective:** *Essay*

13. Students should recognize that Ward's essay is a fairly successful attempt to describe the life of a nineteenth-century cowboy. Most will probably say that the first-hand accounts help bring the essay to life. They may suggest that aspects of the subject could be covered in greater depth, such as the cowboys' home life and the time between cattle drives.
Difficulty: *Challenging*   **Objective:** *Essay*

14. Students may note that the idea of cowboys has been romanticized by movies and music. They should point out that the essay tells what it was really like to be a cowboy. This information provides a deeper understanding of the hardships cowboys faced as they shaped the West.
Difficulty: *Average*   **Objective:** *Essay*

Oral Response

15. Oral responses should be clear, well organized, and well supported by appropriate examples from the selection.
Difficulty: *Average*   **Objective:** *Oral Presentation*

Selection Test A, p. 178

Critical Reading

1. ANS: C	DIF: Easy	OBJ: Literary Analysis
2. ANS: B	DIF: Easy	OBJ: Comprehension
3. ANS: A	DIF: Easy	OBJ: Comprehension
4. ANS: B	DIF: Easy	OBJ: Comprehension
5. ANS: B	DIF: Easy	OBJ: Reading
6. ANS: B	DIF: Easy	OBJ: Literary Analysis
7. ANS: C	DIF: Easy	OBJ: Comprehension
8. ANS: B	DIF: Easy	OBJ: Comprehension
9. ANS: B	DIF: Easy	OBJ: Interpretation
10. ANS: D	DIF: Easy	OBJ: Reading
11. ANS: D	DIF: Easy	OBJ: Interpretation

Vocabulary and Grammar

12. ANS: B	DIF: Easy	OBJ: Vocabulary
13. ANS: A	DIF: Easy	OBJ: Vocabulary
14. ANS: B	DIF: Easy	OBJ: Grammar
15. ANS: C	DIF: Easy	OBJ: Grammar

Essay

16. Students should recognize that a trail boss needed to know about horses, horseback riding, and cattle. He also had to be capable of maintaining order and discipline. Goodnight showed these qualities by requiring that men sign "an article of agreement" and by banning guns, liquor, and gambling.
Difficulty: *Easy*
Objective: *Essay*

17. Students should recognize that all of the informal language is in the cowboys' speech—in the many quotations that Ward uses to make vivid the details of the cowboys' life on the trail. Students may point out that this language has the effect of giving readers a sense of how the cowboys spoke, what they were interested in, and so on.
Difficulty: *Easy*
Objective: *Essay*

18. Students may note that the movies and music portray cowboys in a very romantic way. This essay, however, tells what it was really like to be a cowboy. This information provides a deeper understanding of the hardships cowboys faced as they shaped the West.

Difficulty: *Average*

Objective: *Essay*

Selection Test B, p. 181

Critical Reading

1. ANS: C	DIF: Average	OBJ: Reading
2. ANS: B	DIF: Average	OBJ: Comprehension
3. ANS: D	DIF: Average	OBJ: Comprehension
4. ANS: A	DIF: Average	OBJ: Interpretation
5. ANS: B	DIF: Average	OBJ: Interpretation
6. ANS: B	DIF: Average	OBJ: Reading
7. ANS: C	DIF: Challenging	OBJ: Literary Analysis
8. ANS: A	DIF: Average	OBJ: Comprehension
9. ANS: A	DIF: Challenging	OBJ: Literary Analysis
10. ANS: A	DIF: Average	OBJ: Literary Analysis
11. ANS: A	DIF: Challenging	OBJ: Interpretation

Vocabulary and Grammar

12. ANS: C	DIF: Average	OBJ: Vocabulary
13. ANS: C	DIF: Average	OBJ: Vocabulary
14. ANS: C	DIF: Challenging	OBJ: Vocabulary
15. ANS: C	DIF: Average	OBJ: Grammar
16. ANS: B	DIF: Average	OBJ: Grammar
17. ANS: D	DIF: Average	OBJ: Grammar

Essay

18. Students should recognize that the "article of agreement" suggests that cowboys were rough and inclined to resort to violence and that strict discipline was required to keep cattle drives under control. Students might recognize that Goodnight seems to attribute the absence of shootings on his drives to his agreement, but there is no evidence to suggest that there were shootings on other boss's drives or that the agreement was necessarily what kept Goodnight's drives peaceful.

Difficulty: *Average*

Objective: *Essay*

19. Students should recognize that Ward's essay is a fairly successful attempt to describe the life of a nineteenth-century cattle drive, and most will probably say that the firsthand accounts help to bring the essay to life. They should recognize, however, that by its nature, an essay cannot present a complete picture, and students should suggest aspects of the subject that might be covered in greater depth.

Difficulty: *Challenging*

Objective: *Essay*

20. Students may note that the idea of cowboys has been romanticized by movies and music. They should point out that the essay tells what it was really like to be a cowboy. This information provides a deeper understanding of the hardships cowboys faced as they shaped the West.

Difficulty: *Average*

Objective: *Essay*

"Rattlesnake Hunt"
by Marjorie Kinnan Rawlings

Vocabulary Warm-up Exercises, p. 185

A. 1. horizon
2. clammy
3. marsh
4. region
5. defense
6. casually
7. blunt
8. boldness

B. Sample Answers

1. Yes, good health is more desirable than a lot of money because without it you cannot enjoy anything, including your money.
2. Yes, a scientific principle is usually accepted as a fact because science is based on facts.
3. No; a camouflaged animal has hidden or disappeared into its surroundings, so it would not be easy to find.
4. No, reptiles prefer warmer climates because they need the sun to warm their blood.
5. No, hats of varying styles will come in different shapes, sizes, and colors, because *varying* means "having differing qualities."
6. No, aggressors attack without warning and therefore cannot be trusted with weaker creatures.
7. Yes, you should, because there are no stores and no electricity in the wilds.
8. Yes, a yard filled with vegetation would have plenty of greenery because vegetation is a covering of plants and plants are usually green.

Reading Warm-up A, p. 186

Words that students are to circle appear in parentheses.

Sample Answers

1. where the flat grasslands touched the sky; The morning star rose above the horizon.
2. without a trace of care; "We should stay where we are," Petra said nervously, showing how concerned she was.
3. (western); I live in the Northwest.
4. soggy; The marsh is a good place for ducks.
5. Alicia had never ventured into a marsh before; Alicia's bravery was surprising.

6. (to use in defense against those alligators and poisonous snakes that were surely eyeing her soft flesh); I use a sharp knife to cut tomatoes.

7. those alligators and poisonous snakes that were surely eyeing her soft flesh; Defense is a method of protecting something.

8. Her skin; Her skin felt suddenly dry, and she had run back to the main trail into a worse nightmare.

Reading Warm-up B, p. 187

Words that students are to circle appear in parentheses.

Sample Answers

1. (Snakes); Even strong animals must sometimes play the part of defenders.

2. (hidden); The deer, camouflaged in the forest, escaped from the hunter.

3. (leafy); There is a lot of vegetation in our backyard.

4. the amount of venom it ejects when it bites; How much I study is a varying factor that affects my grades.

5. (of Australia); I have been in the wilds of Yosemite National Park.

6. uncovering other desirable benefits of snake venom; Many scientific discoveries have made life better for all humankind.

7. venom may be useful in preventing heart attacks, strokes, cancer and other diseases; The benefits are desirable because they help people live longer, healthier lives.

8. (snakes); Other reptiles include alligators and lizards.

Writing About the Big Question, p. 188

A. 1. interview; question

2. analyze; understand; investigate; explore; evaluate; discover

3. experiment

B. Sample Answers

1. I went to a scary movie with my brother. I **discovered** that I'm afraid of scary movies. I even had to leave the theater in the middle of the film.

2. My cousin is afraid of mushrooms. She won't eat mushrooms. If she sees one outside, she screams and runs away. I can **understand** not liking the way mushrooms taste, but why run away from something that can't move?

C. Sample Answer

The more we understand something, the less strange and frightening it seems. When I was in preschool, I was afraid of my elementary school building. The gangs of students hanging around frightened me. They made a lot of noise. The first day of school in kindergarten was hard. Once I got to know some of the other students, however, I lost my fear. We should learn to confront our fears.

Reading: Use Resources to Check Facts, p. 189

1. Fact / atlas *or* geographical dictionary

2. Fact / encyclopedia *or* reliable Web site

3. Fact / encyclopedia *or* reliable Web site

4. Opinion

5. Fact / encyclopedia *or* reliable Web site

Literary Analysis: Word Choice and Diction, p. 190

Sample answers are provided; in some cases, the distinction between *technical vocabulary* and *informal language* is negligible.

1. *Technical vocabulary:* "forage"; *Informal language:* none; *Formal language:* the entire passage

2. *Technical vocabulary:* "L-shaped steel"; *Informal language:* "rattlers"; *Formal language:* the rest of the passage

3. *Technical vocabulary:* none; *Informal language:* none; *Formal language:* the entire passage

Vocabulary Builder, p. 191

A. Sample Answers

1. False / An arid region is dry, so crops will not grow there easily.

2. False / The character is facing the knowledge that he will die eventually.

3. True / A desolate, or lonely, location will create a lonely mood.

4. True/ Adequate means sufficient. It is important to make sufficient precautions around dangerous animals.

5. True/ The word *forage* usually refers to food that animals find themselves in fields, etc. Cattle are often fed this way.

6. False/ Windows are almost always translucent — meaning that we can see through them.

B. 1. Only one person plays a game of solitaire.

2. If you seek solitude, you wish to be alone.

3. One person at a time plays a solo.

Enrichment: Dangerous Snakes, p. 192

Sample Answers

Kind of snake: king cobra

1. King cobras live in the highland forests of southern Asia and in the mountains of India.

2. King cobras are brown or black with smooth, shiny skin. They have light-colored spots on the back of the neck and are distinguished by bones around the neck that form what looks like a hood. They are usually about 13 feet long but may grow as long as 18 feet.

3. King cobras eat only meat, lizards, and other snakes.

4. Victims of the king cobra die within 15 minutes of being struck with the snake's venom.

5. The king cobra flattens out the bones around its neck, forming its "hood," before it strikes.

"The Real Story of a Cowboy's Life"
by Geoffrey C. Ward
"Rattlesnake Hunt" by Marjorie Kinnan Rawlings

Integrated Language Skills: Grammar, p. 193

A. Words to be underlined are noted.
1. *compound predicate:* keep, guide
2. *compound subject:* bosses, cowboys
3. *compound predicate:* pay, face
4. *compound predicate:* forbid, punish
5. *compound predicate:* warn, strike
6. *compound subject:* Snakes, reptiles
7. *compound subject:* Sun, temperatures
8. *compound predicate:* must move, suffer

B. Sample Answers
1. We walked through the underbrush and searched for rattlesnakes.
2. Insects and snakes moved about in the bushes.
3. A snake hissed and rattled just ahead of us.
4. We found the snake and caught it quickly.

Open-Book Test, p. 196

Short Answer

1. *Herpetologist* means someone who studies reptiles and amphibians.
   Difficulty: *Average*   **Objective:** *Literary Analysis*
2. It conveys a formal feeling. The words "dispassionate detachment," are formal words.
   Difficulty: *Easy*   **Objective:** *Literary Analysis*
3. You would probably use an atlas because it includes maps with landforms, water, and directions.
   Difficulty: *Easy*   **Objective:** *Reading*
4. The isolated and featureless setting reflects the author's fear at first. Later, her description of the setting becomes less lonely and solitary and more lush, reflecting her change of mood.
   Difficulty: *Challenging*   **Objective:** *Vocabulary*
5. The passage conveys a feeling of triumph. The phrase "upsurgence of spirit" creates a triumphant feeling.
   Difficulty: *Challenging*   **Objective:** *Literary Analysis*
6. She learns that the snake is not frightening but is a living thing like herself, as she states: "a thing that lived and breathed and had mortality like the rest of us."
   Difficulty: *Challenging*   **Objective:** *Interpretation*
7. She realizes that the snake will eventually die.
   Difficulty: *Average*   **Objective:** *Vocabulary*

8. a reliable Web site or an encyclopedia
   Difficulty: *Average*   **Objective:** *Reading*
9. It is more important to know snakes' habits, because if you can think like a snake and if you know what it will do, you can catch it.
   Difficulty: *Easy*   **Objective:** *Interpretation*
10. Beginning: She is fearful and hesitant; she doesn't want to touch the snakes.
    End: She has conquered her fear; she finds snakes fascinating and is even able to touch them.
    Rawlings has learned about the habits of rattlesnakes and learned she could overcome her fear.
    Difficulty: *Average*   **Objective:** *Interpretation*

Essay

11. Students should recognize that at the beginning of her article, Rawlings is afraid of snakes. They might point out that by learning about them and watching them, and, eventually, by picking one up, she becomes less fearful at the end of the article.
    Difficulty: *Easy*   **Objective:** *Essay*
12. Students should identify two facts and should note that Ross provides the information because he wants Rawlings to write an article about his work. He also wants to lessen her fear of snakes.
    Difficulty: *Average*   **Objective:** *Essay*
13. Students should recognize that Rawlings is saying that she has always been afraid of snakes, but that the experience of the past day has reduced her fear dramatically. In discussing the diction, students might recognize that the author uses humorous exaggeration and repetition to emphasize her point.
    Difficulty: *Challenging*   **Objective:** *Essay*
14. Students should point out that Rawlings learns to overcome fear by facing it directly and by learning more about the thing that frightens her. She learns by listening to an expert and faces her fear by trying to catch rattlesnakes. Students may feel that this lesson is one most readers could apply to their own lives in facing and overcoming fears.
    Difficulty: *Average*   **Objective:** *Essay*

Oral Response

15. Oral responses should be clear, well organized, and well supported by appropriate examples from the selection.
    Difficulty: *Average*   **Objective:** *Oral Interpretation*

Selection Test A, p. 199
Critical Reading

1. **ANS:** C	**DIF:** Easy	**OBJ:** Literary Analysis
2. **ANS:** A	**DIF:** Easy	**OBJ:** Literary Analysis
3. **ANS:** B	**DIF:** Easy	**OBJ:** Interpretation
4. **ANS:** A	**DIF:** Easy	**OBJ:** Reading

5. ANS: B	DIF: Easy	OBJ: Comprehension
6. ANS: C	DIF: Easy	OBJ: Reading
7. ANS: A	DIF: Easy	OBJ: Comprehension
8. ANS: A	DIF: Easy	OBJ: Interpretation
9. ANS: D	DIF: Easy	OBJ: Comprehension
10. ANS: B	DIF: Easy	OBJ: Interpretation
11. ANS: C	DIF: Easy	OBJ: Interpretation

Vocabulary and Grammar

12. ANS: B	DIF: Easy	OBJ: Vocabulary
13. ANS: D	DIF: Easy	OBJ: Vocabulary
14. ANS: B	DIF: Easy	OBJ: Grammar
15. ANS: A	DIF: Easy	OBJ: Grammar

Essay

16. Students should recognize that at the beginning of the selection, Rawlings is frightened of snakes. They might point to the statement she makes early on—"it is difficult to be afraid of anything about which enough is known"—in explaining that the more Rawlings learns, the less fearful she becomes. They might also point out that she learns not just by listening to Ross and Will but by watching them and, eventually, by picking up a rattlesnake, carrying it to the truck, and trying to land it in the truck.

Difficulty: *Easy*
Objective: *Essay*

17. Students should identify two or three facts revealed in the essay—for example, that snakes are coldblooded, that they strike only when threatened or hungry, that they are not slimy, and that they live in holes. In citing a fact that Ross demonstrates, they might point to the snake that is "draped limply over the steel L" as evidence that snakes are sluggish when the weather is cool.

Difficulty: *Easy*
Objective: *Essay*

18. Students should point out that Rawlings learns to overcome fear by facing it directly and by learning more about the thing that frightens her. She learns by listening to an expert and faces her fear by trying to catch rattlesnakes.

Difficulty: *Average*
Objective: *Essay*

Selection Test B, p. 202

Critical Reading

1. ANS: A	DIF: Challenging	OBJ: Interpretation
2. ANS: C	DIF: Average	OBJ: Interpretation
3. ANS: A	DIF: Average	OBJ: Interpretation
4. ANS: B	DIF: Average	OBJ: Reading
5. ANS: B	DIF: Average	OBJ: Comprehension
6. ANS: D	DIF: Challenging	OBJ: Interpretation

7. ANS: C	DIF: Challenging	OBJ: Literary Analysis
8. ANS: A	DIF: Challenging	OBJ: Literary Analysis
9. ANS: A	DIF: Average	OBJ: Reading
10. ANS: A	DIF: Average	OBJ: Literary Analysis
11. ANS: B	DIF: Challenging	OBJ: Interpretation
12. ANS: B	DIF: Average	OBJ: Interpretation

Vocabulary and Grammar

13. ANS: D	DIF: Average	OBJ: Vocabulary
14. ANS: A	DIF: Average	OBJ: Vocabulary
15. ANS: C	DIF: Challenging	OBJ: Vocabulary
16. ANS: B	DIF: Average	OBJ: Grammar
17. ANS: A	DIF: Average	OBJ: Grammar
18. ANS: C	DIF: Average	OBJ: Grammar

Essay

19. Students should identify two facts—for example, that snakes are coldblooded and not slimy, that rattlesnakes strike only when threatened or hungry and live in holes. Students should note that Ross provides the information largely because he wants Rawlings to write an article about his work, but the information also has the effect of lessening Rawlings's fear of snakes.

Difficulty: *Average*
Objective: *Essay*

20. Students should recognize that Rawlings is saying that she has always been afraid of rattlesnakes and if she had come upon one before having spent a day learning about them and seeing Ross and Will handle them, she would have been indescribably frightened, but the experience of the past day has reduced her fear drastically. In discussing the diction, students might recognize that Rawlings uses (somewhat humorous) exaggeration and repetition to emphasize her point.

Difficulty: *Challenging*
Objective: *Essay*

21. Students should point out that Rawlings learns to overcome fear by facing it directly and by learning more about the thing that frightens her. She learns by listening to an expert and faces her fear by trying to catch rattlesnakes. Students may feel that this lesson is one most readers could apply to their own lives in facing and overcoming fears.

Difficulty: *Average*   **Objective:** *Essay*

"The Cremation of Sam McGee" by Robert Service
"Alligator" by Bailey White

Vocabulary Warm-up Exercises, p. 206

A. 1. bellow
2. craning
3. stern
4. dread

5. haul
6. raved
7. quality
8. seldom

B. Sample Answers

1. No, a grown alligator would not be able to hide under a pebble because an alligator is a large reptile.
2. Yes, because cattails are marsh plants with brown furry flowers.
3. If a cat is crouched behind a bush, eyeing a bird, the next thing it might do is jump up to try to catch the bird.
4. No, if I wore a long raincoat, my clothing would not get drenched because the raincoat would protect me.
5. Yes, a scream can be described as ghastly, especially if it is frightening.
6. If a boy howled and held his knee, I would suppose that he had hurt his knee.
7. A person must be situated in the driver's seat to drive a car.
8. I am more likely to say *please* when making a request.

Reading Warm-up A, p. 207

Sample Answers

1. (freshness); loyalty
2. He knows the trails by heart. I seldom skip meals.
3. (bed) People might haul luggage to the airport.
4. the trunk of a giant pine; stretching
5. (harsh)
6. The noise came from deep within the animal and echoed though the trees. An alligator might bellow.
7. (fears); great fear or uneasiness, especially about something in the future
8. the sound that had roared through the camp that morning; My uncle raved about the new ice cream parlor on the corner.

Reading Warm-up B, p. 208

Sample Answers

1. a large reptile that lives in freshwater swamps, lakes, and marshes
2. Jenny's request was to first visit the alligator swamp. May I have another slice of pizza, please?
3. too near the tank; located
4. by the cascades of water that the unlikely mammals sent spewing into the audience; I got drenched when I got caught in a rainstorm.
5. to see if she could spot any of the alligators hiding in the cattails; stooped down with the knees bent
6. (tall marsh plants); tall marsh plants with brown, furry flowers.
7. (fright); Joe howled when he stubbed his toe on the leg of the table.

8. (scream); terrifying
9. elter, and raising children.

Writing About the Big Question, p. 209

A.
1. curiosity
2. discover
3. explore; investigate

B. Sample Answers

1. Spending time with small children makes me laugh. I love watching little kids **explore** the world, and I find the **questions** they ask so funny. Lastly, kids make me remember a less complicated time in my own life and that makes me happy.
2. Laughing is a great way to get rid of stress. After spending my lunch hour laughing with my friends, I always feel happier and more awake. A scientist should **experiment** to find out if students do better in the classes they have right after lunch. I wouldn't be surprised if careful **analysis** showed that laughter was the cause.

C. Sample Answer

The funniest things happen when you are trying hard to be serious. My sister and I always crack up during family meetings. My mother is usually talking very seriously about following rules. Even though we understand what Mom is saying, her serious tone just makes us laugh. We should learn to show more respect.

Literary Analysis: Comparing Humorous Essays
p. 210

Sample answers

1. "Alligator": Yes, the alligator comes out of the water to meet Aunt Belle.

   "Sam McGee": Yes, Sam McGee comes back to life after being "cremated."
2. "Alligator": Yes, the writer thinks she hears an alligator bellowing at night.

   "Sam McGee": Yes, the writer describes reality of the icy cold Arctic trails and the dog sleds but also what turns out to be the mistaken view that Sam is dead.
3. "Alligator": Yes, Aunt Belle is going to show the alligator who's boss.

   "Sam McGee": Yes, the writer exaggerates the when he calls the boat he crematorium and when he describes the soaring flames. Sam exaggerates when he says that the roaring fire
4. "Alligator": Aunt Belle is the funniest because she shows off her taming of the alligator.

   "Sam McGee": The narrator is funniest when he describes singing to the corpse and when he calls the corpse his frozen chum, and when he says that he guesses Sam is cooked.

Vocabulary Builder, p. 211

A. Sample Answers

1. Cattails grow in marshes or swamps, not deserts. / On our visit to the wetlands, we found cattails growing everywhere.
2. This sentence makes sense because a crowd roars when a referee makes an unfair call.
3. This sentence does not make sense because the student wouldn't be happy to be in last place. / When she discovered she had come in first place, the student was exultant.
4. This sentence makes sense because it is sad to hear a dog whimper, or whine.
5. This sentence does not make sense because people like to eat delicious things. / Maria loathed mushrooms because she didn't like the way they tasted.

B. 1. B; 2. A; 3. B; 4. C; 5. A

Open-Book Test, p. 213

Short Answer

1. The alligator is afraid of Aunt Belle.
   Difficulty: *Easy*   **Objective:** *Interpretation*
2. A bellow is a sound that is loud and deep and has a vibrating quality.
   Difficulty: *Challenging*   **Objective:** *Vocabulary*
3. Sample answer: Aunt Belle's children are grown, she is lonely, and the alligator keeps her company.
   Difficulty: *Average*   **Objective:** *Interpretation*
4. Sample answer: This information gives the poem a strange, suspenseful feeling.
   Difficulty: *Challenging*   **Objective:** *Interpretation*
5. The speaker continues to carry his friend because he has made a promise and wants to honor the man's last wish to be cremated.
   Difficulty: *Average*   **Objective:** *Interpretation*
6. Sam McGee hated the extremely cold temperatures.
   Difficulty: *Average*   **Objective:** *Vocabulary*
7. Sample answer: "Alligator": The alligator is scared of Aunt Belle, rather than vice versa. "The Cremation of Sam McGee": Sam McGee survives his own cremation. Students' should support their humorous choice with at least one reason or example.
   Difficulty: *Average*   **Objective:** *Literary Analysis*
8. Sample answer: "Alligator": the narrator says that the kids didn't want to miss it if the alligator ate up Aunt Belle. "Sam McGee": Sam McGee says "he'd sooner live in hell."
   Difficulty: *Easy*   **Objective:** *Literary Analysis*
9. Students' responses will vary, but should be supported with a logical reason.
   Difficulty: *Average*   **Objective:** *Literary Analysis*
10. Sample answer: The author of "Alligator" wants you to feel peaceful and at one with nature; the author of "Sam McGee" wants you to feel surprised and amused.
    Difficulty: *Challenging*   **Objective:** *Literary Analysis*

Essay

11. Students may respond that Aunt Belle is unusual because she takes on the challenge of taming an alligator and succeeds; Sam McGee is unusual because he goes to the Yukon even though he hates the cold and seems to survive and enjoy his own cremation. Students should also tell which character they find more humorous and support their opinion with sound reasoning.
    Difficulty: *Easy*   **Objective:** *Essay*
12. Students who choose "Alligator" may identify a theme relating to Aunt Belle's deep connection with nature or the acceptance of aging; those who choose "Sam McGee" may identify a theme relating to the keeping of promises or the harshness of a hostile environment. Students should also note that by using humor to convey these messages, the authors make the messages stronger, more enjoyable, and more memorable.
    Difficulty: *Average*   **Objective:** *Essay*
13. Students should cite one passage from each essay and explain the techniques the author uses to create the humor.
    Difficulty: *Challenging*   **Objective:** *Essay*
14. Students may respond that Bailey White wants us to learn to work with nature rather than against it; or Robert Service wants us to learn to keep promises. Students should say why the lesson is worth learning and support their answer with sound reasoning.
    Difficulty: *Average*   **Objective:** *Essay*

Oral Response

15. Oral responses should be clear, well organized, and well supported by appropriate examples from the selections.
    Difficulty: *Average*   **Objective:** *Oral Interpretation*

Selection Test A, p. 216

Critical Reading

1. ANS: B	DIF: Easy	OBJ: Comprehension
2. ANS: D	DIF: Easy	OBJ: Comprehension
3. ANS: D	DIF: Easy	OBJ: Interpretation
4. ANS: B	DIF: Easy	OBJ: Interpretation
5. ANS: C	DIF: Easy	OBJ: Comprehension
6. ANS: C	DIF: Easy	OBJ: Comprehension
7. ANS: D	DIF: Easy	OBJ: Comprehension
8. ANS: D	DIF: Easy	OBJ: Comprehension
9. ANS: B	DIF: Easy	OBJ: Literary Analysis
10. ANS: C	DIF: Easy	OBJ: Literary Analysis

Vocabulary

11. ANS: C	DIF: Easy	OBJ: Vocabulary
12. ANS: B	DIF: Easy	OBJ: Vocabulary
13. ANS: A	DIF: Easy	OBJ: Vocabulary
14. ANS: A	DIF: Easy	OBJ: Vocabulary

Unit 3 Resources: Types of Nonfiction
274

Essay

15. Students should point to two examples of humor in each essay, state which essay they find more humorous, and offer logical reasons to support their opinions.

    Difficulty: *Easy*

    Objective: *Vocabulary*

16. In comparing White's Aunt Belle with one of Thurber's relatives in "The Night the Bed Fell," students should point to illogical, inappropriate, or unusual situations, the contrast between the character's view of himself or herself and reality, and/or the use of exaggeration to create a sense of humor. Students should present well-supported, logical opinions of the character they find funnier.

    Difficulty: *Easy*

    Objective: *Essay*

17. Students may respond that Bailey White wants us to learn to work with nature rather than against it. Robert Service wants us to learn to keep promises. Students should say why the lesson is worth learning and should support their answer with sound reasoning.

    Difficulty: *Average*

    Objective: *Essay*

Selection Test B, p. 219

Critical Reading

1. ANS: A	DIF: Average	OBJ: Literary Analysis
2. ANS: B	DIF: Average	OBJ: Comprehension
3. ANS: D	DIF: Challenging	OBJ: Interpretation
4. ANS: C	DIF: Challenging	OBJ: Interpretation
5. ANS: B	DIF: Average	OBJ: Interpretation
6. ANS: A	DIF: Average	OBJ: Interpretation
7. ANS: D	DIF: Challenging	OBJ: Reading
8. ANS: A	DIF: Average	OBJ: Interpretation
9. ANS: B	DIF: Average	OBJ: Comprehension
10. ANS: C	DIF: Average	OBJ: Literary Analysis
11. ANS: C	DIF: Challenging	OBJ: Literary Analysis
12. ANS: C	DIF: Average	OBJ: Literary Analysis
13. ANS: B	DIF: Average	OBJ: Literary Analysis
14. ANS: B	DIF: Average	OBJ: Literary Analysis

Vocabulary

15. ANS: A	DIF: Average	OBJ: Vocabulary
16. ANS: B	DIF: Average	OBJ: Vocabulary

Essay

17. Students should cite one passage from each essay and explain the techniques the author used to create the humor.

    Difficulty: *Average*

    Objective: *Essay*

18. In comparing White's Aunt Belle with one of Thurber's relatives in "The Night the Bed Fell," students should point to illogical, inappropriate, or unusual situations, the contrast between the character's view of himself or herself and reality, and/or the use of exaggeration to create a sense of humor. Students should present well-supported, logical opinions of the character they think is portrayed more successfully.

    Difficulty: *Average*

    Objective: *Essay*

19. Students may respond that Bailey White wants us to learn to work with nature rather than against it; or Robert Service wants us to learn to keep promises. Students should say why the lesson is worth learning and support their answer with sound reasoning.

    Difficulty: *Average*

    Objective: *Essay*

Vocabulary Workshop—1, p. 224

Sample Answers

A.
1. put; location
2. device used to create tones on a violin; a bending of the head to show appreciation.
3. associated by being in the same family; told
4. trim and in good shape; are of an appropriate size
5. intend; cruel

B. Some words have more than two meanings. Therefore, definitions may vary, and sentences will vary. Possible responses are shown.

1. junk: Meaning 1 = (noun) things of very little value; Sentence: Dad told me to clean all the old junk out of the garage. Meaning 2 = (noun) a Chinese boat; The men sailed the junk into the harbor.
2. mail: Meaning 1 = (noun) letters and packages sent and received; Sentence: Please sort the mail and put my letters on the table by the door. Meaning 2 = (noun) flexible metal armor worn by knights; The knight put on his mail and prepared for battle.
3. refuse: Meaning 1 = (verb) to decline or respond in the negative; Sentence: If you receive merchandise in the mail that you didn't order, you should refuse to accept it. Meaning 2 = (noun) trash or garbage; Together, they dragged the bags of refuse to the curb.
4. mush: Meaning 1 = (noun) a hash-like food, usually made from corn; Sentence: When we went camping, Dad made a big pot of cornmeal mush. Meaning 2 = (verb) a command given to sled dogs, meaning "Go!"; The dogs took off when the sled driver yelled, "Mush!"

Benchmark Test 6, p. 227

MULTIPLE CHOICE

1. ANS: B
2. ANS: C
3. ANS: A

4. ANS: D

5. ANS: B

6. ANS: A

7. ANS: C

8. ANS: D

9. ANS: A

10. ANS: B

11. ANS: C

12. ANS: A

13. ANS: A

14. ANS: C

15. ANS: D

16. ANS: B

17. ANS: A

18. ANS: C

19. ANS: A

20. ANS: B

21. ANS: C

22. ANS: D

23. ANS: B

24. ANS: B

25. ANS: C

26. ANS: A

27. ANS: D

28. ANS: C

29. ANS: D

30. ANS: A

31. ANS: B

32. ANS: C

33. ANS: D

34. ANS: A

ESSAY

35. Students' essays should state a position clearly and support it with persuasive devices such as appeals to reason and emotions, as well as endorsements by authorities.

36. Students' adaptations should use simple syntax and vocabulary.

37. Students should compare movies or television shows of the same genre. They should include details illustrating both similarities and differences and conclude with a recommendation.

Vocabulary in Context, p. 232

MULTIPLE CHOICE

1. ANS: D

2. ANS: C

3. ANS: B

4. ANS: B

5. ANS: A

6. ANS: B

7. ANS: C

8. ANS: B

9. ANS: A

10. ANS: A

11. ANS: D

12. ANS: D

13. ANS: A

14. ANS: D

15. ANS: C

16. ANS: C

17. ANS: B

18. ANS: B

19. ANS: C

20. ANS: B